Major Themes of the Qur'ān

MAJOR THEMES OF THE QUR'ĀN

by
Fazlur Rahman

Professor of Islamic Thought
University of Chicago

Second Edition

BIBLIOTHECA ISLAMICA
Minneapolis
1989

Bibliotheca Islamica, Inc.
Box 14474
Minneapolis, MN 55414
USA

To my Wife

Acknowledgements

I wish to record my thanks to the following for kindly allowing me to publish in the present work articles or chapters which had previously appeared (in slightly different form) elsewhere: The editors of *Studia Islamica*, Paris; the editors of *Islamic Studies*, Islamabad; and Orbis Books, Maryknoll, N.Y.

I also want to express my gratitude to my publisher, Bruce D. Craig, both for publishing the work and for encouraging me unfailingly; to the staff of Bibliotheca Islamica for expert assistance in the arduous tasks of copy-editing, proofreading, and indexing; and to the Center for Middle Eastern Studies, The University of Chicago, for typing the original draft of the manuscript.

FAZLUR RAHMAN
Chicago, July 2, 1979

FAZLUR RAHMAN. 1919-1988

Fazlur Rahman was born September 21,1919, in what is today Pakistan. His early education was in Islamic schools followed by an M.A. degree from Punjab University, Lahore, in 1942, with a First Class in Arabic. He was awarded the D. Phil. degree by Oxford University in 1949 for his thesis, *Avicenna's Psychology.*

He was Lecturer in Persian Studies and Islamic Philosophy at Durham University from 1950 to 1958.In 1958 he was appointed Associate Professor in the Institute of Islamic Studies, McGill University in Montreal, where he remained until 1961. In 1962 he was named Director of the Central Institute of Islamic Research, in Pakistan, and continued in that capacity until 1968.

In 1969 he was appointed Professor of Islamic Thought at the University of Chicago and, in 1987, the University made him the Harold H. Swift Distinguished Service Professor in recognition of his contributions to scholarship.

The author of ten books and hundreds of articles, in 1983 he was the ninth recipient of the Levi Della Vida award for Islamic scholarship presented by UCLA.

Professor Rahman passed away on July 26, 1988, due to complications of heart surgery. He was sixty-eight years old.

PUBLISHER
Minneapolis, November 11, 1988

Contents

Introduction

Purpose of the Present Work

Muslims and non-Muslims have written extensively on the Qur'ān. The innumerable Muslim commentaries on the Holy Book often take the text verse by verse and explain it. Quite apart from the fact that most of these project tendentious points of view, at great length, by the very nature of their procedure they cannot yield insight into the cohesive outlook on the universe and life which the Qur'ān undoubtedly possesses. More recently, non-Muslims as well as Muslims have produced topical arrangements of the Qur'ānic verses; although these can in varying degree serve the scholar as a source or an index, they are of no help to the student seeking to acquaint himself with what the Qur'ān has to say on God, man, or society. It is therefore hoped that the present work will respond to the urgent need for an introduction to major themes of the Qur'ān.

Except for the treatment of a few important themes like the diversity of religious communities, the possibility and actuality of miracles, and *jihād*, which all show evolution through the Qur'ān, the procedure used for synthesizing themes is logical rather than chronological. In discussing God, for example, the idea of monotheism—which is logically imperative—is made the foundation-stone of the entire treatment, and all other Qur'ānic ideas on God are either derived from it or subsumed under it, as seemed best to establish the synthetic concept of God. Apart from this, the Qur'ān has been allowed to speak for itself; interpretation has been used only as necessary for joining together ideas.

I am convinced that this synthetic exposition is the only way to give a reader a genuine taste of the Qur'ān, the Command of God for man. Even if the chronological order could be feasibly reconstructed passage by passage (which I consider a real impossibility—*pace* Richard Bell!), it would only explicate what is germinal in the original, master idea. This is radically different from the "dissective study" approach—chronological or other—whose usefulness for scholarship is obvious but which must disclaim any pretensions to treat the Qur'ān as what it claims to be: God's message to man. The conventional repetition of such usual "information" about the Qur'ān as the "Five Pillars" or the inheritance laws has kept *understanding* of the Qur'ān at the most superficial level. (Note, however, that this work does include detailed references to chapters and verses so that the reader can verify and think further for himself.)

Modern Western Writings on the Qur'ān

After translations of the Qur'ān, of which A. J. Arberry's *The Koran Interpreted* ranks easily as the best in English (followed by two English translations by Muslims, *The Meaning of the Glorious Qur'ān* by Muḥammad Marmaduke Pickthall and *The Holy Qur'ān* by 'Abdullah Yusuf Ali), earlier modern Western literature on the Qur'ān falls into three broad categories: (1) works that seek to trace the influence of Jewish or Christian ideas on the Qur'ān; (2) works that attempt to reconstruct the chronological order of the Qur'ān; and (3) works that aim at describing the content of the Qur'ān, either the whole or certain aspects. Though this last might be expected to receive the most attention, it has had the least. Perhaps Western scholars consider it a Muslim responsibility to present the Qur'ān as it would have itself presented, retaining for themselves the work of "objective analysis," either in terms of "sources" or in terms of the development of ideas. Muslim scholarship, on the other hand, has two problems: (1) lack of a genuine feel for the relevance of the Qur'ān today, which prevents presentation in terms adequate to the needs of contemporary man; but even more (2) a fear that such a presentation might deviate on some points from traditionally received opinions. This last risk is inevitable; I think it must be undertaken, though with both sincerity and perception.

The three broad categories of Qur'ānic studies are all scholarly; although only the third does true justice to the subject, the other two are very useful in achieving this third task. A grasp of the background of the Qur'ānic passages and of the chronological order (to the extent possible) is crucial for correct understanding of the purposes of the Qur'ān.

Unfortunately, the treatment of the Judaeo-Christian antecedents of the Qur'ān has often been contaminated by the far too obvious desire of its proponents to "prove" that the Qur'ān is no more than an echo of Judaism (or Christianity) and Muḥammad no more than a Jewish (or Christian) disciple! After two early, and excellent, pieces of scholarship (Abraham Geiger's *Was hat Mohammed aus dem Judenthume Aufgenommen* [1883] and Hartwig Hirschfeld's *Jüdische Elemente im Koran* [1878]), there have been a disproportionate number of attempts to "show" that the Prophet Muhammad was literally a disciple of one or another Jewish scholar. Christian scholars have not been quite so immoderate: although one may question many theses in a book like Richard Bell's *The Origin of Islam in its Christian Environment*, it is recognizably a scholarly work.

The logical end of the line for Jewish apologists is John Wansbrough's *Quranic Studies* (1977), which labors to prove (1) that the Qur'ān is truly a work *a la'tradition Juive* because it was produced in an atmosphere of intense Judaeo-Christian sectarian debate and (2) that it is a "composite" work of several traditions (this theory being used to explain certain differences within the Qur'ān, e.g., attitudes towards Abraham); so that (3) as it stands, the Qur'ān is post-Muḥammad.

There are a number of problems with this. Consider first Wansbrough's second thesis, that the Qur'ān is a composite of several traditions and hence post-Prophetic. I feel that there is a distinct lack of historical data on the origin, character, evaluation, and personalities involved in these "traditions." Moreover, on a number of key issues the Qur'ān can be understood only in terms of chronological and developmental unfolding within a single document. Take the question of how the Qur'ān treats miracles. As I explain below in Chapter IV, while the Qur'ānic attitude toward miracles does evolve, it is always cohesive, affirming at later stages that while miracles are no longer necessary, they are always possible. The development is intelligible only in the context of a unified document gradually unfolding itself. It cannot be understood as a composite of different and contradictory elements. A similar case is the Qur'ānic treatment of the problem of diversity of religious communities (treated below in Chapter VIII and more completely in Appendix II).

I also had difficulty with Wansbrough's treatment of retribution, i.e., judgment in history, for he makes a definite disjunction between "historical" and "eschatological" significance in discussing the Qur'ānic terminology. In the Qur'ān there is no disjunction but the closest possible connection. It appears that Wansbrough wishes to equate the Qur'ānic examples of "destroyed nations and civilizations" with the pessimism of the Wisdom literature motif of the transitoriness of the world. In his discussion, Wansbrough refers to C. H. Becker's *Islamstudien*, yet he seems to ignore Becker's direct statement that "[The stories of] 'Ād and Thamūd [in the Qur'ān] do not illustrate the [themes of the] transitoriness of the world and of the destiny of the individual," but rather the fates of nations. I think that the Qur'ān itself is the best argument against Wansbrough's thesis (see below, Chapter III), for it repeatedly admonishes nations to profit by the experiences and mistakes of other nations.

Nor do I feel that Wansbrough has dealt well with the phenomenon of substitution of certain verses by certain others which the Qur'ān itself recognizes and calls *naskh*, abrogation or substitution. Clearly for substitution, there must be a later verse to substitute for an earlier one, a chronological necessity which would be difficult to maintain if the Qur'ān were merely an amalgamation of simultaneous traditions. In that case, there might be adjustments, but they could hardly be called *naskh*.

My disagreements with Wansbrough are so numerous that they are probably best understood only by reading both this book and his. (I do, however, concur with at least one of his points: "The kind of analysis undertaken will in no small measure determine the results!" [p. 21]) I do believe that this kind of study can be enormously useful, though we have to return to Geiger and Hirschfeld to see just how useful it can be when done properly.

With regard to the chronological studies of the Qur'ān, the monumental work of Nöldeke-Schwally, *Geschichte des Qorans*, still sets the standard and cries out for an English translation. R. Blachère's French translation of the Qur'ān and his *Introduction au Koran* both assume Nöldeke's arrangement of the suras; his *Le Probleme de Mahomet* uses a more subjective chronology based on the psychological development of the Prophet, rather than on the German School's principle of development of themes. Richard Bell's translation of the Qur'ān and his companion *Introduction to the Qur'ān* show occasional valuable insights, but develop some rather eccentric

themes. He suggests, for instance, that a certain amount of discon-
nectedness arose in the passages of the Qur'ān because those who
copied it could not distinguish between the front and the back of the
written materials from which they copied! Montgomery Watt has
issued a thoroughly reworked edition of Bell's *Introduction* which I
found very useful despite my disagreements with it on several points.
Rudi Paret's German translation of the Qur'ān is sober and excellent,
as is his *Koran-Kommentar*, where under each verse he gives useful
cross-references to other verses. Paret believes, rightly, I think, that
Bell's type of passage-by-passage chronology is impossible.

The basic work on the history of the Qur'ānic text is again Nöldeke-
Schwally. Blâchere and others, notably A. Jeffery in *Materials for the
History of the Text of the Qur'ān*, have made some valuable
contributions (though care should be exercised in studying Jeffery).
There is, at the opposite pole, along with Wansbrough, John Burton's
The Collection of the Qur'ān (which takes the doctrine of *naskh* much
too far, I think, in speculating that the entire text of the Qur'ān was
"edited, checked and promulgated" by the Prophet himself!); while
Hagarism by Crone and Cook takes its departure from Wansbrough's
thesis as established truth.

The lacunae in Qur'ānic scholarship are most obvious in our third
category, works concerned with the content of the Qur'ān. Most deal
only with certain aspects of the Qur'ān, and none is rooted in the
Qur'ān itself. If they are not purely "scientific," dealing with, say,
foreign terms or commercial terms in the Qur'ān, they exhibit a
controlling, external point of view. None has presented the Qur'ān on
its own terms, as a unity, even those treatments by Muslims
themselves, of which the best mirror is Ignaz Goldziher's *Die
Richtungen der islamischen Koranauslegung*. I have attempted to
elaborate how the Qur'ān might be studied as a unity in the
Introduction to an as-yet-unpublished monograph, *Islamic Education
and Modernity*.

A useful though naturally outmoded work is H. Grimme's second
volume of *Mohammad* (1895), which presents a general overview of the
theology and doctrine of the duties of Muslims as set forth in the
Qur'ān. An extraordinarily sensitive response to Islamic scripture by a
Christian is Kenneth Cragg's *The Event of the Qur'ān*, and his book of
essays *The Mind of the Qur'ān*. Also deserving of notice are Thomas
O'Shaughnessy's "The Development of the Meaning of Spirit in the

Koran,'' in *Orientalia Christiana Analecta* (1953) and S. H. Al-Shamma's Ph.D. dissertation, *The Ethical System Underlying the Qur'ān*.

Finally the remarkable work of the Japanese scholar, T. Izutsu, must be noted. His earlier work, *The Structure of the Ethical Terms in the Koran*, was revised into *Ethico-Religious Concepts in the Koran* in 1966. Between lies a related work, *God and Man in the Koran*. His approach is semantic. Although the books deal primarily with religious ethics and attitude, a good deal of the general Qur'ānic worldview comes under discussion. Though I occasionally disagree with Professor Izutsu on his analysis of certain key terms like *taqwā*, I recommend his work as highly useful.

Qur'ānic bibliographies are collected by William A. Bijlefeld in ''Some Recent Contributions to Qur'ānic Studies,'' *Muslim World*, 64: (1974): 79, n. 1.

Citation of the Qur'ān

In referring to the Qur'ān below, I have followed the verse numbering of the official Egyptian edition rather than that of Flugel's edition. For the most part, I have given my own English rendering of the Qur'ānic verses, though in Chapters I and VI where the quotations are extensive, I have used Pickthall's translation, with some modifications. In general, I take responsibility for all renderings of Qur'ānic passages into English.

Chapter One

God

The Qur'ān is a document that is squarely aimed at man; indeed, it calls itself "guidance for mankind" (*hudan li'l-nās* [2:185] and numerous equivalents elsewhere). Yet, the term *Allāh*, the proper name for God, occurs well over 2,500 times in the Qur'ān (not to count the terms *al-Rabb*, The Lord, and *al-Raḥmān*, The Merciful, which, although they signify qualities, have nevertheless come to acquire substance). Still, the Qur'ān is no treatise about God and His nature: His existence, for the Qur'ān, is strictly functional—He is Creator and Sustainer of the universe and of man, and particularly the giver of guidance for man and He who judges man, individually and collectively, and metes out to him merciful justice.

This "merciful justice" has often been represented as "justice tempered with mercy" by modern writers, but, as we shall soon see, orderly creativity, sustenance, guidance, justice, and mercy fully interpenetrate in the Qur'ānic concept of God as an organic unity. Since all these are relational ideas, we shall have to speak of God a great deal in the following pages. In the present chapter we wish to discuss briefly questions of the necessity of God and of one God, and what according to the Qur'ān these immediately imply (hoping thereby to reduce overlapping to the minimum).

The immediate impression from a cursory reading of the Qur'ān is that of the infinite majesty of God and His equally infinite mercy, although many a Western scholar (through a combination of ignorance and prejudice) has depicted the Qur'ānic God as a concentrate of pure power, even as brute power—indeed, as a capricious tyrant. The Qur'ān, of course, speaks of God in so many different contexts and so frequently that unless all the statements are interiorized into a total mental picture—without, as far as possible, the interference of any subjective and wishful thinking—it would be extremely difficult, if not outright impossible, to do justice to the Qur'ānic concept of God.

First, why God at all? Why not let nature and her contents and processes stand on their own without bringing in a higher being, which only complicates reality and puts an unnecessary burden on both man's intellect and his soul? The Qur'ān calls this "belief in and awareness of the unseen" (2:3; 5:94; 21:49; 35:18; 36:11; 50:33; 57:25; 67:12); this "unseen" has been, to a greater or lesser extent, made "seen" through Revelation for some people like the Prophet (examples: 81:24; 68:47; 52:41; 53:35; 12:102; 11:49), although it cannot be fully known to anyone except God (examples: 72:26; 64:18; 59:22; 49:18; 39:46; 35:38; 32:6; 27:65; 23:92; 18:26; 16:77; 13:9; 12:81; 11:31; 7:188, etc.). God's existence can, however, be brought home to those who care to reflect so that it not only ceases to be an "irrational" or "unreasonable" belief but becomes *the Master-Truth*. This is the task of the Qur'ān: if the task is accomplished, everything has been accomplished; if not, nothing whatever has been achieved.

But in order to achieve this, students also must do something; if they do not, they cannot be called students at all. It is, therefore, not an extraordinary or an unreasonable or a supererogatory demand. The student must "listen" to what the Qur'ān has to say: "Who is humble before the unseen and brings with him a heart such that it can respond [when the truth hits it]" (50:33); "it is a reminder to him/her who has a heart and surrenders his/her ears in witnessing" (50:37). Such verses are everywhere: "These people are [as though] they are being called from a long distance" (41:44). Yet God is not so far that His signals cannot be heard: "*We* created man and We know what the negative whisperings of his mind are and We are nearer to him than his jugular vein!" (50:16).

So near and yet so far! The problem is not how to make man come to belief by giving lengthy and intricate "theological" proofs of God's existence, but how to shake him into belief by drawing his attention to certain obvious facts and turning these facts into "reminders" of God. Hence the Qur'ān time and again calls itself (and also the Prophet) "a reminder" or "The Reminder".

The main points in this ceaseless, tremendous thrust for "reminding" man are (1) that everything except God is contingent upon God, including the entirety of nature (which has a "metaphysical" and a "moral" aspect); (2) that God, with all His might and glory, is essentially the all-merciful God; and (3) that both these aspects necessarily entail a proper relationship between God and Man—a relationship of the served and the servant—and consequently also a proper relationship between man and man. By a natural necessity, as it were, these normative relationships entail the law of judgment upon man both as individual and in his collective or social existence. Once we have grasped these three points, we will have understood the absolute centrality of God in the entire system of existence, to a very large extent *because* the aim of the Qur'ān is man and his behavior, not God.

We shall elaborate in greater detail in Chapter IV that, for the Qur'ān, the whole of nature is one firm, well-knit structure with no gaps, no ruptures, and no dislocations. It works by its own laws, which have been ingrained in it by God, and is, therefore, autonomous; but it is not autocratic, for, in itself, it has no warrant for its own existence and it cannot explain itself.

This lack of rational and moral ultimacy raises the all-important question of whence it derives its being. In particular, the crucial questions must be answered: Why nature and the richness and fullness of its being? Why not just nothing and pure emptiness—which is, on all counts, the easier and the more "natural" of the two alternatives? From the Greeks through Hegel it has often been said that "nothing" is an empty word without any real meaning since "there can be no nothing and we cannot imagine it." But the question then is: Why can we not imagine it? It is certainly theoretically possible that there might be no nature at all. Those who think that nature is "given" and therefore somehow "necessary" are like a child for whom toys are a "given" and therefore somehow "necessary."

This is exactly the meaning of contingency. But a contingent cannot be thought of without that upon which it is contingent, although it is possible to be so immersed in what is contingent that one may not think of that upon which it is contingent—again, like a child who may be so engaged with his toys that he does not care to know what is beyond them. But, according to the Qur'ān, once you think of the whence (and the whither) of nature you must "find God." This is not a "proof" of God's existence, for in the thought of the Qur'ān, if you cannot "find" God, you will never "prove" Him: "The only straight path leads to God—[all] other paths are deviant" (16:9). For reasons that will follow, "find" is not an empty word; it entails a total revaluation of the primal order of reality and throws everything into new perspective with new meanings. And the first consequence of this discovery is that God cannot be regarded as an existent among other existents. In the metaphysical realm, there can be no democratic and equal sharing of being between the Original, the Creator, the Self-Necessary, and the borrowed, the created, the contingent; such a "sharing" rather exists within the second category itself. The Qur'ānic condemnation of *shirk* ("assigning partners to God") has its roots firmly in this metaphysical realm and then, as we shall see, issues forth in the moral field.

God is that dimension which makes other dimensions possible; He gives meaning and life to everything. He is all-enveloping, literally infinite, and He *alone* is infinite. All else carries in the very texture of its being the hallmark of its finitude and creatureliness: "Everything thereon [literally: 'on the earth,' but meaning the whole gamut of nature] is vanishing, there remaining only the Face of Your Lord, the Possessor of Majesty and Generosity" (55:26-27); "Say: If the ocean were to turn into ink [for writing] the [creative] Words of my Lord, the ocean will be expended before the Words of my Lord are—even if we were to bring another ocean like it" (18:109). In the very nature of the case, there can be only one God, for whenever one tries to conceive of more than one, only one will be found to emerge as the First: "And God has said, 'Do not take two gods [for] He is only One" (16:51); "God bears witness that there is no god, but He" (3:18); "Say [O Muhammad!] if there were other gods besides Him, as these people assert, they would all [necessarily] seek their way to the [one] Lord of the Throne" (17:42).

Since nature is well-knit and working with laws that have been made inherent in it, there is undoubtedly "natural causation," and, as we shall see more fully in Chapter IV, the Qur'ān recognizes this. But this does not mean that God creates nature and then goes to sleep; nor, of course, does this mean that God and nature or God and the human will (as will be elaborated in Chapter II) are "rivals" and function at the expense of each other; nor yet does it mean that God operates *in addition to* the operations of man and nature. Without God's activity, the activity of nature and man becomes delinquent, purposeless, and self-wasting. Things and humans are, indeed, *directly* related to God just as they are related to each other, and we must further interpret our statement that God is not an item among other items of the universe, or just an existent among other existents. He is "with" everything; He constitutes the integrity of everything: "Do not be like those who forgot God and [eventually] God caused them to forget themselves" (59:19). And just as everything is related directly to Him, so is everything, *through* and *in* relation to other things, related to God as well. God, then, is the very meaning of reality, a meaning manifested, clarified, and brought home by the universe, helped even further by man. That everything in the universe is God's "sign" will be elaborated in Chapter IV; that His meaningful and purposeful activity is furthered by man will be discussed particularly in Chapter III.

That is how the Qur'ān comes to emphasize and re-emphasize the power and majesty of God. But while this metaphysical truth is the real reason, there is a historical dimension to this emphasis as well and that is the polytheism of the pagan Arabs, who invoked and worshipped many deities besides God. To overcome this the Qur'ān would say:

> O you who believe! Spend of the wealth We have given you by way of sustenance, before the Day comes when there shall be no bargains, nor friendships, nor yet any intercession, and it is the disbelievers who are unjust. Allah alone [is God], there is no God but Him, the Alive, the Sustainer; neither slumber nor sleep overtakes Him. To Him belongs whatever is in the heavens and on the earth—Who can, then, intercede with Him except whom He permits? He knows what is before them and what is behind them, while they encompass none of His knowledge, except what He permits. His Throne envelopes the heavens and the earth and their preservation fatigues Him not—He is the High, the Great (2:255).

Again:

> He is *the* God, other than Whom, there is none; He is the knower of the unseen and the seen, the Merciful, the Compassionate. He is *the* God other than Whom there is none, the Sovereign, the Holy, the One with peace and integrity, the Keeper of the Faith, the Protector, the Mighty, the One Whose Will is Power, the Most Supreme! Glory be to Him beyond what they [the pagans] associate with Him. He is the God, the Creator, the Maker, the Fashioner, to Whom belong beautiful names; whatever is in the heavens and the earth sings His glories, He is the Mighty One, the Wise One (59:22-24).

And once again:

And who other than Him created the heavens and the earth and sent down for you water from the sky, whereby We cause to grow lush orchards—for it is not up to you to cause their trees to grow! Is there, then, a god beside God? Yet these are the people who ascribe partners to Him!

And who other than Him made the earth a firm abode [for you], and set rivers traversing through it, and put firm mountains therein and sealed off one sea from the other? Is there, then, a god beside God? Indeed, most of them do not know!

And who other than Him responds to the distressed one when he calls Him and He relieves him of the distress and Who has made you [mankind] His viceregents on earth? Is there, then, a god beside God? —little do you reflect!

And who other than Him guides you in the darknesses of the land and the sea? And who sends forth winds heralding His mercy [rain]? Is there, then, a god beside God? Far exalted be He above what they associate with Him!

And who other than Him brings forth His creation and then re-creates it? And who gives you sustenance from the heaven and the earth? Is there, then, a god beside God? Say [O Muhammad!]: Bring your proof if you are right [in associating others with God] (27:60-64).

While these passages emphasize God's lordship and power, they equally underline His infinite mercy. As these five verses make clear, God's lordship is *expressed through* His creation; His sustenance and provision of that creation, particularly and centrally of man; and, finally, through re-creation in new forms. His creation of nature *and* man and of nature *for* man is the most primordial mercy of God. His power, creation, and mercy are, therefore, not only fully co-extensive but fully interpenetrating and fully identical: "He has imposed the law of mercy upon Himself" (6:12), and "My mercy comprehends all" (7:156). His very infinitude implies not a one-sided transcendence but equally His being "with" His creation; note that He is nearer to man than is man's jugular vein (50:16). Whenever a person commits a lapse and then sincerely regrets it and "seeks God's pardon," God quickly returns to him—indeed, among His often-mentioned attributes besides the "Merciful" and the "Compassionate" are the "Returner" (as the opposite of "forsaker": 2:37, 54, 160, 128; 5:39, 71; 9:117, 118; 20:122, etc.) and the "Forgiver" (40:3; 2:173, 182, 192, 199, 218, 225, 226, 235; and about 116 other occurrences), which are almost invariably followed by "Compassionate." For those who genuinely repent, God transmutes their very lapses into goodness (25:70).

God is, in fact, that Light whereby everything finds its proper being and its conduct:

> God is the light of the heavens and the earth: the likeness of His Light is that of a niche wherein is set a lamp; the lamp is [encased] in a glass; this glass is [so brilliant] as though it were a pearly star. [The lamp] is lit by [the oil of] a blessed olive tree which is neither Eastern nor Western, and whose oil is apt to catch light even though fire hardly touches it. [God is] Light upon Light and He guides to His Light whom He wills. . . . (24:35).

The anti-God forces, on the other hand, are

> like multiple darknesses in a stormy sea which is covered by one wave upon another and these are themselves covered by [dark] clouds—layer upon layer of darkness. If one were to stretch out his own hands, he is apt not to see them; he whom God has denied His Light, can get no light (24:40).

While God's power and His greatness are, as it were, a tautology—for His power and greatness are the primary meaning of His all-comprehensiveness—the point of their being so often emphasized in the Qur'ān is to show up the dangerous silliness of humans who come either to equate and identify finite beings with the Infinite one, or to posit intermediary gods or powers between Him and His creation, when He is directly and even intimately related with His creation. But even more important for us is the fact that God exercises His greatness, power, and all-comprehensive presence primarily through the entire range of the manifestations of mercy—through being and creation, sustenance of that creation, guiding that creation to its destiny, and, finally, through a "return" to the creatures who, after willful alienation, sincerely wish to be reconciled to the source of their being, life, and guidance.

While we shall treat of creation and the human use of nature more fully in Chapter IV on nature; of guidance in Chapter V on prophethood; and of judgment in Chapters III on society and VI on eschatology, we shall discuss these briefly here to the extent that they relate to God.

First, God does not create as a frivolity, pastime, or sport, without a serious purpose. It is incompatible with the power of the Powerful and the mercy of the Merciful that He should produce toys for amusement or as sheer whim—a blind Fate can do this but God cannot: "Those [are believers] who remember God standing and sitting and lying down and reflect upon the creation of the heaven and the earth [and say]: Our Lord! You have not created all this in vain" (3:191); "We have not created the heaven and the earth and whatever is between them in vain" (38:27); "We have not created the heaven and the earth and whatever is between them in sport. If We wished to take a sport, We could have done it by Ourselves [not through Our creation]—if We were to do that at all" (21:16-17); finally, with regard to the creation of man, "Do you then think that We have created you purposelessly and that you will not be returned to Us? The True Sovereign is too exalted above that" (23:115); "Does man think that he will be left wandering [at his own whim]?" (75:36).

Thus, not only does the Qur'ān part company with atheists and those who believe that the universe is a product of chance and a play of matter, but also with all those who believe that God produced the universe as a sport, including those Sufis who hold literally that God said (according to a famous Ḥadīth-report which they attribute to the Prophet), "I was a hidden treasure, but I wished to be known, therefore I created the creation." As the words of the Qur'ān have it, "If We wished to take a sport, We could have done it by Ourselves," and displaying oneself to oneself, if meant literally, is nothing but a sport. Also, if the world is a sport, all talk of guidance and misguidance and judgment in the Qur'ānic sense (not in the sense of the rules of the sport!) is not only beside the point, but a massive delusion.

The whole matter turns on a faith that is not blind but is rooted in the consideration whether this entire universe, organized and functioning the way it is, could be pure chance or whether it points to a purposeful creator. The Qur'ānic dicta must also destroy belief in the cyclic universes, for no matter how attractive the idea of a cyclic universe may be to many—particularly Greek—thinkers and some modern astronomers, cyclic motion is incompatible with any purposefulness; it belongs more to the world of merry-go-rounds.

While the purpose of man is to "serve" God, i.e., to develop his higher potentialities in accordance with the "command" (*amr*) of God, through choice, and to use nature (which is automatically *muslim*, "obedient to God"), he must be provided with adequate means of sustenance and of "finding the right way." Hence God, Who in His outgoing mercy brought nature and man into being, in His unbroken and sustained mercy has endowed man with the necessary cognition and volition to create knowledge and use it to realize his just and fair ends. It is at this point that man's crucial test comes: will he use his knowledge and power for good or for evil, for "success or loss," or for "reforming the earth or corrupting it" (as the Qur'ān constantly puts it)? This is an extremely delicate task. The question of questions for man is whether he can control history towards good ends or whether he will succumb to its vagaries.

For this reason, God's mercy reaches its logical zenith in "sending Messengers," "revealing Books," and showing man "the Way." This "guidance" (*hidāya*) is also kneaded into man's primordial nature insofar as the distinction between good and evil is "ingrained in his heart" (91:8) and insofar as men have made a covenant with God in pre-eternity to recognize Him as their sovereign (7:172). Man often little heeds these and hence, particularly at times of moral crisis, God sends His messages, for it is the moral aspect of man's behavior which is most slippery and difficult to control and yet most crucial for his survival and success. Hence judgment is an imperative upon this whole process of mercy from creation through preservation to guidance, since it is through guidance that man is expected to develop that inner torch (called *taqwā* by the Qur'ān) whereby he can discern between right and wrong. As we shall detail in Chapters II and III, he is to use the torch primarily against his own self-deception in assessing and judging his actions.

This entire chain—creation-preservation-guidance-judgment, all as manifestations of mercy—is so utterly reasonable that the Qur'ān states surprise and dismay that it is questioned at all. The two points primarily questioned are the beginning and the end: God's role as Creator and His role as Judge.

Even some of those who believe in God (in some sense of "believe") think that judgment, calling to account, is too harsh an idea for a merciful God. But such religious ideologies as have put their whole emphasis on God's love and self-sacrifice for the sake of His children have done little service to the moral maturity of man. It is correct that children cannot be really judged; they can only be punished after a fashion. But it is surely unreasonable to hold that man is still a child even though his *taqwā*-torch is expected to spark and sparkle? There is a world of difference between a child and a mature delinquent—else, when is man supposed to come of age? This picture of a doting father and a spoilt child is hit directly by the Qur'ānic verses that prohibit child-play and frivolity on God's part, as well as those verses (see Chapter III below) that criticize Jews and Christians for laying proprietary claims upon God.

But the most vicious for the Qur'ān are those who formally or substantively deny God's existence: materialistic atheists and "those who assign partners to God." This last phrase is the real high-stress point. Given faith in God, the rest follows in a logical nexus; but if faith in God is not there, then all the rest—preservation of and order in nature (i.e., Providence), guidance, and judgment on "the end of affairs" (*'āqibat al-umūr*; i.e., eschatology)—either become simply dubious or at least become so many discrete issues, each to be discussed separately and accepted or rejected, that the entire chain falls to pieces. This is why God is the cementing piece of the whole chain, giving it meaning.

It is in this context that our earlier outline of the Qur'ān's argument from nature and its orderly working (pp. 3-5) assumes its full significance: the Qur'ān does not "prove" God but "points to" Him from the existing universe. Even if there were no ordered universe, but only a single being, it would still point beyond itself because it is a mere contingent; but there is not a mere single contingent, there is a whole ordered and perfectly working universe. To many, this order, where all parts are interdependent, is less in need of a God than is a single contingent being, for in an ordered whole all parts play a role in supporting it and each other, without the need for an exterior being. Yet, although the parts of any organism are mutually supportive, the organism as a whole does not explain its own genesis. Some contemporary thinkers have suggested that the very concept of "order" in the Universe is meaningless: "order" presupposes a function or a norm with reference to which order is spoken of, and hence any concept of order is related to the subjectivity of our own minds. (My office is ordered if books, files, desk, etc., are in places where they facilitate my work rather than hinder it.) Therefore, the application of the term to the universe is unwarranted.

This argument, which seeks to counter the first, unjustifiably assimilates an objective order to a subjective expectation born of certain human practices. Regularity, correspondence, and proportionate variations in natural phenomena were termed "order" by natural scientists without any necessary reference to expectations born of human practices; which is why this objective order is "discovered." Hence many atheistic and agnostic scientists could recognize a natural order without recognizing God.

Now comes the most crucial point in the thought of the Qur'ān. Is it more rational to believe that this natural order, so vast and so complex, is also a purposive order, or is it more rational to believe that it is pure chance? Can chance order be cohesive and lasting order? Does not chance itself, in fact, presuppose a framework of more fundamental purposiveness? Faith in God, though indeed a faith, for the Qur'ān rests on stronger grounds, in fact, *is* stronger, than many pieces of empirical but contingent evidence. For, it is much less reasonable—indeed, it is *irrational*—to say that all this gigantic and lasting natural order is pure chance. Hence the recurring Qur'ānic invitations and exhortations, "Do you not reflect?" "Do you not think?" "Do you not take heed?" And let us repeat that this "reflecting," "pondering," or "heeding" has nothing to do with devising formal proofs for God's existence or "inferring" God's existence, but with "discovering" God and developing a certain perception by "lifting the veil" from the mind.

A person who is endowed with such perception becomes correctly attuned to reality, for the very basis of being supports him; "he fears nothing but God," i.e., he is not afraid of losing anything except God's support. His personality becomes so fortified that it is immune from any assailant. God is his only helper, the sole refuge; all other imagined havens are hopeless: "Those who have taken friends besides God, their likeness is that of the spider which takes for itself a house, but the weakest of all is the spider's house—if only they knew!" (29:41) The short but emphatic sura 112—which has been rightly regarded by the Islamic tradition as presenting the essence of the whole Qur'ān—calls God "al-Ṣamad," which means an immovable and indestructible rock, without cracks or pores, which serves as sure refuge from floods. To base oneself on anything short of this rock, this basis of all being, is "to be a loser" (as the Qur'ān puts it recurrently), for it means that one has chosen to live in a spider's web. The deeds of men based on other than the rock "have no weight," no matter how highly they themselves might regard them. These deeds are without reference to the ultimate basis of life and the source of all value; they are, therefore, "like motes scattered around" (25:23). Only God gives that value and unity and wholeness to life which make thoughts and deeds worthwhile and meaningful; any partialization of reality, parochialism, fragmentation of truth, is *shirk* ("assigning partners to God") and "God will not forgive *shirk*, but may forgive any sin lighter than that" (4:48).

God, then, becomes the friend of and cooperates with a person who has "discovered" Him. Yet, God's friendship may not be presumed at any point by either any individual or any community, even though the Qur'an speaks of God's promises to individuals and communities. One must exercise *taqwā*, meaning that if one has the proper perception, then one must be constantly "on one's guard" (which is the literal meaning of *taqwā*). One cannot take God for granted, since no individual or community in the world can at any time appropriate Truth; in fact, the very claim, whether made by an individual or a community for itself or by a community on behalf of its real or putative founder, amounts to a confession of lack of *taqwā*. Muhammad, the bearer of the Qur'ānic Revelation, is told in the Qur'an that God can cut off Revelation from him and "seal your heart" (17:86; 42:24). While speaking of the Christian belief in the divinity of Jesus, the Qur'ān says, "Who is to prevent God if He wished to destroy Jesus son of Mary and his mother and whoever lives on the earth—for to God belongs the rule of the heavens and the earth" (5:17).

We now come back to the doctrine of the power of God. This power issues forth in the merciful creativity of God, in terms of "measuring" things, producing them "according to a certain order or measure," not haphazardly or blindly. We shall discuss this "measuring" and "ordering" in Chapter IV, but it should be noted here that in Arabic the term for both power and measuring out is *qadar* and the Qur'an uses *qadar* in both senses. In pre-Islamic Arabia, this term, more often in its plural form *aqdār*, was used to mean "Fate," a blind force that "measured out" or predetermined matters that were beyond man's control, in particular his birth, the sources of his sustenance, and his death. It was a pessimistic belief, but it was not a belief in Fate's predetermination of *all* human acts.

The Qur'ān took over this term but changed the concept of a blind and inexorable Fate into that of an all-powerful, purposeful, and merciful God. This all-powerful God, through His merciful creativity, "measures out" everything, bestowing upon everything the range of its potentialities, its laws of behavior, in sum, its character. This measuring on the one hand ensures the orderliness of nature and on the other expresses the most fundamental, unbridgeable difference between the nature of God and the nature of man: the Creator's measuring implies an infinitude wherein no measured creature—no matter how great its powers and potentialities (as in the case of man)—may literally share. It is precisely this belief in such sharing that is categorically denied by the Qur'ānic doctrine of *shirk* or "participation in Godhead."

Let us make the concept of this measuring more precise: God, not anyone else, has created the laws by which nature works. This does not mean that man cannot discover those laws and apply them for the good of man, for this is what a farmer or a scientist does. The Qur'ān invites man to discover the laws of nature and exploit it for human benefit. God has made certain laws whereby a sperm fertilizes a female egg and, after due process, a baby matures in the mother's womb; and the Qur'ān comments, "So We determined [these laws] and how fine measurers We are" (77:23). This in itself does not mean that man cannot discover the laws of the process whereby a sperm and an egg meet and then, at a certain temperature and with certain materials and other conditions, produce a perfected baby; and then apply those laws to produce a baby in a tube, for example. Many people think that this is "vying with" God and trying to interfere in His work and share His divinity, but the real worry is not that man is trying to displace nature or imitate God, for man is encouraged to do so by the Qur'ān. The fear, on the contrary, is that man may "vie with" the devil to produce distortions of nature and thus violate moral law.

If the Qur'ān expresses power and measuring through the same term, *qadar*, it uses another term, *amr* ("command"), in close association with "measuring" and, so far as nature is concerned, to mean the same thing: the laws of nature express the Command of God. But nature does not and cannot disobey God's commands and cannot violate natural laws. Hence the entirety of nature is called *muslim* by the Qur'ān, for it surrenders itself to and obeys the command of God: "Do they, then, seek an obedience [or religion] other than that to God, while it is to Him that everyone [and everything] in the heavens and the earth submits?" (3:83) "The seven heavens and the earth and whatever is therein sing the glories of God" (17:44; also 57:1; 59:1; 61:1; 13:15; 16:49; 22:18; 55:6; 7:206; 21:19).

From the concept of *qādir*, the powerful and the measurer, there necessarily follows that of *āmir*, the Commander. Just as everything is under His "measurement" (*maqdūr*), so is everything under His Command (*ma'mūr*). The fundamental difference between man and nature is that whereas natural command disallows disobedience, commands to man presuppose a choice and free volition on his part. Hence what is natural command in nature becomes moral command in man. This gives man a unique position in the order of creation; at the same time it charges him with a unique responsibility which he can discharge only through *taqwā*. Hence man is called upon to serve God alone and abandon all false gods, including his own desires and the wishful whisperings of his soul, for all these bar him from an objective perception of the whole reality, narrow his vision, and fragment his being. The following categorical declarations are typical of the very frequent Qur'ānic statements on the subject:

Say, O disbelievers! I serve not what you serve and you are not about to serve what I serve. Neither am I going to serve what you have been serving, nor are you willing to serve what I serve. For you your obedience [or religion], for me, mine! (109:1-6)

To Him belongs whatever is in the heavens and in the earth—He is the High, the Great. The heavens above them are apt to be rent asunder [because of the worship of others than God], while angels glorify the praises of their Lord. (42:4-5)

Say: Shall I take a protector-friend other than God, the Maker of the heavens and the earth, He Who feeds and is not fed? Say: I have been commanded to be the first to surrender [to God]. . . . Say: I fear, should I disobey my Lord, the punishment of a mighty day. (6:14, 15)

The heavens are apt to split asunder and the earth is about to be cleft and the mountains about to go to pieces that they [the Christians, like the Meccan pagans] have called a son for the Merciful, while it does not behoove the Merciful to take a son. (19:90-92)

Say: God guides to the truth; is He who guides to the truth more deserving of being followed or he who cannot find the way unless he is guided to it—what is wrong with you? How do you judge? (10:35)

Did you see the one who has taken his own desire to be his god? Can you be a guardian over him? (25:43)

O people! A parable is being cited, listen well to it. Those [gods] whom you call upon besides God can never create a fly, even if all of them came together to do so. And if a fly were to take away something from them, they can never get it back from it! Both the seeker and the sought are equally helpless. They have not estimated God rightly [in assigning partners to Him]—God is powerful, mighty. (22:73-74)

This, then, is the general picture of God that emerges from the

Qur'ān. What shall we say about the frequent statements of so many Westerners, in some cases even made in the name of scholarship, that the God of the Qur'ān is a loveless, remote, capricious, and even tyrannical power which arbitrarily causes some people to go astray and others to come to guidance, creates some people for hell and others for paradise, without any rhyme or reason? Even the blind Fate of the pre-Islamic Arabs was not quite like this, let alone the creative, sustaining, merciful, and purposeful God of the Qur'ān. Further, the picture is utterly incompatible with the most fundamental outline of the doctrine of God described above. If the Western allegations are correct, they must square with this outline; otherwise, our outline, based on numerous verses of the Qur'ān, must be rejected as false.

There is no doubt that the Qur'ān does make frequent statements to the effect that God leads aright whom He will and leads astray whom He will, or that God has "sealed up" some people's hearts to truth, etc. (2:8, 142, 213, 272; 14:4; 16:93; 24:35; 28:56; 30:29; 35:8), although far more often it says that "God does not lead aright the unjust ones," "God does not guide aright the transgressors," "God guides aright those who listen, are sincere, fear God". (2:26, 258, 264; 3:86; 5:16, 51, 67, 108; 6:88, 144; 9:19, 21, 37, 80, 109; 12:52; 13:27; 16:37, 107; 28:50; 39:3; 40:28; 42:13; 46:10; 61:5: "when they went crooked, God bent their hearts crooked" (61:7; 62:5; 63:6). This means that man does something to deserve guidance or misguidance. Nature and God are not two different factors; God is more of a dimension or meaning than an item among items. Similarly, with regard to man's actions and his destiny vis-à-vis God, God and man are not rivals therein—as the later Mu'tazilite and Ash'arite theologians thought, so that the former made man the sole agent and denied God's role totally in order to make men "completely responsible," while the latter denied any power to man in order to safeguard the "omnipotence of God." The Qur'ān is true to the realities of moral life, for it affirms both sides of the tension, as will become more clear in the next chapter.

If this kind of analysis shows anything, it is that the Qur'ān must be so studied that its concrete unity will emerge in its fullness, and that to select certain verses from the Qur'ān to project a partial and subjective point of view may satisfy the subjective observer but it necessarily does violence to the Qur'ān itself and results in extremely dangerous abstractions. It is notorious how frequently Muslims themselves, let alone Westerners, have mutilated the Qur'ān by projecting their own points of view or that of their "schools" of thought; except that with so many Westerners both unconscious prejudice and deliberate distortion have played roles, as well as the study of verses of the Qur'ān in abstract isolation. The Qur'ān, as the Word of God, is as concrete as the Command or the Law of God—indeed, as God Himself—and represents the depth and breadth of life itself; it will refuse to be straight-jacketed by intellectual and cultural bias.

Yet, we must keep clear of pantheism and relativism, the most attractive and powerful of all spiritual drugs. When we say that God is not an item among items, we certainly do not mean to suggest that God *is* everything or is *in* everything, even though His presence is all-pervasive. When we say that God is concrete and that He cannot be narrowed by interpretations or approaches that are intellectual and cultural abstractions, we certainly do not imply that if all these approaches are mechanically combined, the aggregate could represent the truth. On the point that God is not in things and that creation is other than God, the whole of the Qur'ān upholds this, but verses like "if We wished to take a sport, We could have done it by Ourselves" (21:17) make it absolutely clear that the creation is not some kind of an intra-God drama, although it is witnessed by God as His creation and it witnesses God as its Creator.

As for the point that all paths actually taken by man do not, put together, represent the truth about God, this is evidenced by 16:9: "the only straight path goes to God, while others are deviant." This path is the full recognition of God as God, the path that is of sole interest and importance to man. All others are sectarian and divisive of mankind:

> Those people who have cut up their religion into sects, you have nothing to do with them [O Muhammad!]: their affair is up to God and He shall let them know what they have been doing. He who does one good thing, shall get back ten times of it in reward, while he who does one wrong, will not be requited except equal to it--and they shall not be wronged. Say [O Muhammad!]: My Lord has guided me to the straight path--an upright faith, the religion of Abraham the *Hanif* [one who recognized the unity of religion rather than followed sects]—and he was not one who assigned partners to God. Say: My prayer and my piety, my life and my death are for God, the Lord of the World. There is no partner with Him. This is what I have been commanded and I am the first of those who surrender to God [I am the first of the *muslims*] (6:160-64).

Chapter Two

Man as Individual

Man is God's creature just like any other created being. He is, indeed, a natural creation, for God fashioned Adam out of baked clay (15:26, 28, 33; 6:2; 7:12, etc.), which, when organized into a human being, produces an extract, *sulāla* (reproductive semen). When injected into the womb, this semen undergoes a creative process, described in 23:12-14 (cf. also 32:8, and elsewhere). But man is distinguished from the rest of natural creation by the fact that after fashioning him, God "breathed My own spirit" into him (15:29; 38:72; 32:9, cf. also Chapter V). The Qur'ān does not appear to endorse the kind of doctrine of a radical mind-body dualism found in Greek philosophy, Christianity, or Hinduism; indeed, there is hardly a passage in the Qur'ān that says that man is composed of two separate, let alone disparate, substances, the body and the soul (even though later orthodox Islam, particularly after al-Ghazālī and largely through his influence, came to accept it). The term *nafs*, frequently employed by the Qur'ān and often translated as "soul," simply means "person" or "self," and such phrases as *al-nafs al-muṭma'inna* and *al-nafs al-lawwāma* (usually translated as "the satisfied soul" and "the blaming soul") are best understood as states, aspects, dispositions, or tendencies of the human personality. These may well be regarded as "mental" (as distinguished from "physical") in nature, provided the "mind" is not construed as a separate substance.

When God intended to create Adam in order to establish "a vicegerent on earth," angels protested, saying, "Will You put there a being who will work mischief on the earth and shed blood, while we sing Your glories and exalt Your utter holiness?" God did not deny these allegations against man but replied, "I know what you do not know." He then brought about a competition in knowledge between angels and Adam, asking the former to "name things" (to describe their natures). When the angels could not do so, Adam could (2:30 ff.). This demonstrated that Adam possessed the capacity for creative knowledge that angels lacked, whereupon God asked all angels to prostrate themselves before him to honor him. All angels so acknowledged Adam's superiority in knowledge except one being whom the Qur'ān describes as one of the jinn (18:50), who asserted his own superiority over Adam, disobeyed God's command to honor him, and became Satan. Satan therefore starts his career together with Adam; they are coevals, and the Qur'ān constantly speaks of Satan not so much as an anti-God principle (although he is undoubtedly a rebel against God, and, indeed, personifies this rebellious nature) but rather as an anti-man force, perpetually trying to seduce man away from his natural "straight" path into deviant behaviour (see Chapter VII).

It is this deep-seated moral fact that constitutes the eternal challenge for man and renders his life an unceasing moral struggle. In this struggle, God is with man, *provided man makes the necessary effort*. Man is squarely charged with this effort because he is unique in the order of creation, having been endowed with free choice in order to fulfill his mission as God's vicegerent. It is this mission—the attempt to create a moral social order on earth—which the Qur'ān (33:72) describes as the "Trust." God had offered the Trust to the heavens and the earth but they refused to accept it, being frightened of the burden involved; it was accepted by man, whom the Qur'an tenderly rebukes as "unfair to himself and foolhardy [*ẓalūm* and *jahūl*]"—for man "has certainly not yet fulfilled God's [primordial] command" (80:23).

We shall presently essay the Qur'ān's analysis of the basic human weakness and its remedy but here it may be noted that although Satan "waylays man from all sides," his machinations fail against really virtuous persons. To be sure, no man is immune from the devil's temptations—not even the prophets (22:52; 17:53), nor yet the Prophet Muhammad himself (7:200; 41:36)—yet it is within the reach of any true man of faith and will, let alone the prophets, to overcome them (15:42; 17:65; 16:99). The reason is that such men, amidst all temptations, keep intact their "primordial nature [*fiṭra*] upon which God created man," which "cannot be [logically] altered [although it may be more or less temporarily disturbed]" (30:30). Indeed it is these men who are the cream of all creation, outstripping even the angels, whom they excel in both knowledge and virtue.

It is these men who fully realize that man "has not been created in sport" but has a serious task (23:115) and is answerable for his success or failure, for both God and man have taken a grave risk in this vital affair, the vicegerency of man. The bane of humanity so far is that most men refuse to "look beyond [al-'āqibā]," "do not lay any store by for the morrow," i.e., do not contribute to—and do not even understand or attempt to understand—the long-range moral goals of the human endeavour. They are content to live their lives from day to day, indeed, from hour to hour: "they are like cattle, indeed, worse" (7:179); "they have hearts but cannot understand, they have eyes but cannot see, they have ears but cannot hear" (7:179, and elsewhere). Their primordial nature has been distorted almost beyond recognition; they became "Satan's brothers" (17:27) after God had breathed His own spirit into Adam (15:29; 32:9; 38:72; cf. 95:4-6). "We created man with the best constitution, but then We sent him down to the lowest state of the low, except those who believe and do good works" (95:5). The Qur'ān does not hold to original sin as such but states that Adam and Eve were forgiven their sin after he had received his Lord's Words (2:37).

From here arise a whole series of Qur'ānic verses that speak of "God's sealing up the hearts of men, putting blinds on their eyes, casting chains up to their chins, so that they cannot look down and ponder." The Qur'ān does not hold that God *arbitrarily* seals people's hearts, but usually says that God does so because of the actions of men themselves ("because of their initial infidelity" [6:110; 2:88]; "because of their transgression" [2:59; 6:49], and similar phrases abound in the Qur'ān). Indeed, "We turn man whichever way he wants in turn" (4:115), and, "God does not change the situation of a people until they change it themselves" (13:11; 8:53), i.e., unless men take the initiative. The Qur'ān states repeatedly that every man and woman individually and every people collectively are alone responsible for what they do—a doctrine that underlies the Qur'ānic rejection of redemption. In 29:12 we are told that rich and strong Meccan pagans asked the followers of Muḥammad "to follow our way and [if necessary] we shall bear the burden of your sins," and the Qur'ān adds the former will never bear the latter's burden—although they shall bear manifold burdens of their own!

The idea behind verses about the sealing of hearts appears to be the psychological law that if a person once does a good or an evil deed, his chances of repeating that kind of action increase and of doing its opposite proportionately decrease. With constant repetition of an evil or of a good action, it becomes almost impossible for a person to do the opposite, or even to think of it, so much so that while men's hearts become "sealed" and their eyes "blinded" if they do evil, their doing good produces such a state of mind that the devil himself can have no sway over it. Nevertheless, actions which create a psychological habit, however strong their influence may be, must not be construed as absolute determinants, for there is no "point of no return" for human behavior: genuine repentance (*tauba*) can turn an apparently wholly evil man into a paragon of virtue; on the other hand, although this is much more rare, an apparent paragon of virtue (even a prophet!) can turn into a near devil enmeshed in carnal pleasures:

> Recite to them [O Muhammad!] the news of him whom We had given our signs, but he abandoned them and the devil pursued him so that he became one of the deviants; if We had willed, We would have exalted him through those signs, but he gravitated down to the earth and followed his own desires. (7:175-76)

To hold that the Qur'ān believes in an absolute determinism of human behavior, denying free choice on man's part, is not only to deny almost the entire content of the Qur'ān, but to undercut its very basis: the Qur'ān by its own claim is an invitation to man to come to the right path (*hudan li'l-nās*).

This picture is quite complex, however, and needs to be clarified. The Qur'ān, it is true, often speaks as though man consciously chooses for himself right or wrong ways and follows them, and God only passes judgment upon his actions (e.g., 53:39-40; 76:3; 90:10 ff.; 91:7-10). But the Qur'ān states even more often that when man takes a direction, God entrenches him in it: "So, for him who gives [of his wealth], guards against evil, and confirms goodness, We make good easy for him, but for him who is niggardly, thinks he is self-sufficient, and gives the lie to goodness, We make evil easy for him" (92:5-10)—and for this we have above provided a psychological explanation.

But how or why does a human take a certain road? How does he attune himself to God or turn away from Him? It appears that man does not require much effort to be petty, self-seeking, submerged in his day-to-day life, and a slave of his desires, not because this is "natural" to him—for his real nature is to be exalted—but because "gravitating down to the earth," as we have quoted the Qur'ânic language, is much easier than ascending to the heights of purity. Therefore, God's role, His succor, and His support in the latter case are very crucial: no man can say "I am going to be a good person" and automatically become one. He has to struggle, and in this struggle God is his willing partner. Yet, God may not be taken for granted as though His partnership were automatic; this has to do with both the quality and the quantity of the struggle and it can be described almost literally as God's mercy. In Muhammad's own case, the Qur'ân makes it clear (28:86)—despite his travail in the cave of Hirā'—that "You were not expecting that The Book will be sent down upon you; except that it is a mercy from your Lord" and sometimes even threatens him with the possible cessation of Revelation (17:86): "If We willed, We would take away the Revelation from you and in that case you shall not find any support against Us, but it is a mercy from your Lord" (for a fuller elaboration, see Chapter V). When man "gravitates down to the earth," his conscience becomes dull and he cannot effectively listen to the voice of his true, higher nature "[as though] these people are being called from a distant place" (41:44). Further, a man not only cannot listen, but is irritated by being constantly reminded of the truth; this irritation, when accompanied by false honor and pride—personal, family, national, and historical—changes into positive resistance and rejection of truth—what the Qur'ân terms *kufr*, practically equating it with this special kind of pride. Just as ascending to virtue means God's active cooperation and help, *kufr* means positive desertion by God.

It is in this context that the Qur'ân throws God's indispensability for man into bold relief. Just as God's "remembrance" and presence means the meaningfulness and purposefulness of life, the removal of God from human consciousness means the removal of meaning and purpose from human life: "Do not be like those who forgot God and [eventually] He caused them to forget themselves—these are the unrighteous ones" (59:19). This is as true of the collective life of peoples (as we shall see in the next chapter) as it is of individual life. God's "remembrance" ensures the cementing of personality where all details of life and particulars of human activity are properly integrated and synthesized; "forgetting" God, on the other hand, means fragmented existence, "secularized" life, an unintegrated and eventually disintegrated personality, and enmeshment in the details at the cost of the whole. This is precisely Muhammad Iqbāl's distinction between Godliness and un-Godliness.

> The sign of a *kāfir* is that he is lost in the horizons;
> The sign of a *mu'min* is that the horizons are lost in him.

Further in connection with the role of God vis-à-vis man in the Qur'ān, it should be borne in mind (and we shall expand upon this in Chapter IV) that the Qur'ān speaks of identical phenomena as being caused by God and by nature; these are not two different or duplicate or disparate causalities but are the same. Yet the meaning is different. When the Qur'ān employs the language of nature, it is giving an account; in using the religious idiom in terms of God's causation—which is far more frequent—it is giving the rationale or the meaning of an event. Thus, rains are caused by clouds and winds but they are brought on by God in order to sustain the earth.

Everything caused by natural processes is done by God. Thus, when Muhammad was asked (as happened frequently) why God had chosen *him* rather than "another big person in the two cities," the answer is sometimes, "Do these people apportion the mercy of your Lord?" (43:32); at other times, "God knows best where to place His messengership" (6:124), i.e., God does not appoint or elect people arbitrarily as His prophets. Here is a typical example of natural political processes being represented as God's will (we shall give further examples of this, including the case in reverse, in the next chapter):

> When We wish to destroy a city [or a civilization—the term *qarya* in this context can mean a town like the prophet Shu'aib's or a civilization like the Pharaoh's] *We command* its wealthy ones so they indulge in unrighteousness, and when it is ripe for harvesting [literally: "when the judgment upon it has matured," but the Qur'ān—11:100 and elsewhere—actually uses the metaphor of "harvesting a people"], We destroy it. (17:16)

Last, but not least in significance, it must be constantly remembered that the Qur'ān is not just descriptive but is primarily prescriptive. Both the content of its message and the power of the form in which it is conveyed are designed not so much to "inform" men in any ordinary sense of the word as to change their character. The psychological impact and the moral import of its statements, therefore, have a primary role. Phrases like "God has sealed their hearts, blinded their eyes, deafened them to truth" in the Qur'ān do have a *descriptive* meaning in terms of the psychological processes described earlier; but even more primarily in such contexts, they have a definite psychological *intention*: to change the ways of men in the right direction. Thus, all our clarifications and interpretations of such usages in the Qur'ān—psychological (in the sense of both a process and an intended effect), factual, and moral—operate jointly and must be properly understood and assigned proportionate roles.

There is no doubt that in the later Medieval period, a strong pre-determinism was widespread in Muslim societies (although many Western accounts of it are confused about both its nature and consequently its strength); but this was due not to the Qur'ānic teaching but to a host of other factors. Prominent among these were the overwhelming success of the Ash'arite school of theology (which reduced man to impotence in the interests of saving the omnipotence of God, but whose influence upon Muslims was more formal than real), the broad spread (particularly after the sixteenth century) of doctrines of pantheistic Sufism, and, above all, strong fatalistic doctrines in the world-views of certain highly sophisticated peoples, particularly the Iranians. Under the impact of these influences, the Qur'ānic idea of *qadar* (or *taqdīr*) was interpreted as divine predetermination of everything, including human actions.

That this is a grossly simplistic misrepresentation (which in turn, influenced many Western views of Islam) of the Qur'ānic doctrine of *qadar* is obvious. The term *qadar* actually means "to measure out" and the idea is that while God alone is absolutely infinite, everything else bears the creaturely hallmark of "being measured," i.e., having a finite sum of potentialities—even though the range of these potentialities may be very great, as in the case of man. The Qur'ān is not speaking of the actualization of potentialities but of potentialities per se. According to the Qur'ān, when God creates a thing (*khalq*), He at the same time puts into it its nature, its potentialities, and the laws of its behavior (*amr*, "command," or *hidaya*, "guidance") whereby it falls into a pattern and becomes a factor in the "cosmos."

Since everything in the universe does behave in accordance with its ingrained laws—automatically obeys the "command" of God—the whole universe is therefore *muslim*, surrendering to the Will of God. Man is the only exception to this universal law, for he is the only being endowed with a free choice of obeying or disobeying the Command of God. Just as it is "written into" every other creature, this Command is written upon man's heart:

> [I swear] by man's personality and that whereby it has been formed, God has engraved into it its evil and its good [whereby it can guard itself against moral peril]. He who makes his personality pure, shall be successful, while he who corrupts it shall be in the loss. (91:7-10)

The only difference is that while every other creature follows its nature automatically, man *ought* to follow his nature; this transformation of the *is* into *ought* is both the unique privilege and the unique risk of man. This is why it is so important for man to hearken and hearken well to his nature, despite the intrigues of Satan.

This is also the meaning of the "primordial covenant" that God elicited from all men:

> And when your Lord extracted from the children of Adam—from their spinal cord—their entire progeny and made them witness upon themselves, saying, Am I not your Lord? and they replied, No doubt, You are, we bear witness, [The Lord did this] lest you say on the Day of Judgment, We were quite unaware of this, or lest you should say [by way of excuse for your sins], All that happened was that our forefathers had committed *shirk* [worship of false gods] before us and we as the generations following upon them [were already conditioned by them]—are You, then, going to make us suffer for what those [earlier] falsifiers of truth had done? (7:172-73)

The point is that every person and every people have continuously to search their own consciences, and, because of this engraving upon their heart, which represents the Primordial Covenant, none may take refuge in the excuse that they had been preconditioned by their "hereditary memory," by the set ways of "our forefathers." The primary task of the prophets is to awaken man's conscience so that he can decipher the primordial writing on his heart more clearly and with greater conviction. The Qur'ān, therefore, says with perfect logic that God took a specially strong covenant from prophets: "And when God took the covenant from the prophets—from you [O Muḥammad!], from

Noah, Abraham, Moses and Jesus—We took from them a specially solemn covenant" (33:7).

Since man's real nature is thus "inlaid" in him and is then further strengthened and clarified by God's Messengers, the prophets, no valid excuse can be entertained on his behalf for not *aspiring* to goodness and for "gravitating down to the earth," as the Qur'ān has already idiomatically expressed it. For this reason, a very fundamental feature of the Qur'ān is to reiterate untiringly that all human acts which are apparently perpetrated on another person in a more ultimate sense recoil upon the agent himself. All evil, all injustice, all harm that one does to someone else—in sum, all deviation from man's normative nature—in a much more fundamental way and in a far more ultimate sense one does to oneself, and not just metaphorically but literally. This is true equally of individuals and of peoples. "Self-injustice" (*zulm al-nafs*—all Arab philologists assure us that *zulm* in Arabic originally meant "to put something out of its proper place," so that all wrong of any kind is injustice, i.e., an injustice against the agent himself) is, therefore, a very common term in the Qur'ān, with its clear idea that all injustice is basically reflexive. After recounting all the waywardness and wrongdoings of bygone generations as well as of individuals, the Qur'ān usually says, "We did them no injustice [in destroying them], on the contrary, they did injustice to themselves" (2:231; 65:1; 27:44; 28:16; 2:54; 7:23; 2:57; 3:117; 7:160, 177; etc.).

The basic weakness of man from which all of his major ills spring is described by the Qur'ān as "pettiness [*da'f*]" and "narrowness of mind [*qatr*]," and the Qur'ān ceaselessly reiterates this in various forms and different contexts. Both the pride of man—his identifying himself with the Higher Law—and his hopelessness and despair arise out of this pettiness. His self-destructive selfishness and the greed to which he is a constant prey, his hasty, panicky behavior, his lack of self-reliance, and the fears that perpetually haunt him arise ultimately from the smallness of his mind:

> Man is by nature unstable; when misfortune touches him he panics and when good things come his way, he prevents them from reaching others. (70:19-21)
> Men's personalities have been permeated with greed [or selfishness]. (4:128)
> The successful are those who can be saved from their own selfishness. (59:9; 64:16)

> Say [O Muhammad! to these pagans]: If you were to possess the entire
> treasures of my Lord's mercy and munificence, you would still sit over
> them out of fear of spending [on others] and man is, indeed,
> niggardly! (17:100)

It is because of this pettiness that man is so hasty and panicky and
oblivious of the long-term consequences of his reactions: "Man has
been created out of hastiness" (21:37); "When man prays for goodness, he at once accompanies it with a prayer for evil—and man is
hasty indeed!" (17:11); "Nay, but you covet what is immediate and
abandon what is distant in time to come" (75:20). "Prepare and send
forth something for the morrow" is a constant Qur'ānic reminder
(2:110; 73:20; 2:223; 59:18, etc.).

It is because of this haste that man becomes so full of pride and so
utterly despairing; there is no other being who is so quickly inflated
and deflated as man. The Qur'ān reiterates that when man has been
endowed with blessings, he soon "forgets" God; when natural causes
work for him, in his feelings of smugness and self-sufficiency, he does
not "see" God in these natural causes; but when he falls on evil times,
then either he becomes completely devoid of hope or else he turns to
God only in that hour. He remembers God only in distress, and even in
distress he may not "remember" God and "call upon Him" but may
simply sink into despair:

> When We make man taste mercy from Us and then pull it away from
> him, lo! he despairs utterly and denies [God's blessings] altogether.
> But when he tastes of good things from Us after he had been touched
> by evil, he will certainly say that all evil had gone from him [and he
> had become purged]: he is, indeed, all too easily puffed up with
> pride—except those who are steadfast and do good deeds. (11:9-10)
> Man never tires of praying for goodness to come to him, but should
> evil so much as touch him, he is in total and dire despair. But when
> We make him taste Our mercy after evil has touched him, he will
> certainly say, Well, I deserved it! . . . And when We shower Our
> blessings upon man, he simply becomes indifferent and turns away,
> but when evil touches him, he brings forth lengthy petitions [for
> mercy]. (41:49-51; also see 17:83; 10:12, etc.)

This unstable character of man, this going from one extreme to the
other, arising as it does out of his narrow vision and petty mind, reveals certain basic moral tensions within which human conduct must

function if it is to be stable and fruitful. These contradictory extremes are, therefore, not so much a "problem" to be resolved by theological thought as tensions to be "lived with" if man is to be truly "religious," i.e., a servant of God. Thus, utter powerlessness and "being the measure for all things," hopelessness and pride, determinism and "freedom," absolute knowledge and pure ignorance—in sum, an utterly "negative self-feeling" and a "feeling of omnipotence"—are extremes that constitute natural tensions for proper human conduct. It is the "God-given" framework for human action. Since its primary aim is to maximize moral energy, the Qur'ān—which claims to be "guidance for mankind"—regards it as absolutely essential that man not violate the balance of opposing tensions. The most interesting and the most important fact of moral life is that violating this balance in any direction produces a "Satanic condition" which in its moral effects is exactly the same: moral nihilism. Whether one is proud or hopeless, self-righteous or self-negating, in either case the result is deformity and eventual destruction of the moral human personality.

The model for this is Satan himself: When he refused to obey God's command to honor Adam, he was full of pride, thinking he was far superior to Adam, and he even took God for granted. When he fell, he lost all hope and in total desperation asked God to give him respite till the Last Day, so that he could seduce and beguile Adam's progeny (7:11 ff.; 15:29 ff., etc.); he became a professional evilmonger because he thought his personality could not be recovered.

The Qur'ān, therefore, condemns not only pride and self-righteousness but equally hopelessness and utter despair, which it describes as the hallmark of "unbelievers," those who reject truth: "Do not despair of God's mercy for none despair of God's mercy except unbelievers" (12:87; also 29:23; 15:56; 39:53 and the verses quoted on p. 26, concerning man's loss of hope). Both pride and hopelessness are equally "*kufr*" or unbelief, which is another name for the total loss of moral energy.

Idol-worship is the sure consequence of this condition, for, having lost the transcendental anchoring point of human conduct, one must either "worship one's own [subjective] desires" (25:43; 7:176; 18:28; 28:50; etc.), or if one objectifies one's desires, worships "socialized desires" —self-projections of one's society: "And he [Abraham] said [to his people], You have adopted these idols besides God only as a way to socialize your mutual desires in this world [*mawaddata-bainikum fī'l-ḥayāt al-dunyā*]; but on the Last Day you will disown each other and curse each other" (29:25). When man's moral vision is narrowed and the transcendental dimension is gone, then, from the universally objective moral point of view, it is immaterial whether one worships oneself as God or one's society or nation as God (*pace* Emile Durkheim!). All particularizing of Truth, whether individually subjective or socially (by nation or sect) subjective, numbs moral faculties, and numbs them equally. It is a large price to pay for one's smallness.

We said earlier that to "forget God" is to destroy one's personality, whether individual or social, for only "remembrance of God" can cement personality. We have now found that violating the balance of the tensions of human conduct destroys personality. The "remembrance of God," then, is to work within the framework of these tensions, since all wrong involves a violation of the balance of these tensions, what the Qur'ān also describes as the "transgression of God's limits" (2:187, 229, 230; 4:13; 9:112; 58:4; 65:1).

The "middle road" is not only the best road, it is the only road. Many people think that to be "in the middle" is to be "humdrum" and "banal," and to be "in the mean" is to be really "mean" and "unoriginal" and "un-grand." This is true if the "middle" or the "mean" is construed as something from which both sides are absent, as a negative mean, dry bones from which all flesh is gone. But this is not the mean of the Qur'an; what it has in mind is a positive, creative mean, an integrative moral organism. This is why it is not quasi-automatic but can be achieved only by all the alertness and power one can muster. It is that moment of balance where both sides are fully present, not absent, integrated, not negated.

This unique balance of integrative moral action is what the Qur'ān terms *taqwā*, perhaps the most important single term in the Qur'ān. At its highest, it denotes the fully integrated and whole personality of man, the kind of "stability" which is formed after all the positive elements are drawn in. The term is usually translated by the words "fear of God" and "piety." Though these are not wrong, Muslims are increasingly discarding the term "fear of God" because they think the phrase misleading in view of the false picture, widely prevalent in the West until recently—and present even today—of the God of Islam as a capricious dictator or a tyrant, in the light of which "fear of God" might be indistinguishable from, say, fear of a wolf. The root of the term, *wqy*, really means "to guard or protect against something" and it has also been used in this literal sense in the Qur'ān (e.g., 52:27; 40:9; 40:45; 76:11).

Hence *taqwā* means to protect oneself against the harmful or evil consequences of one's conduct. If, then, by "fear of God" one means fear of the consequences of one's actions—whether in this world or the next (fear of punishment of the Last Day)—one is absolutely right. In other words, it is the fear that comes from an acute sense of responsibility, here and in the hereafter, and not the fear of a wolf or of an uncanny tyrant, for the God of the Qur'ān has unbounded mercy—although He also wields dire punishment, both in this world and in the hereafter.

Considering all the verses in the Qur'ān related to this concept, perhaps the best way to define *taqwā* is to say that, whereas action belongs to man, real and effective judgment upon that action, as well as the standard whereby that action is to be judged, lie outside of him. Similarly, in the case of the collective performance of a society, both the final criterion of judgment upon it and the judgment itself transcend that society. When a man or a society is fully conscious of this while conducting himself or itself, he or it has true *taqwā*. This idea can be effectively conveyed by the term "conscience," if the object of conscience transcends it. This is why it is proper to say that "conscience" is truly as central to Islam as love is to Christianity when one speaks of the human response to the ultimate reality—which, therefore, is conceived in Islam as merciful justice rather than fatherhood.

Taqwā, then, in the context of our argument, means to be squarely anchored within the moral tensions, the "limits of God," and not to "transgress" or violate the balance of those tensions or limits. Human conduct then becomes endowed with that quality which renders it "service to God [*'ibāda*]." Such conduct, as the Qur'ān tells us (6:160), multiplies tenfold (or "manifold," as 4:40 has it), while evil draws its equivalent consequence—if, that is, it is not "forgiven," i.e., if its effects are not obliterated. For, according to the Qur'ān, that which is good remains for the benefit of mankind but that which is false has a transient existence only, even though it looks present: "[When] God sends down water from the heaven, valleys flow with it according to their measures, but the torrent also carries mounting foam on its top; again, the precious metals upon which they [the jewellers] blow fire, seeking to fashion therefrom jewelry or other precious things, generate foam likewise—even so does God cause truth and falsehood to go together in mutual competition. As for the foam, it vanishes quickly, but as for that which is beneficial to mankind, it stays in the earth; even so does God strike parables" (13:16).

On the whole, despite the sad accounts of the human record in the Qur'ān, its attitude is quite optimistic with regard to the sequel of human endeavor. It also advocates a healthy moral sense rather than the attitude of self-torment and moral frenzy represented, for example, by the teachings of Paul and many Sufis, which require some sort of *savior ex machina*. Given a merciful and just God and the solidarity of character called *taqwā*, human well-being is provided for: "If you avoid the major evils that have been prohibited to you, We shall obliterate [the effects of] occasional and smaller lapses" (4:31); "And those [are believers] who avoid major evils and obscenities and when they are under the influence of anger, they exercise forgiveness" (42:37); "Those who avoid major evils and obscenities—except [occasionally] coming to their brink" (53:32); "A work that is really good earns its reward ten times over, while an evil deed draws out an equivalent response" (6:160).

Several other verses also indicate that God will pardon or overlook men's lapses, provided the overall performance is good and beneficial (see 39:34-36—which adds, "Is God not sufficient for man" that he seeks other sources of intercession?). What is essential is that the overall attitude be governed by *taqwā*, which will prevent men from transgression, and should they transgress, will lead them soon to repent and redress the imbalance in their personalities: after talking about the unforgivable abomination wrought by hardened "hypocrites," the Qur'ān goes on, "And there are others who have confessed to their wrongdoing; they have mixed good deeds with bad ones [in following the 'hypocrites']; it may be that God will return to them, for God is forgiving and merciful" (9:102). The door of repentance is ever open, except to those who are bent on doing wrong till the very end, when they think they will repent and ask forgiveness. It is strikingly illustrative of the action orientation and practicality of the Qur'ān that it insists that "last minute" declarations of faith and pleas for forgiveness are absolutely rejected. In the story of Moses, the Pharaoh on the point of death asks God's forgiveness, but his appeal is severely rejected (10:90-91); also God is apt to accept repentance only from those who commit evil inadvertently and repent promptly. Repentance cannot be accepted from those who continuously perpetrate evil, even if when death overtakes one of them, he says, "I now repent of sins to God" (4:17-18; also 10:54).

We have already said that the Qur'ān rejects "saviorship." As a corollary, it equally rejects intercession. Although the Hadīth literature is loaded with references to intercession of the prophets on behalf of the sinful of their communities, particularly the Prophet Muhammad's intercession on behalf of his community (and in popular Islam, "saints" will do so much effective intercession that they even surpass the prophets), the Qur'ān seems to have nothing to do with it. On the contrary, it constantly speaks of how God will on the Day of Judgment bring every prophet as a *witness* over the deeds of his community, a witness whereby the people will be judged: "What about when We bring a witness from every community and We bring you [O Muhammad!] to bear witness upon these people?" (4:41; cf. 28:75).

The whole temper of the Qur'ān is against intercession, for, to begin with, "God does not require from any person what is beyond his [or her] power" (2:233, 286; 6:152; 7:42; 23:62); secondly, as we have repeatedly underlined, God's "mercy comprehends everything" (7:156; 40:7). According to the orthodox Muslim belief, as it crystallized in the second and third centuries of Islam (the eighth and ninth centuries of the Christian era), intercession is not possible with regard to infidels or non-Muslims in general (on the fate of Jews and Christians some Muslim theologians like Ibn Taimīya have advocated a non-committal attitude), but it will be effective on behalf of sinful Muslims. This belief was originally opposed by the Mu'tazila (who subsequently, however, fell in line with the orthodox view on the point—so strong is the psychological factor involved in the ideas of intercession and redemption) yet here is a clear-cut verse of the Qur'an negating, beyond doubt, any intercession even on behalf of Muslims: "O you who believe! spend [for the welfare of the poor] from what We have provided you before the arrival of a Day on which neither trade shall benefit, nor any friendship, nor any intercession" (2:254; cf. also 2:48, 123; 6:51,70; 39:44, 23).

However, the Qur'ān also says that no one shall intercede with God "*except whom He permits*" (2:255; 10:3; 20:109; 34:23; 53:26) and it is to these words that the orthodoxy attached the idea that intercession is permissible *on the assumption that God would permit Muhammad* to intercede on his community's behalf. But as Ibn Taimīya has pointed out, the clause about permission in this context cannot be taken literally; it is simply a rhetorical device meant to portray the majesty of God, before Whom all are helpless except by His mercy: "Picture the Day when the [Holy] Spirit and the angels shall stand [before God] in rows—none shall be able *to speak* except he whom the Merciful permits and who speaks the truth" (78:38). Not only is intercession with permission an unintelligible concept, but, as verse 78:38 shows, if the Qur'ānic words are to be taken literally, nobody will even be able to speak, let alone intercede, without God's permission. The Qur'ān is portraying a sense of the overwhelming majesty of God through such rhetorical phrases (cf. also 78:37: "The Lord of the heaven and the earth and whatever is between them, the Merciful Whom none shall be able to address").

But let us now return to the question of the "accounting" of actions and "balancing" of deeds which will take place in assessing the total performance of an individual or a society, an "accounting [*hisāb*]" upon which will depend the fate to be meted out to humans. It is correct that the concept of "accounting" and "balancing" so vividly portrayed in numerous Qur'ānic passages has as its sociohistorical background the commercial life of Mecca; but this interesting fact is trivial in religious terms. There what matters is the *quality* of an act, what the Qur'ān calls its "weight." A man may be able to realize an ambitious personal good but its beneficial effects may be limited to him alone, not enhancing the fate of others or even affecting their fate adversely. If the effect on others is adverse, then his action, being totally alienated from God, is an act of *kufr*, of rejection of truth; if it affects well only him, it is still an act of *khusrān*, of loss. A person may perform a heroic deed for "his own people" but in contradiction to the principles of justice and in "transgression of the limits of God"; such an action would also emanate from the state of mind the Qur'ān terms *kufr* for it counteracts the purposes of God for man, and the true purposes of man himself.

God did not create either man or the universe "in sport [*'abath*]" (23:115); also: "We have not created the heaven and the earth and what is between them purposelessly [*bātilan*, 38:27; cf. also 3:191] but with a serious purpose." That purpose is the "service of God," i.e., the implementation of the divine imperative for man, for this "service" is for man's own benefit, not for God's: "Whatever good a person earns is for his own benefit and whatever evil he earns is only against himself" (2:286; cf. 4:111; 2:79, and various other entries in the Qur'ānic index under ᶜamal and its derivatives, and kasb and its derivatives; cf. also the discussion of "self-injustice," above, pp. 25-28).

Nor can man be left alone, therefore (75:36), but he must be constantly invited to goodness; for when "left alone" with his own subjective desires, he is apt to misjudge the quality and validity of his own performance:

> Say: Shall We inform you of those who are the greatest losers in [consequence of] their actions, while *they* think they have made wonderful achievements? These are the ones who rejected their Lord's signs and denied that they would face Him [with their answerability]—thus will their deeds have come to nothing and We shall not consider them of any weight on the Day of Judgment. (18:103-5)
>
> When it is said to them: Do not corrupt the earth [with your negative deeds], they say: We are only doing reform! Beware! They are the corruptors but they do not know that. (2:11-12)

Special victims of self-deception are human institutions, organizations, and more particularly religious communities; the Qur'ān says, addressing Muslims, "This is not a matter of your subjective desires or wishful thinking, nor that of the People of the Book, for whosoever perpetrates evil must get its requital and he has no friend or helper besides God" (4:123).

Given the depth of human self-deception, how important it is that man be "awakened" to his real nature, to be responsible before God, to think thoughts and do deeds that would be consequential, for upon this depends the whole destiny of man and of God's purposes for man. The layers of "heedlessness are indeed thick and manifold and it is all-important that "man make his sight keen," before it is too late (50:22). In this context, the warnings of the Qur'ān assume the most severe and threatening tone:

> We have created many of the jinn and humans for hell: they have minds but they do not understand therewith; they have eyes but they do not see therewith; they have ears but they do not listen therewith. These are like cattle, indeed even more difficult to guide—for these are the heedless ones. (7:179)

"Empirical" knowledge itself is of little benefit unless it awakens the inner perception of man as to his own situation, his potentialities, his risks, and his destiny:

> Have they not travelled around the earth, so that they might come to possess hearts whereby they can understand or ears wherewith they can listen? For it is not the [physical] eyes that become blind but the hearts in people's breasts [that lose perception]. (22:46)

This is why the Qur'ān appears to be interested in three types of knowledge for man. One is the knowledge of nature which has been made subservient to man, i.e., the physical sciences. The second crucial type is the knowledge of history (and geography): the Qur'ān persistently asks man to "travel on the earth" and see for himself what happened to bygone civilizations and why they rose and fell. The third is the knowledge of man himself, since "We shall show them Our signs in the horizons [external nature] and within themselves, so that Truth becomes clear to them—is your Lord not a sufficient witness over everything?" (41:53). This knowledge is "scientific" knowledge, for it is based on observation by "the eyes and the ears"; yet this scientific knowledge has finally to "strike the heart" and to kindle a perception in man which will transform his scientific and technological skills in accordance with the moral perception that will, one hopes, be born in him. Without this perception, scientific and technological knowledge could be—indeed, must be—positively dangerous, and in its critique of the materially prosperous Meccans, the Qur'ān makes this very point: "They know well the externalities of the worldly life, but they are so ignorant ['heedless'] of the ultimate consequences" (30:7).

When one talks about the comparative weightiness of human deeds, one speaks essentially of their consequences for man's destiny. We recall once again the metaphor of the "foam that mounts upon the torrent" but which quickly becomes nothing, leaving no consequences behind, while "that which benefits mankind stays in the earth." Further:

> Did you not see how God strikes the parable of a good word like a luxuriant tree whose root strikes deep into the earth and whose top hits the sky? It gives its fruit all the time by permission of its Lord—and Allāh strikes parables for men on the chance that they will take admonition. The parable of a heinous word [on the other hand] is

that of a heinous tree that has been rooted out without finding any place to stay. (14:24-26)

It is in this sense that all evil deeds, especially worship of false gods, are very often termed *dalāl* by the Qur'ān. This term is usually translated as "misguidedness," which is correct provided we clearly understand that "misguidedness" and "wrong path" signify primarily that "one will not get anywhere," no matter how long or how hard one walks—indeed, one will fall into a pit. That is to say, *dalāl* is sterile, inconsequential, *in vain*, and its equivalent term, *bāṭil*, is also used in this sense by the Qur'ān. The results of evil deeds are often portrayed in the Qur'ān by powerful and lively symbols of burning in hell-fire, whose "hissing sound" can be heard from afar by the sinful and which burns even rocks.

Some Muslim thinkers, past and present, have explained both the punishment of hell and the joys of paradise as non-physical, "spiritual" states. There is considerable support for this in the Qur'ān itself, provided the "spiritual" is not supposed to negate the physical, for there is no pleasure or pain which is purely spiritual or purely physical. Also, it is important to point out that the Qur'ān makes it clear in more than one place that torture in hell would depend upon the nature of man's awareness of the sterility of his deeds:

> Whenever a [new] community shall enter [hell-fire] it shall curse its sister [which preceded it], until when all sink into it together, the last community [in time] shall say of her predecessor: O God! these people led us astray [by their example], so give them double punishment in hell; upon which God will say, Each one of you is receiving double punishment, but you are not aware. (7:38)
>
> [God shall say to an evil-doer,] you never realized this [result of your actions], but now that We have lifted the veil, your sight today is very keen! (50:22)

Torture in hell, then, basically consists of the realization that the mountains one thought one had built have suddenly shrunk to a particle of sand and the Qur'ān frequently says that on the day of accounting all false gods will have been *"lost,"* "will come to nothing"—will simply not be there (6:24, 94; 7:53; 10:30; 11:21; 16:87; 41:48; 7:139; 11:16; 22:62; 29:67; 47:3). This establishes the equation of *bāṭil* and *ḍalāl* ("being lost" and that which is "in vain," "unreal," and "inconsequential"), and their contrast with *hadāya* and *ḥaqq* ("getting somewhere" and "the truth," that which is "real" and therefore "stays" and "does not vanish").

Chapter Three

Man in Society

There is no doubt that a central aim of the Qur'ān is to establish a viable social order on earth that will be just and ethically based. Whether ultimately it is the individual that is significant and society merely the necessary instrument for his creation or *vice versa* is academic, for individual and society appear to be correlates. There is no such thing as a societiless individual. Certainly, the concepts of human action we have discussed, particularly that of *taqwā*, are meaningful only within a social context. Even the idea of "being unjust to oneself [*zulm al-nafs*]," so that individuals and particularly societies are eventually destroyed, really means destruction of the right to exist in a social and historical context. When the Qur'ān talks about the death of individuals like Pharaoh or Korah, it is basically talking about the self-destructiveness of a way of life, of a society, of a type of civilization.

Whenever there is more than one human being, God enters directly into the relationship between them and constitutes a third dimension which can be ignored by the two humans only at their own risk:

> Do you not see that God knows everything in the heavens and the earth? There is no secret cliquing of three but that God is their fourth, nor of five but that He is their sixth, nor of less than these or more but that He is with them wherever they be. (58:7)

This verse is one of the Qur'ān's recurrent criticisms of the small but frequent conspiratorial meetings of the opponents of Islam (whether Meccan pagans or Madinan hypocrites), and while the immediate meaning is that no matter how secretly they talk, God knows what they say, the more general idea obviously is that God is present wherever two or more persons are present. God's presence is not merely cognitive, for His condition entails other consequences—most importantly, judgment upon cumulative human activity. This is the meaning of the frequent Qur'ānic reminders that God is ever wakeful, watching, witnessing, and, so far as societies are concerned, "He is sitting in a watch tower" (89:14), and "no atom in the heavens or the earth ever escapes His notice" (10:61; 34:3).

The Qur'ān's goal of an ethical, egalitarian social order is announced with a severe denunciation of the economic disequilibrium and social inequalities prevalent in contemporary commercial Meccan society. The Qur'ān began by criticizing two closely related aspects of that society: the polytheism or multiplicity of gods which was symptomatic of the segmentation of society, and the gross socioeconomic disparities that equally rested on and perpetuated a pernicious divisiveness of mankind. The two are obverse and converse of the same coin: only one God can ensure the essential unity of the human race as His creation, His subjects, and those responsible finally to Him alone. The economic disparities were most persistently criticized, because they were the most difficult to remedy and were at the heart of social discord—although tribal rivalries, with their multiple entanglements of alliance, enmity, and vengeance, were no less serious, and the welding of these tribes into a political unity was an imperative need. Certain abuses of girls, orphans, and women, and the institution of slavery demanded desperate reform.

Looking first at the economic sphere: Mecca was a prosperous commercial town, but it had a subterranean world of exploitation of the weak (the tribeless, slaves, and hirelings), and a variety of fraudulent commercial and monetary practices. The Qur'ān bears eloquent testimony to a situation characterized by selfish and callous uncharitableness and boastful conspicuous consumption on the one hand and grinding poverty and helplessness on the other:

> Competition in accumulating wealth keeps you preoccupied until you visit your graves. Nay, you shall find out soon; nay, nay, you shall find out soon. (102:1-4)
>
> Woe betide every fault-finder, back-slider, who collects wealth and counts it. He thinks his wealth will bestow eternal life upon him! Nay, he shall certainly be thrown in *huṭama* and do you know what *huṭama* is? It is God's fire that He lights and that descends upon the hearts [of callous miserly people]. (104:1-6)

The Qur'ān is certainly not against earning wealth. On the contrary, it sets a high value on wealth, which it terms "the bounty of God [*fadl Allāh*]" (62:10; 73:20; 5:2; cf. 24:22; 27:16; 30:23) and "good [*khair*]" (2:105,215,272-73; 11:84; 22:11; 38:32; 50:25; 68:12; 70:21). It counts peace and prosperity among the highest blessings of God:

> How accustomed have the Quraish [the mercantile tribe of Mecca] become to their winter journey [to Byzantium] and their summer journey [to the Indian Ocean] [so that they take them for granted]. Let them, then, serve the Lord of this House [the Ka'ba] Who has given them plenty instead of hunger, and peace instead of war. (106:1-4)

But the abuse of wealth prevents man from pursuing higher values and renders it "a pittance of this world" and a "delusion of this world" (3:14, 185, 197; 4:77; 9:38; 10:23, 70; 13:26; 16:117; 28:60; 40:39; 42:36; 43:35; 57:20). The Meccans' singleminded pursuit of wealth is said to be "the height of their knowledge" (53:30), since they knew only the "exterior of life, being heedless of its higher ends" (30:7).

In the absence of concern for the welfare of the poor, even prayers became hypocritical:

> Did you see the one who gives the lie to the Faith? It is he who maltreats orphans and works little for the feeding of the poor. Woe betide, then, those who pray, yet are neglectful of their prayers—those who pray for show and even deny the use of their utensils [to the poor]. (107:1-7)

This lack of consideration for the economically needy is the ultimate expression of pettiness and narrowness of mind—the basic weakness of man.

The Meccans contended that they had earned their wealth, which they, therefore, rightfully owned and which they could spend or dispose of as they wished. The Qur'ān insisted, first, that not all wealth earned was rightfully the earner's; the needy had also a "right" in it: "In their wealth there is a definite right of the indigent and the deprived" (70:25; also 51:19). Secondly, the Qur'ān told the Meccans that even the wealth they rightfully owned they could not spend just as they wished, for they could not become islands of plenty in a sea of poverty: "Does man think that none can put reins on his wealth when he says, 'I have thrown away stacks of money [on such-and-such]' ?" (90:6). The people of the prophet Shu'aib tell him, "Shu'aib! do your prayers order you that we should give up those [idols] which our fathers worshipped or that we should desist from doing with our wealth whatever we please?" (11:87; cf. also 2:272; 30:38,39; 76:9).

The Qur'ān exhorted Muslims "to spend in the cause of Allāh" and thus "establish credit with God, so that God may repay you manifold," rather than invest money in usury in order to suck the blood of poor people (30:39; 2:245; 5:12,18; 57:11,18; 64:17; 73:20). In a lengthy Madinan passage (2:260-74), the Qur'ān states that expenditure on the needy is like a single grain that grows seven ears of corn, each ear containing a hundred or more grains, that those who spend in order to show off or who want recognition from their beneficiaries are like rocks upon which there is a thin layer of earth which is easily washed away by a torrential rain, leaving the bare rock that grows nothing, while those who spend "seeking God's pleasure" are like the highlands which, if watered by rains, bring forth plenty but which even in the absence of rains get enough dew because of their height to grow a crop. It then states: "Satan inspires you with [fear of] poverty [for investing in society] and commands you obscenities; God, on the other hand, promises you forgiveness and prosperity [for such investment] (2:268)." Indeed, the Qur'ān holds that one major cause of the decay of societies is the neglect into which they are cast by their prosperous members:

> When God tests man and raises his position and gives him plenty, he says, My Lord has favored me; but when God tests him and puts strict reins on his means of sustenance, he says, My Lord has forsaken me! Nay [it is not so], but you do not do good to orphans nor work for the weal of the poor; you [wrongfully] devour inheritances wholesale and are excessively attached to wealth. (89:15-20)

Two important measures taken were the banning of usury and the imposition of the *zakāt* tax. The ground for the banning of usury was prepared in the Qur'ān:

> The wealth you invest in usury so that it should grow at the expense of other people's wealth, does not grow in the sight of God, but whatever wealth you spend on welfare [*zakāt*]—supporting sincerely the cause of God—it is multiplied several-fold. (30:39)

It should be noted that the repeated phrase concerning social expenditure that it "grows several-fold" has the practice of usury in view, since usurious deals increased the invested sums "many many-fold [*ad'āfan muḍā'afa*]" (3:130). It was then banned (2:275-78) with a stern warning that God and His Messenger would wage war against violators; the alleged equation between usury and "lawful commerce" was rejected; and the antithesis between usury and welfare spending was once again underlined. Creditors were asked to recover only their capital sums, but "if you forego even that it would be better for you—if you only knew."

The prohibition of usury was essential for the public welfare; the medieval lawyers of Islam, however, drew the conclusion from this that all forms of interest are banned, a stand to which even today the vast majority of Muslims still cling, despite the fundamental change in the role of modern banking in the context of a "development economy." It is some measure of the current confusion in thought that numerous educated Muslims use Keynesian or Marxist arguments to support their position.

With regard to distributive justice, the Qur'ān laid down the principle that "wealth should not circulate only among the rich" (59:7). Although these words were spoken in the context of the distribution of booty among the poor Meccan immigrants to Madina to the exclusion of more well-to-do Madinese, who consequently raised complaints, they point to a central theme in the general economic policy of the Qur'ān. Thus, after the Qur'ān denounced the Meccans for hoarding wealth and exploiting the poor classes, in Madina the *zakāt* tax was imposed. Its purposes are detailed in 9:60:

> The *zakāt* is [not for the rich but] only for the indigent and the poor, those who collect the tax, those whose hearts are to be won over [for Islam], for [ransoming] war-captives, for the relief of those who are in chronic debt, for the "cause of God" [*jihād* and social welfare purposes like education and health] and for the wayfarer [facilitating travel].

These categories of expenditure, including social welfare in a wide sense and comprising relief from chronic indebtedness, wages for the administrative service (tax-collectors), diplomatic expenditure ("for the winning of hearts"), defense, education, health, and communications, are so broad that they comprise all the activities of a state. Yet, the Muslims came to understand these functions characteristically narrowly under a hidebound tradition, and *zakāt* became, in the course of time, necessarily defunct.

At the sociopolitical level, the Qur'ān aims to strengthen the basic family unit comprising parents and children with aged grandparents, on the one hand, and the larger Muslim community, on the other, at the expense of the tribe. Filial loyalty is emphasized (2:83; 4:36; 6:151; 17:22; 29:8; 31:14; 46:15). The bond of the community is strewn over all the pages of the Qur'ān, especially in the Madinan suras. All Muslims are declared to be "brothers" (49:10). They are together as impregnable "as a building reinforced with lead" (61:4). They give priority to needy Muslims over themselves even if they themselves are in need, and "whosoever is saved from the pettiness of his own self, they are the successful ones" (59:9).

There may, of course, arise serious tensions between natural blood ties (including filial piety), on the one hand, and loyalty to truth, righteousness, or the community on the other, in which case unflagging concern for the latter is uncompromisingly demanded. The story of Abraham and his idolatrous father is told several times, of how the former forsook the latter despite his tender feelings for him, for the sake of God. Although Abraham is said (6:76; 19:42; 60:4, etc.) to pray on behalf of his father, it is also stated (9:114) that Abraham only prayed for his father "because he had promised him," hinting that if one's parents are entrenched in unrighteousness, even prayers on their behalf may not be a good thing. A stark announcement is made in 29:8: "We have certainly admonished man to be good to parents, but should they exert pressure upon you to associate others with Me [in worship] of which you have no knowledge, then do not obey them." Again, the oft-repeated story of Noah and his idolatrous son who perished in the Flood has the same import.

Similarly, on the question of doing justice and giving truthful evidence, the command is clear:

> O You who believe! establish justice, being witnesses for God—even if the evidence goes against yourselves or against your parents or kinsmen; and irrespective of whether the witness is rich or poor, under all circumstances God has priority for you [over your relatives]. (4:135)

Nor can one take an unfair attitude even towards enemies: "Let the enmity of a people [towards you] not determine you upon an unjust course; be fair, it is closer to *taqwā*" (5:8; cf. also 5:2). Finally, in *jihād* for Islam, any consideration of blood relationship is sternly warned against:

> Say [O Muhammad! to Believers]: If your fathers, your sons, your brothers, your spouses, your clans, the wealth which you have acquired, the trade whose decline you fear and your houses with which you are so pleased—if all these things are dearer to you than God, His Messenger, and struggling in His Cause, then wait till God brings down His judgment; God guides not an unrighteous people. (9:24)

The Muslim community is, then, constituted by its ideology, Islam, whose aim is to "command good and forbid evil" (3:104,110; 9:71)—which includes all specific commands and prohibitions and in fact represents the social dimensions of *taqwā*. To carry on their collective business (government), the Qur'ān asks them to institute *shūrā* (a consultative council or assembly), where the will of the people can be expressed by representation. *Shūrā* was a pre-Islamic democratic Arab institution which the Qur'ān (42:38) confirmed. The Qur'ān commanded the Prophet himself (3:159) to decide matters only after consulting the leaders of the people. But in the absence of the Prophet, the Qur'ān (42:38) seems to require some kind of collective leadership and responsibility. The Qur'ān will tolerate strongman rule only as a temporary arrangement if a people is immature, for how can a society whose people remain immature produce mature leaders? The efforts of several Muslims in the nineteenth and twentieth centuries to justify and propagate the idea of a strongman rule, therefore, run in the very teeth of the Qur'ān.

At the same time, the Qur'ān sternly prohibits dissension and cliquing, whether it is the work of groups or of political parties (this does not mean that political parties are prohibited; only cliquing), saying firmly:

> Do you not see those to whom cliquing [*najwā*] had been prohibited but they [constantly] return to what was forbidden to them, and they clique with sinful and aggressive thoughts and in order to defy the Messenger. . . . O you who believe! if you hold secret meetings, do not hold them for sin, transgression, and defiance of the Messenger. . . . Secret meetings [cliquing] are inspired by Satan so that the generality of the Believers might come to grief. (58:8-10; see also 58:7; 4:114)

Political parties, which in themselves can be salutary, must not degenerate into forces divisive of the community, but must consult with each other as well. The perils of democratic demagoguery must be avoided.

That is why, with all its concern for a liberal pluralism of institutions and basic individual freedom, the Qur'ān, under certain conditions, admits that the state, when representing society, is paramount. Rebellion is punishable by the severest penalties:

> The punishment of those who take up arms against God and His Messenger and devote themselves to [corruption], creating discord on the earth, is that they should be killed or hung on the cross or their hands and feet should be severed from the opposite sides or they should be exiled—such should be their disgrace in this life, and in the hereafter there is greater chastisement for them, except those who repent before you lay your hands upon them. (5:33-34)

When there is dissension and in-fighting between Muslim groups, the Qur'ān mandates arbitration; if one party rejects arbitration, it must be reduced by force of arms (49:9; see also 49:10). Again, a certain management or censorship of news in the public interest is called for where open propagation of news will demoralize the public:

> And when news about peace or war reaches them [the "hypocrites" of Madina], they broadcast it [in order to demoralize the people]; but if they had left it to the Messenger and to those who are in authority from among themselves, they would know how to dispose of the matter. (4:83)

As a general rule, Muslims are asked to "obey God, the Messenger, and those who are in authority from among yourselves [duly elected or appointed authority]" (4:59).

But it must not be imagined that protest or rebellion is never allowed. Indeed, according to the Qur'ān, all Messengers after Noah were rebels against the established order. The real criterion for the Qur'ān is what it constantly calls "corruption on the earth" (*fasād fi'l-ard*), which can mean any state of affairs that leads to general lawlessness—political, moral, or social—when national or international affairs are out of control. The Qur'ān comments on the situation contemporary to the Prophet, probably referring to the international situation caused by the Perso-Byzantine wars (the sura opens with a reference to a battle in which the Byzantines were defeated):

> Chaos [corruption] has become rampant on land and sea, thanks to what the hands of men have earned, so that [God] might make them taste something of what they have done; perchance they may return [to the right path]. Say, Travel over the earth and see for yourselves the end of those before you, most of whom assigned partners to God. (30:41-42; among other references to "corruption" or "corruption on the earth" and "reform" or "reforming the earth" are 2:11, 27, 205; 8:73; 7:56, 85; 11:116; 12:73; 13:25; 16:88; 17:4; 26:152; 28:77)

The essence of all human rights is the equality of the entire human race, which the Qur'ān assumed, affirmed, and confirmed. It obliterated all distinctions among men except goodness and virtue (*taqwā*):

> O you who believe! let not one group of men among you deride another, for they may be better than them; nor one group of women deride another, for they may be better than them, nor slander each other, nor call each other names—how bad it is to call [each other] by bad names after all of you became Believers. Whoever does not desist [from this], they are the unjust ones. O you who believe! avoid most suspicion, for some suspicion is sinful, and do not pry into others' affairs and do not backbite each other; would any one of you like to eat the flesh of his dead brother?—how distasteful would it be to you! So fear God—indeed, God is forgiving and merciful. O people! We have created [all of] you out of male and female, and we have made you into different nations and tribes [only] for mutual identification; [otherwise] the noblest of you in the sight of God is the one most possessed of *taqwā* [not one belonging to this or that race or nation]; God knows well and is best informed. (49:11-13)

The reason the Qur'ān emphasizes essential human equality is that the kind of vicious superiority which certain members of this species assert over others is unique among all animals. This is where human reason appears in its most perverted forms. It is also true that the distance between human potentialities and their actual realization displays a range exemplified by probably no other species of living being: barring natural defects, there is hardly any difference, for example, between one specimen of earwig and another. But as we ascend the scale of evolution, the distances between potentialities and their actualities proportionately increases: among higher animals, like certain types of dogs, the gap is surprising.

But it is in man that the gap is most yawning and this is why the Qur'ān talks of God's Messengers, their conscience and sensitivity, the acuteness of their intelligence, and their godliness on the one hand, and on the other the bulk of mankind, who "are like animals, indeed, even more incapable of guidance, since they are so heedless!"(7:179). Further, man can exploit inherited or reflected power and glory in which no part whatever may be played by personal achievement—indeed, which may even lead to personal decadence, something quite irrational and yet man alone is capable and culpable of it.

To offset all these artificial but powerful sources of discrimination between man and man, it is necessary that man constantly remind himself that we "are all children of Adam and Adam was of dust" (as the Farewell Pilgrimage address of the Prophet has it), that in the darkness of the earth there are no distinctions and that while in the light of the heaven there are distinctions, *their* basis is that intrinsic worth which is called *taqwā*.

With perfect justification have the lawyers of Islam emphasized four fundamental freedoms or rights—life, religion, earning and owning property, and personal human honor and dignity (*'ird*), all of which it is the duty of the state to protect (for life, 5:32; for religion and belief, 2:256; for property, all verses pertaining to the earning of wealth quoted earlier on the issue of economic justice and those on *zakāt*; for personal honor, all verses referring to man's nobility and dignity, and the story of the creation of Adam itself in 2:30 ff.). Any large-scale violation of these, including, of course, demeaning man through sheer poverty, would constitute "corruption on the earth." However, for the Qur'ān, there is equally "discord and corruption on the earth" when the opposite happens, i.e., when people do not carry out their obligations, upon which the Qur'ān lays even greater stress. "Obligations" and "rights" are the obverse and converse of the same coin; the one obviously cannot subsist for any length of time without the other. Indeed, the Qur'ān is a document that primarily exhorts to virtue and a strong sense of moral responsibility, suggesting that a comprehensive sense of responsibility can very well take care of all human rights; but the converse is not so true—indeed, a society that begins to understand "rights" in terms of permissiveness and lawlessness spells its own inevitable doom.

Through its more specific social reforms, the Qur'ān aimed at strengthening the weaker segments of the community: the poor, the orphans, women, slaves, those chronically in debt. In understanding the Qur'ān's social reforms, however, we will go fundamentally wrong unless we distinguish between legal enactments and moral injunctions. Only by so distinguishing can we not only understand the true orientation of the Qur'ānic teaching but also solve certain knotty problems with regard, for example, to women's reform. This is where the Muslim legal tradition, which essentially regarded the Qur'ān as a lawbook and not *the religious source* of the law, went so palpably wrong.

To take the example of polygamy: the Qur'ān says, "If you fear that you cannot do justice to orphans, then marry from among [orphaned] women such as you like, two, three, or four. But if you fear you will not be fair [to your wives], then [marry] only one; that is the safest course" (4:3). In 4:2 the Qur'ān accuses many guardians of orphan boys and girls (the abundance of orphans was a necessary consequence of frequent wars) of being dishonest with the orphans' properties—a theme which the Qur'ān had already begun to address in Mecca (6:152; 17:34) and emphasized even more in Madina (2:220; 4:2, 6, 10, 127; for the general welfare of orphans, see 2:83, 177, 215; 4:8, 36; 89:17; 93:9; 107:3; for their share in booty and that of the poor in general, see 8:41; 59:7). It then says that since guardians do not deal honestly with orphaned women's properties, then they may marry them, up to four, *provided they can do justice among them.* That this is the correct interpretation of this text is clearly borne out by another passage of the same sura which appears to be earlier than 4:3: "They ask you [O Muhammad!] concerning women. Say: God gives you His decision concerning them, and what is being recited to you in the Book concerning orphan women to whom you do not give their due, but you would rather marry them, and [also concerning younger] and weaker children" (4:127). This shows that this question arose within the special context of orphan girls; but the Qur'ān also states, "You shall never be able to do justice among women, no matter how much you desire to do so" (4:129).

There is apparently a contradiction between permission for polygamy up to four; the requirement of justice among co-wives; and the unequivocal declaration that such justice is, in the nature of things, impossible. The traditionalist interpretation was that the permission clause has legal force while the demand for justice, though important, is left to the conscience of the husband (although traditional Islamic law gave women the right to seek remedy or divorce in case of gross injustice or cruelty). The weakness of this position from the viewpoint of normative religion is that something should be left to the good conscience of the husband, even though in the nature of things it is certain to be violated. Muslim modernists, on the other hand, tend to give primacy to the demand for justice plus the declaration of the impossibility of justice, and say that permission for polygamy was meant to be only temporary and for a restricted purpose.

The truth seems to be that permission for polygamy was at a legal plane while the sanctions put on it were in the nature of a *moral ideal towards which the society was expected to move*, since it was not possible to remove polygamy legally at one stroke. We encounter a similar phenomenon with regard to slavery: the Qur'ān legally accepted the institution of slavery, since it was impossible to legislate it away at one stroke, but strongly recommended and encouraged emancipation of slaves (90:13; 5:89; 58:3), and, in fact, asked Muslims to allow slaves to purchase their freedom by paying an agreed sum in installments (24:33); the classical Muslim lawyers, however, interpreted this as a "recommendation," not a command.

That appears to have been the usual procedure in Qur'ānic legislation. Generally speaking, each legal or quasi-legal pronouncement is accompanied by a *ratio legis* explaining why a law is being enunciated. To understand a *ratio legis* fully, an understanding of the sociohistorical background (what the Qur'ānic commentators call "occasions of revelation") is necessary. The *ratio legis* is the essence of the matter, the actual legislation being its embodiment so long as it faithfully and correctly realizes the *ratio*; if it does not, the law has to be changed. When the situation so changes that the law fails to reflect the *ratio*, the law must change. Traditional lawyers, however, while recognizing the *ratio legis*, generally stuck to the letter of the law and enunciated the principle that "Although a law is occasioned by a specific situation, its application nevertheless becomes universal." For example, it is said (2:282) that in a credit transaction, the credit, large or small, should be written down and there should be two witnesses to the deed; the witnesses can be two reliable adult males or, if two are not available, then one male and two women "so that if one of the two women should be forgetful, the other would remind her." The reason for having two female witnesses instead of one male is that women would be more "forgetful" than men, since women in those days were normally not used to dealing with credit. According to the traditionalist understanding, the law that two female witnesses equal one male is eternal and a social change that enabled a woman to get used to financial transactions would be "un-Islamic." The modernist, on the other hand, would say that since the testimony of a woman being considered of less value than that of a man was dependent upon her weaker power of memory concerning financial matters, when women became conversant with such matters—with which there is not only nothing wrong but which is for the betterment of society—their evidence can equal that of men.

A similar problem is that of the general equality of men and women. The Qur'ān says, "And for women there are rights [over against men] commensurate with the duties [they owe men]—but men are one degree higher" (2:228). It is certain that, in general, the Qur'ān envisages division of labor and a difference in functions (although there is nothing in the Qur'ān against women earning wealth and being economically self-sufficient; indeed, the Prophet's first wife owned a business and the Qur'ān recognizes the full and independent economic personality of a wife or a daughter). The question is whether the verse quoted is a statement of inherent inequality. We are told that "Men are in charge of women because God has given some humans excellence over others and because men have the liability of expenditure [on women]." (4:36). This shows that men have a functional, not inherent, superiority over women, for they are charged with earning money and spending it on women. We have said in the previous chapter that the Qur'ān speaks often of the superiority of some men in wealth, power, etc. and also of the superiority of some Messengers over others, but that this superiority is not inherent but purely functional. If a woman becomes economically sufficient, say by inheritance or earning wealth, and contributes to the household expenditure, the male's superiority would to that extent be reduced, since *as a human*, he has no superiority over his wife.

Religiously speaking, men and women have absolute parity: "Whosoever does good deeds, whether male or female, while being believers, they shall enter Paradise" (4:124; 40:40; also 16:97). Often when people of virtue and *taqwā* are mentioned, the Qur'ān mentions males and females separately:

> Those who have surrendered to God of males and females, those who believe of males and females, those who are sincere of males and

females, those who are truthful of males and females, those who are patient of males and females, those who fear God of males and females, those who give in charity of males and females, those who fast of males and females, those who preserve their private parts [from indecency] of males and females, those who remember God often of males and females—God has prepared for them forgiveness and great reward. (33:35)

Infanticide of girls, to which some Arabs resorted for reasons of poverty or honor, was abolished: "And when the girl buried alive shall be asked for what sin she was slain?" (81:8); again:

When one of them is given good news of [the birth of] a girl, his face darkens as he tries to suppress his chagrin. He hides from people because of the evil the good news meant to him [and he wonders] whether he shall keep her in disgrace or shove her into the earth—beware! evil is what they judge. (16:57-58; also 43:17; 17:31; 6:140, 151; 60:12)

It is strongly suggested (6:137) that Arab pagans used to justify the killing of their children on the authority of their gods.

The Qur'ān also prohibited the marriage of widows with their stepsons (4:23; cf. also 4:19). Essentially, the Qur'ān views the marital relationship as sustained by natural feelings of "love and mercy" (30:21) and it is stated: "They [our wives] are garments unto you and you are garments unto them" (2:187). Kind and generous treatment of women is laid down:

O You who believe! it is not permissible for you that you inherit from your womenfolk against their will; nor must you pressure them in order to make away with part of the wealth you have gifted them, except when they commit a clear obscenity [i.e., adultery]. And live with them in goodness; even when you dislike them [for certain things]; it is quite possible that you may dislike a thing, but God has put a great deal of goodness in it. But when you do want to divorce a woman in favor of another [whom you want to marry], and you have already given your [existing] wife a large amount of wealth, do not take anything away from it—will you take it back as a pure falsehood and a clear sin? How will you take it back when you have fondly met each other in intimacy, and they have gotten solemn promises from you? (4:19-21)

The question of the feeding of the infant after a divorce is discussed in

2:233 but in 2:229-32 the question of divorce itself is discussed. This passage clearly reveals how anxious the Qur'ān is to preserve a family by allowing remarriage, no doubt for the sake of children—something which contrasts oddly with the historic practice of the Muslim community:

> Divorce is lawful twice; after that either you keep your wife in goodness or set her free in kindness. And it is not permissible for you to take back anything from her that you have gifted to her, except if the couple fears that they will not be able to observe the limits of God [i.e., that they will continue to quarrel and harm each other after divorce]; if you fear this, then there is nothing wrong if she gives up a part [of those gifts] willingly. These are the limits of God, do not transgress them; and whosoever transgresses God's limits, they are the unjust ones. If the husband does divorce her [i.e., for the fourth time], she shall not be lawful to him afterwards until she marries another husband; if this latter should divorce her [or he dies], then there is no harm if the original couple return to each other, provided they think they can observe God's limits. These are God's limits which He makes clear to people who are capable of knowledge. When you divorce women and they have completed their term [the waiting period of three months after divorce], then either keep them in goodness or set them free in goodness, but do not keep them in order to harm them and to transgress against them—whosoever does that, he has *committed injustice against his own self* [for this phrase, see pp 26-28]. Do not take God's commands frivolously. . . . When you divorce women and they have completed their term, do not pressure them against remarrying their [former] husbands, if they have come to a mutual understanding in goodness. This is what those among you are being admonished who [really] believe in God and the Last Day—it is cleaner for you and purer, and God knows but you do not. (2:229-32)

In its laws of inheritance (see 4:7-12, 176), the Qur'ān prescribed shares for daughters and other females, but laid down the share of a daughter at half of the share of a son. Modernist Muslim opinion is divided as to whether, under the changed conditions of today, the daughter should get an equal share with her brother, the opponents of change contending that since the daughter when she marries, also gets a dowry from her husband (without which a marriage cannot be valid), the apparent inequality in inheritance shares means a real equality. The question must obviously be studied further in the light of today's realities.

To resume our account of the general social philosophy of the Qur'ān, human history basically consists of a constant process of the making and unmaking of societies and civilizations according to certain norms which are essentially moral; their source is transcendental but their application is entirely within collective human existence. These norms are called "God's Sunna" (practice or law for mankind which is unalterable):

> [Look at] the example of those [Messengers] we sent before you [O Muhammad!], and you will find no change in Our law. (17:77)
>
> This has been God's practice with regard to bygone peoples, and God's Command [law] is irrevocably determined. (33:38)
>
> This has been God's practice with the peoples of yore, and you shall certainly not find any change in God's practice. (33:62)
>
> Are these people [Muhammad's opponents], then, awaiting only the fate of earlier communities? For they shall surely find no deviation, no change whatever in God's law [or practice]. (35:43; see also 8:38; 15:13; 18:55; 40:85; 48:23)

This is the Qur'ān's concept of "judgment in history," which descends upon peoples and nations rather than individuals (who will primarily be judged on the Last Day). When the Qur'ān speaks of judgments upon peoples on the basis of their collective performance, it talks in much more cut-and-dried terms than when it talks about the last judgment upon individuals. In the latter case, God is forgiving and merciful, even if an individual has made many mistakes. But although God gives nations respite to see if they will mend their ways and improve their performance (13:32; 7:183; 22:44, 48; 3:178; 68:45), when their "term is come, they can neither hasten it, nor postpone it." Certain past nations have been so obliterated that "neither the heavens nor the earth wept for them, nor were they given respite" (44:29). The whole earth is not destroyed for the sins of certain nations, so some are "reaped off while others keep standing" (11:100; cf. 10:24). But when a nation perishes or is swallowed up by a morally clean and virile civilization, its good members are visited by the same doom as its bad ones if the former have not tried to halt the rot:

> Why, then, did those possessed of excellence and virtue [*baqīya*] among the peoples who preceded you [Muslims] not prevent [their co-nationals] from corrupting the earth—except very few whom We saved—but those who sank into decadent ways had to pay for them for they were criminals. (11:116)

This, then, is the essence of the Qur'ān's goal: to prevent people from "corrupting the earth" by "falling into decadent ways." Thus it is said of the Jews, with an implicit threat of punishment, "Why did their rabbis and learned men not dissuade them from uttering sinful sayings and consuming wealth earned through foul means? Evil is what they used to do" (5:63). Sins of omission of this order are as bad as grave sins of commission. This is why Muhammad came to warn his people, and through them others, for although a Messenger immediately addresses his people, once delivered, his Message becomes universal. This is why the Qur'ān insists on the "indivisibility of prophethood" (as we shall see in Chapter V and in Appendix I). This task of preventing the rot, or curing it once it has set in, was the function of each community instituted by every Messenger; through Muhammad it devolved upon the Muslim community, which is charged with "being witnesses upon mankind" and "calling to goodness and prohibiting evil" (2:143; 3:104, 110)—a task for which, as we shall see, the necessary instrument of *jihād* was provided.

The weakening of moral fiber is often represented by the Qur'ān as a natural process: "Too long an age has passed over them, so their hearts have become hardened [i.e., their conscience has become dull]" (57:16); "We have created many generations [of them], and their age has become prolonged" (28:45; also 25:18). It is in this context that the Qur'ān says to Jews and Christians, "O People of the Book! Our Messenger has come to you clarifying [matters of right and wrong] to you during an extensive gap of Messengership among you—lest you should say, No [new] giver of good tidings and warner has come to us" (5:19).

This renewal of conscience is absolutely essential if a community is to continue its task. In this connection, the Qur'ān makes particular targets of Jews and Christians (although it definitely prefers the latter to the former [5:82]) for their exclusivist claims: "They say: None shall enter the Garden except Jews (as the Jews say) and Christians (as the Christians say)" (2:111); "They say, Become Jews or Christians, if you want guidance; say, Guidance is God's guidance [not of Jews or Christians]" (2:135; also 2:120; 5:18). And the measure of their self-righteousness is that "Christians say Jews have nothing to stand on and Jews say Christians have nothing to stand on—and yet both of them recite the Book" (2:113). The Qur'ān also told Muslims repeatedly that they are not indispensable for God unless they exert themselves to further His purposes: "If you turn back, God will substitute another people for you, and they will not be like you" (47:38; also 9:39).

The specific forms of vice that can kill a society can be many, as we have said: economic oppression and exploitation of the poor; or political and social oppression of the poor and subject classes, in which case eventually "the inheritance of the earth" comes to the weak and the oppressed, as was the case with the Jews versus Pharaoh (7:137; 28:5). Or, there may be vices of idolatry and permissiveness, as with the people of Noah and Lot. When the rot sets in, there is either a successful reaction against it from within or a power is imposed from without, the former being more common. However, even in this case, a fresh start has to be made and the new generation has usually to build the edifice of a clean civilization once again.

The Qur'ān sometimes talks as though there is an essential discontinuity between a decrepit and decayed civilization and its successor: often no ready-made and quick succession can be assured to a decaying civilization. God would rather clean the slate and make a new beginning than tolerate a symbiosis of decadent and the virile. The Qur'ān definitely seems optimistic about the future, while rather grim about the past: "When a new community enters [Hell], it curses its sister(s) [fore-runners]" for leaving bad precedents for future generations (7:38); the phrase "Then we created an altogether new generation" occurs repeatedly (6:6; 23:31, 42; 38:3) as well as "We gave the inheritance of the earth" to new and more deserving people (21:105; 33:27; 28:5; 7:128, 137; 39:74; 44:28).

The real "inheritor" (owner) of the earth is, of course, God, but He puts deserving nations in charge of running its affairs until they lose the capacity to do so (15:23; 19:40; 3:180; 57:10). It is absolutely imperative for successor civilizations and their bearer communities to study well and learn from the fate of earlier ones that have perished; or they will assuredly meet with the same fate, for "God's law does not change" for any people. This is perhaps one of the most insistent ideas in the Qur'ān, which constantly exhorts people to "travel on the earth and see the end of those before them [or you]" (3:137; 6:11; 7:84, 86, 103, 128; 10:39, 73; 12:109; 16:36; 27:14, 51, 69; 28:40, 83; 30:9, 42; 35:44; 37:73; 40:21; 43:25; 47:10).

Those who are people of excellence and virtue *and at the same time actively try to prevent others from committing moral suicide* are certainly saved by God: the conviction that active goodness (not passive) must finally succeed lies at the very root of the Qur'ānic moral world-view. We shall elaborate on it while discussing phophethood, but we may refer here to the numerous Qur'ānic passages using the verb "We saved" or "We save" (*anja'inā, najja'inā, nunjī*).

This "deliverance" or "success," however, has nothing to do with the Jewish doctrine of the "remnant" in the Old Testament; one must guard against over-stretching antecedents to the Qur'ānic concepts or locutions in earlier Semitic religious documents. Thus, in his anxiety to show that the Qur'ān upholds the Jewish doctrine of the "remnant" (we have in this chapter already quoted evidence from the Qur'ān to contradict this idea), John Wansbrough in *Qur'ānic Studies* (cf. the Bibliographic Introduction above) refers on page 4 to certain alleged verses of the Qur'ān containing the words *baqiya, bāqiya,* and *bāqiyūn* (although quite apart from the fact that the last never occurs in the Qur'ān, it is grammatically absurd and should be *bāqūn*), which are supposed by him to mean "remnants" in the Old Testament sense.

There is no truth in this statement: there is only one such verse in the whole Qur'ān, "We made his [Noah's] progeny to survive him" (37:77)—but even there it means not Noah's physical progeny but his ideological followers. (As we learn from 11:46, his son was not saved from the Flood, for God told Noah, "He does not belong to your family for his deeds are unrighteous.") For the rest, no word in the Qur'ān derived from the root *bqy* means "surviving remnants"; in 26:120 the active participle plural is used in the accusative, again referring to the people of Noah, but it means not the surviving remnants, but on the contrary "the remnant that was destroyed." *Bāqiyāt* means "good deeds that survive the doer" (18:46; 19:76), while *bāqiya* in the singular means "Abraham's teaching that survived in his progeny" (43:28), or "anything that remains" (69:8). As for *baqīya,* of its three uses (2:248; 11:86, and 11:116), none means "remnant" and the last of the three, which Wansbrough actually quotes as an example of the Jewish "remnant" and which we have translated as "people possessed of excellence and virtue," would become absurd if translated as "remnant": consider "people possessed of remnant!" The entire idea of the "remnant" is, in fact, eliminated by the Qur'ān's telling the Muslims that if they will not struggle and fight in God's cause, He will find a substitute; they will not be indispensable for His plan.

Such is also the case with the so-called "election" theory in the Qur'ān, on which Wansbrough and others insist: "Divine justice is here mitigated by what seems clearly to be a reflex of the Biblical election tradition" (*Qur'anic Studies*, p. 4). We have said enough on the interplay of the naturalistic and non-naturalistic (religious) idiom of the Qur'ān in the preceding chapter to require no repetition here: God's blessings on a person, or more obviously on a city, or His choice or election of a person or a nation, can equally be and, indeed, *are* stated by the Qur'ān in terms of natural causes. Certainly there is no irreversible election in the Qur'ān: when God told Abraham He was going to appoint him leader of men (whether He had chosen him or Abraham had earned this by various deeds, including his willingness to sacrifice his son) and Abraham asked about the destiny of his progeny, the answer was, "My promise does not extend to unjust ones" (2:124). Again, the Qur'ānic reply to the question about why God "chose" Muḥammad as Messenger is a "naturalistic" one (6:124), while it is also said, "Do these people distribute the mercy of Your Lord?" (43:32); the Qur'ān mentions (6:83-86) seventeen Biblical personalities from Noah and Abraham onwards and says, "We chose them and guided them to the right path" (6:87), but read in the next verse, "But if they had associated [anyone with God], all their previous deeds would have come to naught." What does "election" mean in the face of this and other evidence?

In fact, "choice" and "election" are, for the Qur'ān, other names, a different idiom, for the natural processes. In the preceding chapter we have tried to point out the significance of this idiom in the Qur'ān; it can also be seen in the Qur'ānic account of the decline and decay of nations. This process has a thousand and one specific causes, but the basic cause is undoubtedly the moral perversion on the part of some and moral apathy on the part of others which is the exact opposite of *taqwā* or keen moral perception and motivation. In general, man appears incapable of wielding peace, prosperity, and power; something impels him to commit one of the various forms of *fasād fi'l-ard*, so that he loses all these three—which are, indeed, also the supreme object of his desire and priceless blessings of God: "Rather, we gave them and their forefathers prosperity, so that too long a time has passed over them" (21:44; also 25:18; 43:29). The moral diseases caused by perversions of the search for peace, prosperity, and power and the resulting process of decay and destruction are also called the "command of God": "When We want to destroy a town [i.e., a civilization], We command its luxurious ones, so they commit unrighteousness in it—and when the judgment becomes ripe upon it, we destroy it utterly" (17:16).

When a people is set in negative and evil ways so that it loses the capacity to discern and therefore cannot make right judgments, it can no longer define its purposes and goals but is simply adrift. At this critical juncture God sends a Messenger who invites its members to truth and goodness—which, of course, they cannot recognize and hence reject. However, the Message does trouble them, particularly because they are afraid that some among them, particularly men without the means of a luxurious life, might accept it. Hence they start to resist with devices and strategies which the Qur'ān calls *makr*, a term denoting a stratagem within the process of a struggle: "And so did We cause in every town [i.e., society or civilization] the foremost of its criminals to resort to devices and stratagems; they only victimize themselves therewith, however, but they do not know" (6:123). Just nothing seems to work, though, for "God is the best executor of stratagems" (3:54; 8:30; 10:21; 27:50); "even though their stratagems might be capable of crushing mountains out of existence" (14:46).

What, then, is the real stratagem? Not to let the power of discernment and correct judgment die; to keep the keenness of the sense of moral responsibility [*taqwā*] alive—this is the purpose of studying the fate of past nations:

> How many a town have We destroyed because it did wrong [to itself]; it was laid waste with its roofs crumbling down to its foundations, its defunct wells and its desolate castles hewn out of rocks and strengthened with lead. Have these people not traveled on the earth so that they might come to possess hearts [i.e., minds] wherewith they can understand or ears wherewith they can hear—for it is not [the physical] eyes that become blind but the hearts that are set in breasts. (22:45-46)

Physical avenues of information may remain intact—in fact, may improve vastly—but "the heart," the instrument of perception and discernment, is dulled; the inputs and outputs of computers continue—indeed, become ever more efficient; only the capacity to ask the right questions, the humanly relevant questions, fails.

When a people becomes decadent and its civilization decrepit, it becomes a burden on the very earth from which it had once sprouted with so lush a promise. It may prolong its existence somewhat by various devices, but its exit is inevitable "for none can defeat God" (8:59; 22:51; 34:5, 38; 9:2-3; 6:134; 10:53; 11:20). This phenomenon, which has a certain inevitability about it (judging from the Qur'ān), is on the whole good, although it involves a certain loss for mankind, since the very struggle brings fresh blood to the veins of an aging humanity—it is as though dead earth has quickened and blossomed once again. This struggle between good and evil, fresh and stale, new and decrepit, between the vigor of moral youth and the dotage of senility, is of positive benefit, for it keeps the perennial moral values alive:

> But for the fact that God repels some people at the hands of others, churches, synagogues, places of God's worship and mosques—wherein God's name is so frequently mentioned—would be razed; but God must help those who help Him and God is, indeed, powerful and mighty. These are the ones [those who help God and God helps them] who, when We establish them on the earth, shall establish prayers, pay *zakāt*, command the good, and prohibit evil, and to God belongs the ultimate end of all issues [i.e., His command is eventually successful]. (22:40-41, on the occasion of the earliest pronouncement by the Qur'ān of *jihād* by the Muslims against pagan Arabs; cf. also 2:251)

From the foregoing it must not be imagined that wealth and its earnings are bad *per se*: we have said this before but it must be re-emphasized. What is all-important is how one pursues wealth and wields it. We have already quoted 30:7 and 53:30 to the effect that Meccan traders "knew the externalities of life" very well but were heedless of "its ends" and that this was "the height of their knowledge." In fact, the Qur'ān insists that when a society declines morally, its prosperity also departs; so long as it preserves a keen perception of the Message, it prospers: "Whoever turns away from My reminder [or remembrance] shall have a highly straitened life and [also] on the Last Day we shall raise him up as blind" (20:124); again:

> If the People of the Book were to believe and develop *taqwā*, we would remove their evils, and cause them to enter the luxuriant gardens. If they were to establish the Torah, the Gospel, and what has been sent down to them from their Lord [the Qur'ān], prosperity would be

showered upon them [literally: "they would have eaten"], from above and from beneath them. (5:64-66)

Had the people of the towns [the pagan Arabs of Mecca and elsewhere] believed and developed *taqwā*, we would have opened up for them the blessings of the heavens and the earth. (7:96)

In discussing evolution and discontinuity of civilizations, we have already said that although the Qur'ān often speaks of the discontinuity of civilizations, i.e., of making a fresh start with an altogether "new generation" of people, it is on the whole optimistic about the future because "the inheritance of the earth is given to good people." A word also must be said about the legacy of civilizations for their successors. Here again there is a tension between two opposite directions. On the one hand, the history of civilizations is cumulative and evolutionary because while the "foam on the top of a torrent disappears, that which is beneficial to mankind [the alluvium] settles down upon the earth" (13:17). This means that while the negative side of men's conduct departs, the constructive side does leave a positive legacy for mankind. On the other hand, the evil legacies of earlier peoples do affect the quality of performance of later ones. In a sense, every earlier civilization is a forerunner of or an example for later ones; hence the tremendous responsibility to future generations. It is not clear whether this influence is due to the fact that later civilizations actually learn of the earlier ones—and try to vie with their foolish deeds—or whether their legacy becomes embedded in the unconscious of the later ones and becomes, as it were, part of their moral genes—in which case it is cumulative and the entire historic movement is like a spiral, not a cycle. The Qur'ān does state that successor communities will accuse their predecessors of having had a negative influence upon them:

> When a [new] community enters [Hell], it shall curse its sister[s] [i.e., its predecessors], until when all have reached down into its depths, every successor shall say of its predecessor, Our Lord, these people misled us, so give them double punishment in the Fire; God will reply, Each one of you is experiencing double punishment, but you do not realize it. (7:38; also 38:59 ff.)

A part of humanity influencing others in evil ways through example, pressure, or even education is a frequent theme in the Qur'ān, for those who influence and educate and form or inform others' minds bear a direct responsibility for the conduct of those they affect: "Those who have disbelieved shall say [on the day of judgment], Our Lord! show us those two who led us astray from among the humans and the jinn, so that we put them underneath our feet that they be among the lowest [inhabitants of Hell]" (41:29). It is against this background that such frequent Qur'ānic terms as "guidance," "right guidance," "Truth," "the right way," and "the straight path" become invested with their full-blown significance: the whole fate of man, whether he will be "successful" or "shall perish," depends on whether he can and does "take the right path"—something that most men take very lightly, as though it did not make any difference to the future of humanity.

A particularly insistent theme is that the stronger constantly attempt to influence or pressure the weaker to take a certain course of conduct, against the better judgment of the latter. The genesis of this theme, of course, lies in the society of Mecca, where generally (although not exclusively—see Appendix II) the early adherents of Muḥammad were the socioeconomically weaker classes who were under constant pressure from the "aristocrats [al-mala']" to abjure the Prophet:

> Those who have disbelieved say to the believers, Follow our way, and we shall bear [the burden of] your sins—but they will never bear any of their sins; they are only lying. They shall, of course, bear their own burdens, and additional ones, too [for trying to hoodwink the weaker members of their society]. (29:13; also 7:75)

The Qur'ān vividly portrays the accusations brought on the Day of Judgment by the weaker ones against the stronger and influential ones:

> The weak shall say to those who thought they were big, But for you we would have been believers. Those who thought big of themselves shall say to the weak, Did *we* block your way to the Guidance after it came to You? Indeed, you yourselves were criminals! The weak shall reply, Rather, it was your cunning strategies day and night [that prevented us from believing]—when you [constantly] commanded us to disbelieve. (34:33)

The corruption of religious leaders, who were expected to be the source of spiritual force and regeneration, is the last step in the process of decay of a community. The natural path their corruption takes is the easy conscience by which they come to compromise truth with the wayward "whims [*ahwā*]" either of the rich or of the community at large. In either case, they first yield to pressure and subsequently their consciences become easy and they compromise, with money or popularity or both. We have already referred to verses where religious leaders fail to give the erring community the correct advice because this would be unpopular. The Qur'ān also often accuses Jewish religious leaders and occasionally Christian of corruption. Against Jewish scribes and rabbis the common charge is that they "sell God's words for a paltry sum of money" (2:41, 79, 174; 3:77, 187; 16:95):

> Then a generation succeeded [the earlier Jews] which inherited the Book but which accepts the paltry benefits of this world [and corrupts religion] and says, We will be forgiven [by God], but should they have another opportunity to accept such paltry benefits, they will take them. Has the Covenant of the Book not been taken from them that they shall not speak about God but truth and they have already studied [that truth] in that Book? (7:169)

Further,

> O you who believe! many a learned Jew and Christian monk consumes the properties of people by false means and blocks the path of Allah— but those who hoard gold and silver and do not spend them in God's cause, let them have the good tidings of a painful punishment. (9:34)

The Qur'ān is adamant that every community or nation gets what it deserves by "what its hands have earned": "What would God gain by punishing you if you are grateful [for His blessings] and believe [in Him]?" (4:147); "God is not the one who would destroy towns [i.e., civilizations or peoples] unjustly while their people are active in goodness" (11:117; also 6:131; 10:13). God does nothing but operate through those unchangeable laws that govern the rise and fall of peoples: "God does not change the condition of a people until they change it themselves" (13:11; 8:53). There is a religious sense in which everything is authored by God, since God is the extra dimension in all nature, but in ordinary parlance it is correct to say that man does everything to himself and for himself, and is responsible for it.

Against this background there was brought into existence the Muslim Community (*umma muslima*), which was formally instituted in

Madina about eighteen months after the Hijra when the permission for *jihād* was enunciated:

> [This is] the Community of your forefather Abraham, who already named you Muslims [i.e., those who surrender to God] before this; let the Messenger [Muhammad] be a witness over you in this regard and let you be the witnesses over mankind. So establish prayers, pay *zakāt* and hold fast to God Who is your Protector—what an excellent protector and what an excellent helper! (22:78)

About the same time the Qur'ān says, "Even so have we constituted you as a median community [i.e., between the imperviousness of Judaism and the liquidity of Christianity] that you be witnesses to mankind and that the Messenger be a witness over you" (2:143). They were defined as "The best community produced for mankind who command good and forbid evil and believe in God" (3:110; also 3:104) and their function was to be, "Those who, if we give them power on the earth, shall establish prayers, pay *zakāt*, command good, and forbid evil" (22:41).The Qur'ān also clarified that by "prayers" it does not simply mean standing up facing the Ka'ba and making certain gestures with the body and the tongue; although prayers are undoubtedly among the cardinal duties of a Muslim, they are a mere farce without a wholistic view of Islam:

> It is no virtue that you turn your faces east and west [in prayer]. Virtuous are they who believe in God, the Last Day, the angels, the Book [in a generic sense, i.e., all Revealed Books], the prophets, who give of their wealth—despite their love for it—to needy kinsmen, orphans, the poor, the wayfarer, those who ask for financial help and for ransoming war captives, who establish prayers, pay *zakāt*, fulfil their pacts when they make them, are steadfast in hardship, adversity and war—these are the true [Believers]. (2:177)

Throughout these characterizations of the task of the Muslim Community, the words "commanding good, forbidding evil, establishing prayer, and paying [and, of course, collecting] *zakāt*" recur. There is no doubt that the Qur'ān wanted Muslims to establish a political order on earth *for the sake of creating an egalitarian and just moral-social order.* Such an order should, by definition, eliminate "corruption on the earth [*fasād fi'l-ard*]" and "reform the earth." To fulfil this task, to which every people whose vision is neither truncated nor introverted pays at least lip-service, the Qur'ān created the instrument of *jihād*—indeed, 22:41, describing this function of the Muslim Community, follows directly upon the verse laying down the principle of *jihād* for the first time.

The Qur'ān also envisaged, or at least called for, cooperation between like-minded communities: "O People of the Book! Come [let us join] on a platform [literally: a formula] that may be common between us—that we serve naught except God" (3:64). It should be noted that the proposition "that we serve naught except God" is a statement of the *platform*, not of the *task* that has to be performed on earth and whose details are supposed to flow from this platform or formula of "service" to one God. It should also be noted that this invitation is for cooperation in building a certain kind of ethico-social world order and is not of the nature of contemporary forms of "ecumenism," where every "religious" community is expected to be nice to others and extend its typical brand of "salvation" to others as much as it can! For Islam, there is no particular "salvation": there is only "success [*falāḥ*]" or "failure [*khusrān*]" in the task of building the type of world order we are describing. It is striking, indeed, that even in "ecumenism," Christianity, which never envisioned any social order, thinks inevitably in its own terms and will envisage inter-confessional relationships only within the parameters of those terms which primarily surround the cult of Jesus.

But when human religio-social endeavor is envisaged in the terms in which we have understood the Qur'ān, *jihād* becomes an absolute necessity. How can such an ideological world-order be brought into existence without such a means? Most unfortunately, Western Christian propaganda has confused the whole issue by popularizing the slogan "Islam was spread by the sword" or "Islam is a religion of the sword." What was spread by the sword was not the religion of Islam, but the *political domain* of Islam, so that Islam could work to produce the order on the earth that the Qur'ān seeks. One may concede that *jihād* was often misused by later Muslims whose primary aim was territorial expansion and not the ideology they were asked to establish; one must also admit that the means of *jihād* can vary—in fact, armed *jihād* is only one form. But one can never say that "Islam was spread by the sword." There is no single parallel in Islamic history to the forcible conversion to Christianity of the German tribes *en masse* carried out by Charlemagne, with repeated punitive expeditions against apostates—although, of course, locally and occasionally isolated cases of such conversions may well have taken place.

Jihād, indeed, is a total endeavor, an all-out effort—"with your wealth and lives," as the Qur'ān frequently puts it—to "make God's cause succeed" (9:40). We shall elaborate in Chapter VI on the nature of this endeavor and the purpose of this order, although as we have hinted, the concept of the ultimate end of this endeavor (*al-ākhira*) is pivotal to the whole system of Qur'ānic thought. The concept of *ākhira* implies that man needs not *just* economic justice; economic justice itself is for a higher end, for man does not live from hour to hour and from day to day like animals but his vision must see through the consequences of his actions and aim at the end which constitutes the meaning of positive human effort. This is the end which cannot be achieved without *jihād*, for it is God's unalterable law that He will not bring about results without human endeavor; otherwise those who endeavor and those who do not would become indistinguishable (3:142; 4:95; 9:16, 24, 86; 29:6-8; 61:11; 47:31).

Chapter Four

Nature

The Qur'ānic cosmogony is minimal. Of the metaphysics of creation the Qur'ān simply says that the world and whatever God decided to create in it came into existence by His sheer command: "Be" (2:117; 3:47, 59; 6:73; 16:40; 19:35; 36:82; 40:68). God is, therefore, the absolute possessor of the universe and its unquestioned commander, just as He is its merciful sustainer. Because of His unconditional mastery, when God wished to bring the heavens and the earth into existence, He said to them: "Come hither, voluntarily or involuntarily" (41:11). And so it is that, as we shall see shortly in more detail, all nature obeys God by an "automatic volition"—except for man, who has opportunity equally for obedience or disobedience.

This is why the Qur'ān regards the whole universe as "Muslim," because everything therein (except man, who may or may not *become* "Muslim") has "surrendered itself to God's will" (3:83), and everything glorifies God (57:1; 59:1; 61:1; also 17:44; 24:41, etc.). The only hint in the Qur'an about the "unfolding" of the universe is: "Did the disbelievers not see [i.e., know] that the heavens and the earth [i.e., all space] were one undifferentiated mass [*ratq*] and then We unfolded them?" (21:30). The entire process of creation is said to have taken "six days" (7:54; 10:3; 11:7; 25:59), after which God established Himself on the "Throne" (7:54; 10:3, etc.).

From His throne God manages the affairs of the world; He sends down commands through angels and the Spirit, and these ascend back to Him with reports. The Qur'ān speaks often of this double movement (22:5; 70:4; 34:2; 57:4; cf. 97:4). Time, for the Qur'ān, is certainly relative and depends on the type of experience and status of being of the subject. In 32:5 we are told that one day of the ascension of angels equals one thousand years of "earthly" time, while in 70:4 the span given equals fifty thousand years of the time of ordinary experience.[1] It is often said (e.g., 2:259; 17:52; 20:104; and 23:112-114) that on the Day of Resurrection sinners will think that their time in this world, or the time until the Resurrection, lasted but a few days. And some people, awakened after sleep lasting several years or even several centuries (as in the case of the "young men of the cave" in sura 18), thought their sleep had lasted only "for an hour" or "for a day or part of a day." However these difficult passages are to be interpreted, the figures of one thousand or fifty thousand years of ordinary time being equal to one day "there" are surely not to be taken literally.

But if the Qur'ān has little to say about cosmogony, it makes frequent and repeated statements about nature and natural phenomena, though these statements invariably relate nature to God or to man, or to both. Often they portray God's unlimited power and majesty and invite man to believe in Him, or depict His infinite mercy and require man to be grateful to Him. In both cases, nature's magnitude and utility for man, as well as the stability and regularity of natural phenomena, are stressed. If you sow seeds and nurture the saplings, you can expect to reap the harvest; otherwise not. If you build a ship and place it on the sea, and the winds are favorable, you may anticipate profitable trade; otherwise not. The working of natural causes, therefore, is inevitable and undeniable.

Besides natural causation, however, there is another, more ultimate causation, bestowing upon natural processes in their entirety a significance and an intelligibility that natural processes viewed in themselves do not yield. This higher causation is not a duplicate of, nor is it in addition to, natural causation. It works within it, or rather is identical with it—when viewed at a different level and invested with the proper meaning. As we shall see presently, the Qur'ān uses both natural causation language and divine causation or religious language,

---

1. Theodor Nöldeke (*Geschichte des Qorāns*, revised by Friedrich Schwally [Leipzig, 1909], Part 1:106) and Régis Blachère (*Le Coran* [Paris, 1966], p. 614) think 70:4 is a later insertion. Nöldeke even says this verse "actually looks like a gloss." If these scholars are saying that this verse was inserted by later Muslims, they are definitely wrong. Richard Bell (*The Qur'ān* [Edinburgh, 1937], p. 604) says: "Vv. 4, 5 are an insertion designed to obviate the difficulty of the delay in the coming of the event," referring to the "punishment about to fall" mentioned in verse 1, and promised, according to Bell, in 52:7-8. Bell's view is based on the assumption (which I consider false) that verse 1 refers to a terrestrial punishment promised to the Meccans rather than the punishment of hellfire, which is clearly referred to in verses 15-18. There is thus no convincing evidence that verse 4 is a later insertion.

in different contexts and clearly with different purposes in view.

The most fundamental disparity between God and His creation is that, whereas God is infinite and absolute, every creature is finite. All things have potentialities, but no amount of potentiality may allow what is finite to transcend its finitude and pass into infinity. This is what the Qur'ān means when it says that everything except God is "measured out" (*qadar* or *qadr*, *taqdir*, etc.), and is hence *dependent upon* God, and that whenever a creature claims complete self-sufficiency or independence (*instighnā*, *istikbār*), it thus claims infinitude and a share in divinity (*shirk*). When God creates anything, He places within it its powers or laws of behavior, called in the Qur'ān "guidance," "command," or "measure" whereby it fits into the rest of the universe: "He gave everything its creation and then guided [it]" (20:50); "He who created [things] and [created them] well, and who measured [them] out and thus guided [them]" (87:2-3); "Lo, to Him belong both creation and commanding" (7:54); and, "Indeed, We have created everything with a measure" (54:49; cf. 15:21). If things should break their laws and violate their measure, there would be not an ordered universe, but chaos. The Qur'ān speaks frequently of the perfect order in the universe as proof not only of God's existence but also of His unity (21:22; cf. also the moving passage at 27:60-64).

It should be noted that this "measuring" has a strong holistic bias in terms of patterns, dispositions, and trends. Nor is the resulting total performance conceived of in terms of particular events and acts. It is, therefore, *not* a theory of predetermination, although it does mean a kind of "holistic determinism." This is clear from the references where "measured" does not mean "predetermined" but "finite" or "limited." The following passage must be understood in the same light:

> And the sun moves [along its course] to its resting place—that is the measuring [or determination] of the All-Mighty, the All-Knowing. And for the moon We have appointed certain stations, until it returns like an old curved stick. It is nót for the sun to overtake the moon, nor for the night to overstrip the day, each coursing in its own orbit. (36:38-40)

This *qadar* or "measure" also operates at the holistic level in the sphere of human moral actions, which by definition are free. Judgment in history, for instance, concerns the total performance of a people; in the Last Judgment, it is primarily the total performance of individuals that comes under review. The difference between nature and man is that in the case of man the particular moral actions take place by free choice.

Nature is in fact so well-knit and works with such regularity that it is the prime miracle of God, cited untiringly in the Qur'ān. No being short of God could have built this vast and stable edifice:

> He who created seven heavens one on top of another—you shall not find in the creation of the Merciful any dislocation. Look again—do you see any gap? Look again and again—your sight will return to you frustrated [in the attempt to find any discontinuity or irregularity] and fatigued. (67:3-4)
>
> And you see the mountains and think them solid [and stationary] but they are fleeting like clouds—the creation of God *who has well-completed [the creation of] everything.* (27:88)

References to phenomena like the regularity of the day following the night and the night following the day, the rainy season when the earth is quickened following the dry season when it had been parched and dead, are strewn through the pages of the Qur'ān.

This gigantic machine, the universe, with all its causal processes, is the prime "sign" (*āya*) or proof of its Maker. Who else but an infinitely powerful, merciful, and purposeful Being could have brought into existence something with dimensions so vast and an order and design so complex and minute? Yet, man, the Qur'ān complains recurrently, is ordinarily apt to "forget" God so long as "natural" causes work for him; it is only when natural causes fail him that he "discovers" God. What superficiality and short-sightedness! A man in dire thirst in a desert is desperately searching for water and, taking a mirage to be water, runs after it. When he gets to the point where he thought there was water, he finds no water—indeed, nothing—but in that moment of utter disillusionment he "finds" God (24:39). The situation is cited as a parable for unbelievers who deem their life-record to be full of weighty and consequential deeds; these deeds, in the final analysis, will turn out to be no more than a mirage. Again, when people sail in a ship and the waters are calm and the winds favorable, they forget in their revelry that there is God. But suddenly a storm overtakes them and angry waves whipped up by strong winds encircle them, so that they think there is no escape. In that moment of utter helplessness, they cry out to God in all sincerity. After deliverance by God, they once again become rebellious and do negative deeds (10:22ff.; cf. 29:65ff.).

People belittle or ignore or even rebel against God, because they view the processes of nature as having self-sufficient causes, normally regarded by them as ultimate. They do not realize that the universe is a sign pointing to something "beyond" itself, something without which the universe, with all its natural causes, would be and could be nothing.

The first problem is that people do not take the ordered universe to be a sign or a miracle at all, but rather look for the interruption or suppression of natural processes in order to find miracles of God. Secondly, and far more importantly, the universe as a sign vanishes into nothing when "put beside" God, for beside God nothing at all has any inherent warrant to exist. That the earth supports people and does not sink, and the heavens holding this immense space do not shred is itself a miracle (34:9; 50:6ff.; 51:47ff.; also 13:2ff. and all verses that speak of the heavens and the earth having been firmly built and well-knit). Indeed, there could have been just empty nothingness instead of this plenitude of being, pure inanity instead of this richness of existence, *but for the primordial act of God's mercy.* This plenitude of natural being is therefore itself "supernaturally" miraculous and the greatest of all miracles "for those who sincerely ponder and surrender their ears to listen." Mercy is as ultimate an attribute of God as power, and is in a definite sense synonymous with creation. While nature therefore is *autonomous* in the sense that it works by its own innate laws, it is certainly not *autocratic,* for it does not contain its own ultimacy or final rationale as an integral part of its being.

Nature with its incomprehensible vastness and regularity should serve as God's sign for humans, since none but an infinite and unique Being could have created it. This may be called a "natural sign." If, however, some or even most people are not persuaded by the normal workings of nature, God is capable of diverting, suppressing, or temporarily suspending the efficacy of natural causes. Such portents as floods, hurricanes, violent earthquakes, or torrential rains falling where there is normally little or no rain, are unusually distinctive signs, coming often at some point when a people is irretrievably on a wicked course of action. That is why, when the Meccans repeatedly demanded such fateful "signs" from the Prophet, the Qur'ān told them not to "anticipate" them, for when they come the people upon whom they are visited shall no longer have any respite (21:40; 32:29; 6:8, etc.). Such signs are not contrary to the course of nature but are prodigies that may be called "portent signs" or "historical signs."

Other signs are apparently *against* the course of nature, as when fire became cool and safe for Abraham when he was thrown into it to be burnt, or when Moses' rod turned into a serpent. These may be called "supranatural miracles." Such signs are miracles par excellence, manifested at the hands of a Messenger of God to support the truth of the Messenger's claim and teaching. The Qur'ān is emphatic that no prophet can work miracles without divine permission and active help: "It is not up to a Messenger to produce a sign unless it be by God's permission" (40:78). Thus, all Jesus' miracles are said to have been produced "by God's permission" (3:49, etc.). This is not just a defense of Muhammad when he appeared to be unable to produce this kind of miracle. The basic reason for this statement in the Qur'ān is that, since people mistakenly attribute the occurrence of natural events to their natural causes alone without recognizing the presence of God in them, when a "supranatural miracle" occurs, it must be such that there is no doubt that it is authored by God.

Before proceeding further with our account of natural and supranatural signs or miracles, we will do well to keep two important points in mind. First, although a "sign" in the religious sense points beyond itself to its Author, and the transition is in this sense rational or at least reasonable, it is nevertheless not equivalent to rational proof. In order to determine the meaning of a sign, one must have, in addition to reason, a certain disposition, i.e., the capacity for faith. This is why for many naturalists the universe is not a sign pointing beyond itself, but is the ultimate reality ("We die and we live and we die only through [the natural process of] Time"—45:24). The Qur'ān, indeed, insists throughout that to read the signs correctly and to understand the Qur'ān requires a mental-cum-spiritual attitude so that one may "really hear, really see, and really understand." For that matter, the signs do not become subjective for the Qur'ān because many do not "see" them, any more than the sun becomes subjective because animals habituated to darkness cannot see it.

The second important point is that although many people have confused signs, particularly supranatural or revelational signs (or verses of the Qur'ān), with magic or sorcery, the two are not the same; the first is real, the latter illusory. The former has a permanence after being efficacious which the latter does not except in its psychological dimension. Magic is therefore evil, because it conceals and distorts reality; while a sign shows reality in its full plenitude. When opposing Moses, Pharaoh's magicians only "beguiled the sights of men" (7:116); "Lo, their ropes and sticks created the impression upon him [Moses], due to their magic, that they were moving" (20:66). Magic is a kind of trickery (20:64; 20:69) and requires some training and expertise (7:109, 112; 10:79; etc.). But, with all its unreality, magic does have a psychological effect which is real, as for example when the two angels Hārūt and Mārūt (2:102) are said to have taught people magic whereby they separated husbands from their wives—this effect, of course, being "with the permission of God."

The Meccans (and sometimes the Madinan Jews) had asked the Prophet to produce miracles like those of earlier prophets, in order to vindicate his claim. The Qur'ān gives several types of responses. The workings of nature from the heavens to the earth, various phenomena on land and sea, the human mind itself—in fact, all natural phenomena—are pointed to as genuine signs. This claim appears to rest on the assumption, or rather seeks to prove, that the same God who created nature and displayed His wisdom therein so clearly has also revealed the verses (āyāt, also meaning "signs") of the Qur'ān.

This would be evident, if only the opponents would ponder on both nature and God seriously and sincerely. Just as no one but God could have created nature, so no one but God could have produced the Qur'ān. The opponents of the Prophet are sometimes challenged to "produce even a single sura of the Qur'ān," and the conviction is expressed that they would not be able to do so even with their combined endeavor and with help from other sources (2:23; 10:38; 11:13; 17:88; 52:33ff.). Just as nature represents the inexhaustible "words" or *logoi* of God, so does the Qur'ān (18:109ff.), for, like nature, the Qur'ān flows through the mind of the Prophet *with God's permission*, and if God should so will, He could close down the flow of the revelation from the Prophet's heart (42:24; etc.).

The parallel (or even the identity) between the revelation of the Qur'ān and the creation of the universe has been pointed out by several medieval Muslim authors who have noted the numerous passages in which the revelation of the Qur'ān and the creation of nature are coupled. Of course, both are also mentioned often in other contexts—e.g., the revelation of the Qur'ān in relation to the revelation of earlier scriptures. The point made, I think correctly, is that the Qur'ān and nature are mentioned together so often not fortuitously but because of an intimate connection between the two, as seen, for example, in 3:108ff., where after a brief reference to what will happen to the wicked and the good on the Last Day, the Qur'ān says: "These are God's signs that We recite to you in truth . . . . And to God belongs whatever is in the heavens and in the earth."

> Indeed, in the creation of the heavens and the earth and the succession of day and night are signs for people of wisdom—those who remember [or mention, i.e., by reciting the Qur'ān] standing and sitting and lying on their sides, and who ponder over the creation of the heavens and the earth [exclaiming]: Our Lord, You have not created all this in vain! (3:190ff.)

> These are the verses of the Book. That which has been sent down to you from your Lord is the Truth; yet most people do not believe. It is God who has raised the heavens without any pillars that you can see; then He established Himself on the Throne and subdued the sun and the moon—each running to a designated term (13:1 ff.; and cf. such other passages as 10:1-3; 12:102-5; and 20:1-6).

The verses of the Qur'ān are *āyāt* or "signs" because they come from the same God who created the universe. But the Qur'ān refers to its verses as *tabyīn al-āyāt*, "the clarification of the signs [of God]," or speaks of "bringing them home" to the mind, as "We bring home the *āyāt* [*nuṣarrif al-āyāt*]" (6:65), or "We detail the *āyāt* [*faṣṣalna'l-āyāt*]" (e.g., in 6:97-98). Often we read: "We explain [or clarify] to them the *āyāt* [that are already there] [*bayyannā'l-āyāt*, or *nubayyin'l-āyāt*]," as in 2:118, 219, 266; 3:118; 5:75. When the term *āyāt* refers to verses of the Qur'ān, these *āyāt* are usually said to be "recited" (*natlūhā*, or *tutlā*, etc.); they are often said to be "clear *āyāt* [*āyāt bayyināt*]." This latter expression is applied to signs other than the Qur'ānic verses only three times, once in reference to a "portent sign," i.e., the destruction of the people of Lot (29:35), and twice in reference to historical or supranatural signs involving Moses and the Jews (2:211; 17:101); it seems never to be applied to nature, presumably because natural signs lie buried beneath natural causation until the Qur'ānic verses resurrect them and clarify them as signs of God.

Thus (although the point should not be over-stressed), whereas natural miracles are, in this sense, weak for most of mankind and in the

Qur'ān are usually called simply *āyāt*, the historical (portent) miracles, the supranatural miracles, and much more patently the revelation, are called *āyāt bayyināt* or simply *bayyināt*: "clear, manifest, and indubitable signs."

Most people are so obdurate, however, that even these "indubitable signs" are not sufficient to convert them, although they should be much more convincing than the natural *āyāt*. The *bayyina* is most effective as a sign, of course, for those who witnessed it originally and directly (e.g., the prophets), and their firm conviction clearly and once and for all sets them apart from the disbelievers (6:57; 8:42; and especially 11:17, 28, 63, 88). The Qur'ān asks: "Is one who has a clear proof (*bayyina*) from His Lord like him whose evil deeds [merely] appear attractive to him?" (47:14). A *bayyina* thus clearly distinguishes the truth of the one to whom it is given from the falsehood of his opponent, even though this falsehood seems to be the truth to the disbelievers. What falsely appears to be the truth will disappear, but a *bayyina* never will. Also, whereas an *āya* is either perceived or *not* perceived, a *bayyina* is either perceived or *mis*perceived and misidentified either as sorcery or some other form of trickery; but it cannot simply be denied. In 98:1-4 the Prophet himself, together with the Qur'ān, is termed a *bayyina*. This short sura, called "al-Bayyina," also expresses the view, repeated elsewhere in the Qur'ān, that religious dissensions and sects are caused by *bayyināt*, when people, who cannot deny them, differ widely as to their exact nature, source, and meaning.

A term even stronger than *bayyina* is *burhān*, which means "a demonstrative proof" and contains a factor of compelling rationality. It is close to *bayinna* and like it is confined to portents, supranatural miracles, and revelation and reason, or rather, reason-in-revelation; but whereas *bayyina* is clear or manifest and, in this sense, passively irresistible, *burhān* is rationally and psychologically compelling. The Qur'ān itself is termed *burhān* (4:174). In 2:111; 21:24; 23:117; 27:64; and 28:75, the term apparently means a convincing (rational) account being asked from disbelievers and polytheists in defense of their religious stand. A highly interesting use of *burhān* is in 12:24, where Joseph is depicted as having desisted from unlawful sexual intercourse with the Egyptian lady and finally resisted her powerful charms after the mutual sexual fascination of both had turned into excitement, "because he [Joseph] saw a *burhān* from his Lord." *Burhān* is, therefore, a kind of rational (and not just "logical") proof capable of controlling and diverting the course of extremely powerful instincts.

But the strongest type of *āyā* or "sign," also close to *burhān* in its usage, is *sultān*, literally meaning "authority" or "power" but used in the Qur'ān for a kind of sign or proof that might be described as a "knock-down proof." While a *bayyina* is clear and irresistible to an open and unprejudiced mind, and a *burhān*'s demonstrative power might overcome some prejudices, a *sultān* has a power that is psychologically almost coercive, in that it might cause those who were fairly determined in their rejection of the truth to accept it anyway. It must be emphasized that the differences among all these terms appear to be largely of quantity or degree of pursuasive power.

Sultān is perhaps best translated as "that which overwhelms without leaving any real alternative." The root in its second form as used in the Qur'ān means "to cause someone to overwhelm or overpower someone else by physical force" (4:90; 59:4), and this power is attributed to God. In his commentary on 55:33 ("O species of jinn and men! If you [think you] are able to penetrate the corners of the heavens and the earth, then [go and] penetrate—you shall not [be able to] penetrate except on the basis of a *sultān* [i.e., the authority or power rooted in knowledge]"), al-Tabarī says that the original meaning of *sultān* is "a clear proof or argument [*bayyina, hujja*]," but that it also comes to mean "physical possession or coercive power [*mulk, milk*]," since this latter type of force also comes to constitute some sort of "clear proof."[2]

While it is correct to say that *sultān* in 55:33 means clear proof or argument rooted in sure knowledge, in the general usage of the Qur'ān, the inference seems to be the other way around. The term certainly can mean physical, overwhelming power, as al-Tabarī himself also admits. Satan will reply to those who, on the Last Day, will accuse him of misleading them in this world: "I had no power [*sultān*] over you; I only invited you [to evil] and you accepted my invitation" (14:22). A similar conversation will take place on the Last Day between those who were weak in this world and those strong and rich ones whom the former will accuse of having led them astray (37:27-30). All these uses of the term *sultān* seem to mean or directly imply sheer

---

2. Abū Ja'far Muhammad ibn Jarir al-Tabarī, *Jāmi' al-bayān fī tafsir al-qur'ān* (Cairo, 1321 A.H./1903-4 A.D.), 27:71.

physical power. This meaning must be logically prior, since it can easily be understood how overwhelming physical power can be changed into overwhelming rational or spiritual power, rather than vice versa.

In most other Qur'ānic contexts, however, *sultān* does mean a powerful, even overwhelmingly powerful, proof, reason, or sign (miracle). It can take the form of a supranatural miracle (23:45), or a revelation that can be recited or read (37:156ff.). It can also mean a reason justifying a punitive course of action: "Whosoever is killed without reason, we have given his next of kin the authority [or justification] [to retaliate]" (17:33); and, "Do you want [by your wrongdoing] to give God a clear justification against you?" (6:81). Or, a strong reason is given in defense against punitive action, as when Solomon said about the hoopoe: "I shall punish him severely or I shall slaughter him, unless he brings me some clear [or overwhelming] justification [for being absent]" (27:21).

Although we often find in the Qur'an that *sultān* was either demanded of the prophets or was given to them, and we have seen that the Qur'ān itself is described as *sultān* on several occasions, the more common usage appears when prophets are portrayed as accusing their opponents of "worshipping besides God that for which God has sent down no authority [*sultān*]," or when it is said that what they worshipped besides God "were mere names given by them [to their deities] without God having sent down any authority for them" (3:151; 6:81; 7:33, 71; 12:40; 53:23). W. Montgomery Watt,[3] following Richard Bell,[4] has interpreted the statement in 53:23 that certain pagan deities are "mere names" given to the deities by their worshippers, to mean that the Qur'ān is asserting that what the pagans worshipped actually did not exist. Watt and Bell claim that this was the final position of the Qur'ān regarding the pagan deities, after it had earlier adopted the view that what the Meccans worshipped as deities were really angels—a view held to be exemplified by 53:27.

This interpretation seems to me to be a capital mistake, apparently concocted to bolster Bell's theory of incessant revision of the Qur'ān by the Prophet—albeit "under divine guidance." Nowhere does the Qur'ān suggest that the pagan deities were nothing but mere names.

3. W. Montgomery Watt, *Muhammad at Mecca* (Oxford, 1953), p. 104, and *Companion to the Qur'ān* (London, 1967), p. 245.

4. *The Qur'ān*, p. 541.

What the Qur'ān is obviously saying to the pagans—not only through Muhammad but also through Abraham, Joseph, and others—is that when the pagans called various objects deities, they were *merely calling names* without any substance of truth or justification. That pagan deities, far from being just *nothing*, were in fact real objects—either human or otherwise—is brought out clearly in several parts of the Qur'an, e.g., when Joseph says to his prison companions:

> O my two prison companions! Are *several* Lords better or one all-powerful God? You worship besides Him only names you yourselves and your forefathers have given [i.e., names as deities are unreal, but names as objects *are* real], and for which [i.e., the deity-names] God has revealed no authority [*sultān*]. (12:39 ff.)

To resume our account of the demands of Muhammad's opponents for "signs" or miracles: the Qur'ān's usual response is to point out the complexity, the regularity, and the order of nature itself, and to emphasize that the universe and all that is in it could not have brought themselves into existence. Nor were they created in sport, but with a serious purpose (3:191; 38:27). This answer appears on the surface to be aimed not so much at vindicating the truth of Muhammad's message, as at proving God's almighty power and purposefulness. In view of the relationship between the "verses" (*āyāt*) of the Qur'ān and the "signs" (*āyāt*) of nature, however, the Qur'ānic response involving nature becomes directly relevant to the truth of the Qur'ān itself.

There is also evidence to show that the Qur'ān claims that certain "historical" or "portent" signs support the truth of the Prophet's message. We read: "These people [the Meccans] say: Why does he [the Prophet] not bring a sign from his Lord? Has there not come to them the clear proof contained in the earlier Books?" (20:133); and, "Indeed, it is in the Books of the men of old. Is it not a sign for them that the learned ones of the Children of Israel recognize it [the Qur'ān]?" (26:196ff.).

A clear portent-type sign is mentioned in 13:31: "The disbelievers continue to be afflicted [with misfortune] because of what they do, or it alights near their door—until God's promise is [eventually] fulfilled." The idea here is that the misfortunes (famines, battles, etc.) of the Meccans are a foretaste of what is to come later as divine chastise-ment. Al-Tabarī tells us, from numerous authorities, that the verse points specifically to the misfortunes suffered by the Meccans as a result of Muslim attacks on their caravans, resulting in the surrender of Mecca to Islam.[5] According to this interpretation, in its prediction this verse parallels 30:1-6, which refers to a victory of Persia over Byzantium while predicting (e.g., in the statement, "It is a promise of God") a reversal of the fortunes of war.

But what the Meccans and Jews specifically demanded from Muhammad were *supranatural* miracles like those of earlier prophets. They demanded, for example, that an angel should be sent down to him, that he should become very rich suddenly or come to possess huge orchards, that he should bring down the heavens or ascend to heaven and bring back a book they could recite, etc. (6:8, 50; 11:31; 25:7; etc.; cf. also 17:90ff.). The Qur'ān replies that angels would be sent down to them if those to whom the message is being brought were angels; that Muhammad has never claimed to be a master of treasures but only a Messenger of God; that God could, if He wished, bring about these things at the hands of a prophet, but that a prophet cannot do these things on his own (6:9, 36, 110; 17:95; 7:188; 11:12). But there are also other answers: that previous nations *had been* shown miracles at the hands of *their* prophets exactly as they had demanded them, but the people still rejected the prophets; that if Muhammad were to bring a thousand miracles to the Meccans or to the Jews, it still would do them no good; that if Muhammad were to bring down a book from the heavens *in concreto* so the people could touch it, they still would not accept him (3:183ff.; 6:7; etc.). Indeed, 17:59 states categorically: "And nothing has prevented Us from sending miracles [*ayat*] except that earlier peoples disbelieved in them." The Jews had asked Moses to perform much greater miracles than they were demanding from Muhammad, for they asked Moses to show God to them physically (4:153).

One reason Muhammad did not have miracles of the older supranatural type is that they were out of date. Still, the Prophet was uneasy that supranatural miracles were not available to him. On this the Qur'ān comments rather sharply:

We know, indeed, that what they say grieves you [O Muhammad], but the wicked ones are not just rejecting you; they are rejecting the signs

5. Al-Ṭabari, *op. cit.*, 13:89-91.

[āyāt] of God. Messengers before you have been repudiated [by their peoples], but they bore with patience their repudiation and their persecution until Our succor came to them. . . . If their rejection [of your message] weighs heavily upon you, then, if you can, seek out a hole into the earth or [climb up] to the heavens by a ladder and bring them a miracle [āya]! If God had so willed, He would have united all people on [this] Guidance—so do not be among the ignorant ones. (6:33-35)

The concepts of the regularity and autonomy of nature on the one hand and of the non-ultimacy of nature on the other do not appear in the Qur'ān exclusively, or even perhaps most importantly, in connection with the doctrine of miracles, but for two other purposes. The argument of the non-ultimacy of nature is often employed to prove the destructibility of nature and the possibility of its eventual re-creation for the purpose of the final accountability of, and judgment upon, man. Those to whom the stability of natural phenomena seems to afford a snug haven from accepting total moral responsibility and final judgment must know that the God whose great sign this universe is can create other forms of existence and life as well. The dawning of the consciousness that this life is only one of an infinite number of possible forms of life that God is capable of creating should be a potent factor, even for the dullest minds, in removal of the veil of nature that separates man from God. Indeed, the myriad forms of life in this universe betoken a Being of infinite power and wisdom. If God could create this universe and all that is in it, then He can replace it with another level of existence where people will be judged according to their deeds in this life and assigned their true destinies.

The Qur'ān also portrays vividly in several suras (e.g., 81 and 99) the chaos that will occur at the end of time when God suspends the laws of nature He established at the time of creation. Before God's power, which is exercised in the cause of justice and mercy, nothing whatever can stand. The entire earth shall be in His grasp on the Last Day and the immense magnitude of the heavenly space "shall be wrapped up" in His right hand (39:67). Has God been so fatigued with this first creation that He cannot create another (50:15)? Destruction is not for the sake of destruction alone, but to bring about a rearrangement of physical and moral elements and factors, a new level of creation.

Similarly, the argument involving the regularity of nature is very often employed to prove the utility of nature for man. Nature exists for

man to exploit for his own ends, while the end of man himself is
nothing else but to serve God, to be grateful to Him, and to worship
Him alone. The utility, serviceability, and exploitability of nature by
man are spoken of in numerous verses:

> It is He who has created all that is in the earth for you [or: has created
> what is in the earth for all of you]. (2:29)
>
> Do you not see that God has made subservient to you what is in the
> heavens and the earth? (31:20)
>
> God it is Who has subjected to you the sea that ships may sail therein
> by His command, that you may earn of God's bounty [through trade]
> and that you may be grateful. And He has made subservient to you all
> that is in the heavens and the earth, coming from Him; therein are
> signs for people who reflect. (45:12 ff.; cf. also 14:32 ff.; 16:12-14;
> 22:65; 29:61; 31:29; 35:13; 39:5; 43:12 ff.)

Though all such verses portray God's power, their primary intent is
to show God's use of His power for the betterment of man. Man is
invited to use this opportunity for the good and not to "corrupt the
earth [*fasād fī'l-arḍ*]," a phrase often repeated in the Qur'ān. The
creation of the universe was a serious affair, not a sport or a triviality:
'And We have not created the heavens and the earth and what is
therein purposelessly—that is the view of those who reject [God] or
who are ungrateful" (38:27; cf. 3:191). Nature is the grand handiwork
of the Almighty, but it does not exist just to show off His might and
power. It is to serve man by meeting his vital needs.

The purpose of man's creation is that he do good in the world, not
substitute himself for God and think that he can make and unmake the
moral law at his own convenience and for his own selfish and narrow
ends. This is the difference between physical laws and the moral
law—the one is to be used and put to service; the other must be obeyed
and served. For God says: "Do you think, then, that We created you in
sport and that you shall not be returned to Us [charged with
responsibility]?" (23:115).

Chapter Five

Prophethood and Revelation

In Chapter I, we spoke in general terms of the necessity of prophethood and Revelation, for which the basis is the mercifulness of God and the immaturity of man in ethical perception and motivation. The prophets were extraordinary men who, through their sensitive and impregnable personalities and their reception and steadfast and fearless preaching of the Divine Messages, shook men's consciences from a state of traditional placidity and hypomoral tension into one of alertness where they could clearly see God as God and Satan as Satan. As we have repeatedly said in several preceding chapters, the Qur'ān recognizes this as a universal phenomenon: all over the world, there have been God's Messengers whether or not named in the Qur'ān (40:78; 4:164). These Messengers or prophets are "sent to their peoples" at first but the message they deliver is not just local; it has a universal import and must be believed in and followed by all humanity—this is what the indivisibility of prophethood means.

It is imperative that the prophet succeed in getting the support of his people, for otherwise his message has little chance of getting through to others and even when it does, it may be gravely distorted. The prophets are, therefore, squarely charged with doing everything to get their message across; the Qur'ān often speaks of a confrontation, on the Day of Judgment, between the prophets and their peoples: "We shall certainly ask those to whom the Messengers were sent and We shall equally question the Messengers, and We shall surely relate to them [what transpired between them] on the basis of sure knowledge and We are never absent" (7:7). The Prophet Muhammad is urged to proclaim the Message without any "reservations in your mind" (7:1) and "loudly and uncompromisingly" (15:94; cf. also 5:67, and the confrontation of Jesus with Christians, 5:116-117). From every community a "Witness," i.e., the prophet sent to them, will be brought forth (16:84, 89; 28:75). The Prophet Muḥammad shall declare, "O my Lord! My people have abandoned this Qur'ān" (25:30).

From the earliest days of Islam, Muslims have held that this succession of Divine Messengers came to an end with the Prophet Muḥammad: "Muḥammad is not the father of any of your men, but he is God's Messenger and the Seal of the Prophets" (33:40). This interpretation appears correct, but to an outsider the belief appears dogmatic and in need of rationalization. Medieval Muslim thinkers, theologians, philosophers, and historians, have formulated several arguments to this end, mainly on the two different but allied bases that there has been an evolution in religion, of which Islam is the final form, and that an examination of the content of religions shows that Islam is the most adequate and perfect religion—a theme which itself has complicated and varied proofs.

Several Muslim modernists have held passionately that with and through Islam and its revealed book, man has reached rational maturity and there is no need for further Revelations. In view of the fact that man is still plagued by moral confusion, however, and that his moral sense has not kept pace with his advance in knowledge, in order to be consistent and meaningful, this argument must add that man's moral maturity is conditional upon his constantly seeking guidance from the Divine Books, especially the Qur'ān, and that man has not become mature in the sense that he can dispense with divine guidance. It must further be held that an adequate understanding of divine guidance does not depend any more upon "chosen" personalities but has become a collective function.

The proposition of the finality of the mission of Muḥammad does appear to be corroborated by the fact that no global religious movement has arisen since Islam—not that there have been no claimants, but that there have been no *successful* claimants. However, Muḥammad's being the last Messenger of God and the Qur'ān's being the last Revelation obviously place a heavy responsibility upon those who claim to be Muslims. Such a claim is not so much a privilege but an obligation; yet it has been taken by Muslims to be a privilege.

For God's envoys to mankind, the Qur'ān uses the terms *nabī* and *rasūl*. The *nabī*, "a giver of news," does not mean in the Qur'ān (as it mostly did in the Bible) "one who gives news about the future," but "one who gives news from God"; he comes from God to warn against evil and to give good tidings to those who are good. Hence the terms "giver of good tidings" and "warner" appear frequently in the Qur'ān, particularly in the earlier period. *Rasūl* means "messenger," one sent by God to mankind—although in the Qur'ān, as we shall see in this chapter, this term is sometimes also applied to the Angel of Revelation, one who is sent by God to the Prophet and in this latter meaning the term *safara* (plural of *safīr* meaning "ambassador") is also used once (80:15). Traditionally, Muslim Qur'ān commentators have made a distinction, saying that *nabī* means a divine envoy without a law (*sharī'a*) and, presumably, without a revealed book, while *rasūl* means one with a law and a revealed book.

Although such sharp distinctions are somewhat doubtful, since the Qur'ān describes some religious personages both as *nabī* and as *rasūl* (e.g, 7:158; 19:51, 54), there is no doubt that some distinction is intended, for example, in a verse like "And We did not send before you any *rasūl* or *nabī*" (22:52). It also appears that the frequency of use of *nabī* increases from the later Meccan period through the Madinan period. On the whole, *rasūl* does signify something weightier than *nabī*, for a *nabī* can be auxiliary to a *rasūl* as Aaron was to Moses (19:51, 53), although *rasūls* (or, strictly speaking, *mursal*, "the one sent") can be jointly commissioned (36:13, 16). Although prophecy is indivisible (2:136), not all prophets are equal, for "We have made some Messengers more excellent than others" (2:253; also see 17:55) and Muhammad is exhorted to "be patient [under trial] as the Messengers with determination and steadfastness were patient" (46:35).

The most celebrated prophets are those whose own stories and those of their peoples have been told and retold in the Qur'ān. These include personages from the Bible, Noah, Abraham, Moses, Jesus, and Shu'aib (the Prophet of Midyan)—particularly the first four—and two from the Arab tradition, Sālih of the tribe of Thamūd and Hud of that of 'Ād; indeed, the two ancient Arab tribes were called by the Arabs *al-'Arab al-'āriba*, the "primal Arabs." This mixed prophetology presumably existed in Arabia before Islam, although the process whereby it was achieved and the period of the formation of the tradition are not known. But the existence of the tradition does show that the Arabs had come to achieve a prophetology that was independent of the Biblical tradition. The chronology of the major prophets as it can be ascertained from suras 7 and 11—which give their accounts systematically, especially sura 11, which has a developed and patterned style—is: Noah, Hūd, Ṣālih, Abraham (whose contemporary is Lot), Shu'aib (who is placed "not much after" Lot and Abraham, 11:89), Moses, and Jesus. Except for Noah, the two Arabian prophets are more ancient than the entire Biblical tradition.

All Messengers have preached essentially the same message, that there is one, unique God to Whom alone service and worship are due, Who in the final analysis alone must be loved and feared. All others are "false gods" who can claim no share in the Divinity; all else is God's servant ('abd) and necessarily under His law and command. This is the Qur'ānic doctrine of *tauhīd* or monotheism which we have tried to elaborate in Chapter I; the reader is urged to grasp as well as possible the meaning of this doctrine which is central to the Qur'ān—without which, indeed, Islam is unthinkable—yet which seems to have degenerated alike with non-Muslims and most Muslims into a mechanical formula and has lost much of the content, let alone the depth and intensity of the feeling, which this doctrinal preaching generates. For non-Muslims, unfortunately, one great obstacle to a true understanding and appreciation of the *tauhīd* of the Qur'ān is the stereotyped belief that the Qur'ān "borrowed" it from the Jews, as though it were a matter of indifference whether one studies this or that form of monotheism!

Muhammad, like all other prophets, is a "warner and giver of good tidings" and his mission is to preach—constantly and unflinchingly. Since this message is from God and is direly needed by men for survival and success, it has to be accepted by man and implemented. His preaching, therefore, is no conventional speech-making but has to "bring home" the crucial message. If the message is not accepted and the mission does not succeed, then the preacher may have discharged his duty, but God has definitely failed and humanity is doomed. But if God's purposes are frustrated and humanity doomed, has the preacher "discharged his duty"? His duty is to *succeed* in implementing the message in order "to reform the earth and remove corruption therefrom," and to institute an ethically-based social order wherein "good shall be commanded and evil prohibited" and "God's sovereignty shall be upheld."

This trend represents the basic thrust and the real élan of Muhammad, both inside and outside the Qur'ān. He must be constantly on the move in order to persuade his people to accept the

Divine Message. "Warn your immediate clan" (26:214), the Qur'ān advises him on strategy. He does; but he cannot let pass any opportunity of influencing others as well, and particularly of enlisting the support of the powerful elder statesmen of the Quraish, who, once won to his cause, can turn the tide in its favor. He is a Messenger in a desperate hurry, for he sees his society in a desperate situation—"During the day, you perform a long out-reach, indeed" (73:7), the Qur'ān says to him, and "We are going to put upon your shoulders a heavy Call" (73:5); therefore, he is to "stand through the night—except a small portion of it—in intimate prayer to your Lord" (73:2). This "heavy Call" replaces that "burden which was breaking your back" (94:2-3), i.e., the tormenting realization of the acute problems in his society in particular and human society in general and his search for solutions through prayer and contemplation in the Cave of Hirā': "He [God] found you probing in the dark and guided you to the right path" (93:7).

In his unrelenting endeavor to further God's cause, the Prophet was once reprimanded by the Qur'ān. While he was conversing with al-Walīd ibn al-Mughīra, an influential Meccan, he was approached with a question by a blind early convert to Islam, ibn Umm Maktūm. The Prophet was irritated at this intrusion and ignored the blind man. The Qur'ān said:

> He frowned and turned his back that the blind man approached him. What do you know [O Muhammad!] if perchance the blind man has a pure heart? Or, he remembers God and this remembrance benefits him? As for him [the influential Meccan] who proudly considers himself self-sufficient, you seek him out on purpose—and it will do you no harm if he does not become pure. But as for him who comes running to you—and he fears God—you ignore him. Nay! This Qur'ān is but an admonition; whosoever will, let him take it. It is in noble documents, sealed and pure, in the hands of Divine Messengers [the Angels or Agencies of Revelation]. (80:1-15)

This restless and unhalting campaign had attracted some devoted followers, mainly from the lower and disenfranchised classes but a number also of well-to-do merchants and religiously sensitive personalities, some of whom had already been experiencing spiritual ferment. But since the message of Muhammad apparently threatened the larger vested interests of the Meccan mercantile aristocrats—in the economic field as well as the religious—most of them rejected it. Not long after the message began to be preached publicly, the persecution of Muslims started. The weaker classes in the new community particularly came under trials and dire pressures. The new message in many cases also divided families and set brother against brother and son against father—a phenomenon most disastrous for Arab tribal society, whose solidarity rested on blood ties and affiliation pacts. As the struggle went on, the Meccans became more and more perturbed and distressed and tried to persuade Muḥammad's uncle, Abū Ṭālib— who had not accepted his nephew's message but had given him protection—either to cause Muḥammad to desist or to withdraw his support from him; these repeated attempts were all unsuccessful.

At times this situation naturally affected the Prophet's own inner life and made him pause to think whether the whole effort was worthwhile, or had any real prospects of success. On the one hand was the utter conviction that the message was from God and that he must execute it—otherwise his own society was doomed to perish; on the other, the actual situation was so distressing and prospects of success so problematic that if a dilemma had real horns, this one surely did. We must remember that Muḥammad was not by temperament an aggressive or obtrusive man—indeed, a close study of his character reveals a naturally pensive, introverted, shy, and withdrawn personality who had been impelled by an inner urge born of an acute perception of the existential human situation to enter the arena of historic action. This explains why the Qur'ānic revelations, particularly in the early stages, are characterized by a staccato-like abruptness and consist of very short expressions like sudden volcanic outbursts or the passage of a huge river through a gorge. The Angel of Revelation spoke directly through Muḥammad's heart.

Under these conditions of exceptional strain, the Qur'ān expresses itself in various ways. The Meccans are frequently denounced as possessing no understanding; they are deaf and dumb and blind and their hearts are sealed (2:8, 18, 171; 6:39; 8:22; 10:42; 27:80) and other dramatized expressions to that effect, (e.g., 36:8-9); "they are like cattle, in fact, much more misguided" (7:179); "To Hell have We destined many of the jinn and the humans" (7:179). A second important channel of expression for the Qur'ān is to relate the situation of pagan Mecca to that of the peoples and cities of earlier prophets, which met their doom when they refused to mend their ways in accordance with the invitations of their prophets.

A third important way of dealing with this mood of frustration, agony, and apparent helplessness is the consolation that the Qur'ān offers: "We have not sent down the Qur'ān upon you that you should be miserable" (20:2); "Will you, then, melt away your soul after them out of grief that they do not believe in this teaching?" (18:6); similarly in Madina: "Do not waste yourself away for the unrighteous ones" or "the disbelieving ones" (5:26, 68). In the later Meccan period, the prophet Shu'aib is reported as saying to his people, "O my people! I have delivered to you the Message of my Lord and I have admonished you; how shall I waste myself on a disbelieving people?" (7:93). Muḥammad is told that he is only a "Warner," "a reminder"; "your task is only to preach"; "you are not a warden over them"; "you cannot force them"; "God it is Who can make those hear whom He wills—you cannot cause the dead to hear in their graves" (35:22; 11:12; 88:21; 3:20; 5:92, 99; 88:22; 50:45); "If God had so willed, He would have caused the whole world to come to guidance and made them one community" (5:48; 6:35; 10:99). In moments of unusual exasperation the Qur'ān tells him that if these people do not believe and mend their ways, they will be doomed, either before his eyes or after his death: "Either We shall show you something of the punishment which We have warned them of, or We shall bring your life to a term" (10:46; in the same vein: 13:40; 40:77; 43:41-42).

But these moments pass, and the basic élan of the inevitable success of God's cause and vindication of the Truth reasserts itself. Divine succor and final victory belongs to God's Messengers and those who support them: "We do, indeed, help our Messengers and the believers *in this life* as well as on the Day when the Witnesses shall stand up" (40:51). In sura 21, devoted to earlier prophets, one prophet after another is named and his vindication described; about Noah (with whom the series of great prophets begins) it is said, "We helped him against the people who had given the lie to Our signs" (21:77). So about Moses, Aaron, and their followers, "We gave them help and they were the victors" (37:116).

Earlier prophets had faced similar situations of exasperation and distress, until they cried out, "When *will* God's help come? Lo! God's help is at hand" (2:214). God's help is certainly conditional upon the efforts of the prophets and their followers—which is their help to God (the Qur'ān recurrently emphasizes this mutuality; cf., for example, 47:7; 22:40, etc.)—but in the end victory will be theirs: "It is God's party that is victorious" (37:173; 5:56). And when success began to come, it was naturally seen as proof of the truth of the prophet's mission and as a harbinger of total success (for if in a situation of apparent helplessness, God did promise eventual success and vindication, there is all the more justification for success to be regarded as prefiguring further success). The crescendo is reached in the following verse, "These people [the pagans] want to extinguish God's Light by blowing at it with their mouths, but God will not have it otherwise except to complete His Light, even though the disbelievers dislike it" (9:32; also 61:8).

It is because of this basic line of thought concerning the final victory of good over evil that the Qur'ān refers constantly to the vindication of Noah, who was saved from the flood; of Abraham, who was saved from fire; of Moses, who was saved from Pharaoh and his hordes; and of Jesus, who was saved from execution at the hands of the Jews (hence the rejection by the Qur'ān of the crucifixion story). Muhammad must equally be vindicated: he will not only be saved but his Message will be victorious. Hence he must proclaim the Message loudly and without reservations—even though he is by temperament a reserved and withdrawn person and the Message is revolutionary: "Proclaim loudly what you are commanded and become indifferent to [the machinations of] those who assign partners to God" (15:94); "This is a Book that has been sent down to you, so let there be no heaviness in your heart about it—that you should warn [people] by it" (7:2); "O Messenger! proclaim [unreservedly] what has been sent down to you from your Lord; for if you do not; you have not proclaimed His Message; and God will protect you from people" (5:67).

Finally, to this genre belong those verses and incidents where the Messenger is said to have contemplated some sort of compromise which his opponents pressed for soon after it became clear to them that he was totally serious about his mission. Under pressure from the Meccans and entreaties from his protecting uncle, Abū Tālib, his inclination is understandable, particularly in view of the hardship his movement had created for many families, his native sensitivity of character, and his inborn instinct of mercy, to which the Qur'ān also testifies abundantly: "You are no sorcery-stricken person, by God's blessing; you shall have [on the contrary] an unending reward—and you are, indeed, of a great moral character" (68:2-4); "We have not sent you except as a mercy for the whole world" (21:107). Though grieving over the defeat in the Battle of Uḥud, due to the clear mistake of his followers, he generously forgave them and the Qur'ān comments, "By the mercy of God you were lenient to them, for if you had been rough and harsh-hearted, they would have deserted you" (3:159).

These compromise rapproachements were repeatedly sought by the Meccans:

> They wish you would soften up a little, so they would, too. (68:9)
>
> They nearly seduced you away from what We had revealed to you in attributing to Us something else—in that case they would have befriended you. But for the fact that We made you firm, you had almost yielded to them some ground—in that case We would have given you a double punishment in this life and a double punishment in the hereafter, and you would have found no helper against Us. (17:73-75)

This last passage seems to be connected with a plot to expel the Prophet from Mecca, as is shown by the verse immediately following (17:76), "They almost drove you out from your hometown in order to expel you therefrom—in that case they would not have survived except for a little while." (There were, of course, other plots to kill him, for example, by burning him alive [21:68; 29:24] or by lapidation [11:91; 18:20; 19:46; 44:20; 36:18], or assassinating him in sleep [27:49], for it is certain that often the Prophet's own situation is mirrored in the accounts of earlier prophets. These plots are generally confirmed by the Prophet's biographers.) Further, in the same vein:

> We never sent any Messenger [rasūl] or any prophet [nabī] but that when he thought, Satan intruded into his thoughts; but God erases [or abrogates] what Satan has intruded and then makes His own verses firm—God is knowing, wise. (22:52)
>
> Are you perchance going to abandon part of what is being revealed to you and your breast is going to be straitened for it [for fear of non-acceptance], since they would say Why has a treasure not been sent down upon him or an angel has not come with him? (11:12).

But whatever fears or thoughts—or even actual gestures—of compromise the Prophet might make, they were soon "abrogated" or "erased" by God, as verse 22:52 makes clear. The well-known story that after mentioning the pagan goddesses once (53:19-20), the Prophet described them as "exalted swans whose intercession [with God] is to be hoped for [*tilka' l-gharāniq al-'ūlā, wa inna shafā'ātahunna la-turtaja*]," only to abrogate these words in 53:21-23, is perfectly intelligible, for this incident occurred at a time of great trial and persecution for his followers, whom he had ordered to emigrate temporarily to Abyssinia. There are other indications that certain verses were replaced by others:

> We do not abrogate a verse or cause it to be forgotten but that We bring a better one in its place. (2:106)
>
> God obliterates whatever [verses] He chooses and confirms others, for with Him is the Mother of all Books. (13:39)
>
> And when We substitute one verse for another—and God knows best what He sends down—they say, You are but a forger; surely most of them are ignorant. (16:101)

For the Qur'ān, it is neither strange nor out of tune nor blameworthy for a prophet that he is not always consistent *as a human*. It is nevertheless as a human that he becomes an example for mankind, for his *average* level of conduct is still so high that it is a worthy model for mankind. Prophets are humans who must constantly struggle inwardly, but in this inward struggle truth and righteousness prevail; if prophets did not struggle and suffer inner travail, they could not become examples for other humans (for the humanness of Muhammad and the other prophets, see, e.g., 3:79; 14:11; 18:110; 21:34; 41:6; 17:93-94). We are told (2:260) that Abraham, the exemplar of all prophets, asked God to "show me how You can revive the dead," and when God asked him, "Do you not believe?" Abraham replied, "Yes, but still I want to set my heart at complete rest [about the matter]." Similarly, Abraham arrives at monotheism by a gradual process of eliminating astral gods (6:76). This is a major reason why a human who is God or becomes God is simply anathema to the Qur'ān. To struggle and to succeed—the success being seen as coming from God—is the hallmark of a man of God.

Let us return to the "substitution" of certain verses for others. This is the original meaning of "abrogation [*naskh*]" in the Qur'ān; it does not mean the juristic doctrine of abrogation which later developed in

Islam and which is an attempt to smooth out apparent *differences* in the import of certain verses. We have already seen that certain verses were replaced by others at God's command, i.e., through Revelation. The Qur'ān makes it clear that when Meccans asked him to make adjustments in the Qur'ānic doctrine so that they could accept it, the Prophet told them that it was up to God, not him:

> When Our clear verses are recited to them, those who do not expect to meet Us [on the Day of Judgment] say, Bring a different Qur'ān or change this one. Say, It is not up to me to change it by myself; I only follow what is revealed to me. I fear, if I disobey my Lord, the punishment of a mighty Day. Say, If God so willed, I would not be reciting it to you, nor would He be making it known to you—do you not reflect that I have lived amongst you [a long part of] my life before this? (10:15-16)

There is abundant evidence in the Qur'ān that while the Prophet did at times wish that developments would take a certain turn, God's Revelation went a different way: "Do not move your tongue with [i.e., ahead of] the Revelation, hastily anticipating it. It is upon Us to bring it together and to recite it—so when We recite it, let you follow its recitation. Then it is also Our task to explain it" (75:16-19).

That Muhammad neither anticipated his becoming the Prophet, nor deliberately prepared himself to become one is also clearly demonstrated in several passages:

> He who has laid the obligation of the Qur'ān upon you, will certainly bring you to a [satisfactory] end; say, My Lord knows best who has brought guidance and who is clearly astray. You never did expect that the Book would be given to you—it is only a mercy from your Lord. (28:85-86)
> Even so did We send to you [or inspire you with] a spirit of Our Command [or Word]; you did not know before this what the Book is, nor Faith—We have made it a Light whereby We guide whomsoever We will. (42:52)
> You did not recite before this [the Qur'ān] a Book, nor did you write it down with your right hand [like the scribes]—in that case the disbelievers would be able to doubt the authenticity of your Revelation. (29:48)

It is certain that Muhammad's religious experience was sudden, as if a dead person had become alive: "Is he who was dead and whom We gave life and a Light whereby he moves about among people, like him who wanders about in multiple darkness whence no exit is afforded him?'' (6:123).

As we have tried to clarify in Chapters II and IV, the Qur'ān uses both naturalistic and religious idioms to describe *all* world phenomena, with no question of a contradiction between the two. On the contrary, the religious idiom *presupposes* the naturalistic language and, far from supplanting it, *envelops* it: winds and clouds do *cause* rains but it is God who *brings* rains and Who is working within the natural causes. The religious idiom is *ultimate after the demands of natural causation have been satisfied as explanatory formulae.* We would therefore have to say that in a naturalistic sense, Muḥammad did prepare himself for Prophethood (though not consciously), for he had an intense, natural, inborn sensitivity for moral problems confronting man; this sensitivity was increased by his having been orphaned so early in life. The tribe of the Quraish was the most powerful in Arabia; it first opposed him vehemently, but once it turned in his favor, Islam was truly launched on a world career.

All this naturalistic account is true, and yet the Prophet did not create his natural capacities any more than anybody else does; therefore, when all the natural factors collaborate towards a single, powerful *telos*, they must be referred to God. Besides, as we have already noted, Muḥammad had no conscious effort or desire to become Prophet, "If God so willed, I would not be reciting it to you (10:16)." For this reason, when Muḥammad's opponents asked him why he had come to be Prophet and "Why was this Qur'ān not sent down upon some big man in the two cities [of Mecca and Ṭā'if]?" (43:31), the Qur'an gives both kinds of reply: "Do *they* distribute the mercy of your Lord?" (43:32)—which is couched in a religious idiom—and "God knows where to put His Messengership" (6:124)—which is cast in a naturalistic idiom. The Prophet himself was always only too conscious that his Prophethood was not of his own making and that even his natural capacities could not *cause* Revelation, which was a sheer mercy of God: "Do they say that he [Muḥammad] has forged [the Qur'ān] as a lie upon God? If God wills, He shall seal up your heart [so that there will be no more Revelation]" (42:24); again, "If We willed, We would surely remove the Revelation We have given you; then you will find no one who can help you with it despite Us!" (17:86).

Before we begin to talk about the nature and mode of Muhammad's revelatory experience and the Qur'ān itself, we must discuss the celebrated event of the *Mi'rāj*, the "Ascension," of the Prophet, which according to tradition took place late in the Meccan period on the eve of his immigration to Madina. There is a highly detailed description of this experience—in fact, two experiences:

> The one of powerful sinews and strong muscles [the agent of Revelation] taught him [Muhammad]: he established himself on the highest horizon, then he drew near and descended so that he was at two bow-lengths or even nearer [to Muhammad]. He then revealed to God's servant [Muhammad] whatever he revealed. His [Muhammad's] heart has not lied about what it saw—will you then doubt what he actually saw? He had seen him another time also when he had descended—near the furthest lote-tree where the Garden of Abode is located, when there enveloped the lote-tree what enveloped it! The Prophet's eye did not blink, nor did it go out of control—he witnessed one of the greatest signs of his Lord. (53:5-18)

It is obvious from this passage (1) that the reference is to experiences at two different times; (2) that in one experience the Prophet "saw" the Angel of Revelation at the "highest horizon," and he possessed extraordinary, almost suppressive strength, while on an earlier occasion he had "seen" him at the "furthest lote-tree—where the Garden of Abode is located"; (3) that instead of the Prophet "going up" in Ascension, in both cases the agent of Revelation "came down"; (4) that the experience was spiritual and not physical-locomotive: "his *heart* did not lie about what it saw"; (5) finally, that these revelatory experiences involved an expansion of the Prophet's self by which he enveloped all reality and which was total in its comprehensive sweep—the reference in both cases is to an ultimate, be it the "highest horizon" or the "furthest lote-tree."

This last point is confirmed by two other relevant passages:

> Glory be to Him who caused His servant [Muhammad] to travel one night from the Sacred Mosque to the "remotest Mosque" whose environs We have blessed, that We may show him of Our signs. (17:1)
>
> This [the Qur'ān] is the speech of a noble Messenger [the Angel of Revelation] who is powerful, who has a firm station with the Lord of the Throne, and who is obeyed and trusted There. Your companion

[Muhammad] is not mad—he has seen him [the Angel of Revelation] at the clearest horizon and the latter is not niggardly [but generous] in giving news of the Unseen. (81:19-24)

Like the first passage, these two passages also mention something ultimate as the object of the Prophet's experience: the "remotest mosque" in the first passage and the "clear horizon" in the other. This latter passage bears certain striking resemblances to the first of the three passages in that both describe the agent of Revelation as a powerful being and speak about the "horizon" as the furthest point of experience. There may also have been more than two experiences because the "remotest mosque" mentioned in what is probably the latest of the three passages (17:1) is not spoken of in the other two. Since the experiences are spiritual in nature, the entities mentioned in these passages obviously cannot be physical, although it must be remembered that when a spiritual experience is of great intensity, where the distance between subject and object is almost completely removed, "voices" are "heard" and "figures" "seen" by the subject and the inner experience takes on a quasi-concrete form. We shall see presently that although the standard revelatory experience of the Prophet was a matter of the "heart", this experience nevertheless automatically took the form of words, as is the case with all spiritual experiences of great intensity.

Before we discuss in closer detail the nature of the Spirit or the agent of Revelation that descended upon Muḥammad, it would be well to point out the kinds of accusations that were hurled at Muḥammad by his opponents. He was occasionally called a soothsayer (*kāhin*: 52:29; 69:42); in pre-Islamic Arabia members of this profession were consulted for oracular statements on certain important matters. (The Qur'ān, of course, rejects this.) More often, he was called a poet (*shā'ir*: 36:69; 21:5; 37:36; 52:30; 69:41). Many Arabs believed a poet to be invaded by some spirit when he delivered poetry; the precise nature of that spirit is not known, but it most probably involved some disturbance of consciousness or the supervening of a supernatural consciousness (the root *shu'ūr* means consciousness or awareness beyond the ordinary). The Qur'ān strongly denies this and criticizes poets:

We have not taught him poetry nor is it proper for him—this is but a Reminder and a clear Qur'ān. (36:69)

Shall I inform you of those upon whom Satans descend? They descend upon every sinful liar. They listen carefully [to their inspiring Satans] but most of them tell falsehoods. Poets are followed by us wayward ones. Do you not see that they wander aimlessly in every valley and that they say what they do not do—except those who believe and do good deeds. (26:221-27)

"Wandering aimlessly in every valley" is probably a reference to the uncontrolled and extravagant poetic imagination as well as to the pre-Islamic poets' uninhibited singing of their sexual freedom. This passage is not, therefore, a condemnation of all poetry but only of undisciplined imagination. The Qur'ān is itself highly poetical, particularly in its vivid and powerful diction and in the masterful artistry and expressiveness of its portrayals; but it is not poetry of the kind the pagans condemned in it.

Besides the accusations that he was a soothsayer or a poet (which seem peculiar to Muḥammad among all prophets in the Qur'ān), he is also called a sorcerer (*sāḥir*) or a victim of sorcery (*mashūr*), and a man possessed with some evil spirit (*majnūn*); the last two, besides being frequently attributed to Muḥammad, are also attributed generally to all earlier prophets by their peoples (51:52). The Pharaoh especially accused Moses of being a sorcerer (also once of being possessed by an evil spirit [26:27]) and twice the Jews said the same of Jesus (5:110; 61:6). But besides Muḥammad, only Moses is said to have been called *majnūn*, and that only once. Against Muḥammad it is also urged that he was too well versed in certain earlier Books: That they should say, "You have studied well" (6:105), and that he is a "well-taught mad man" (44:14).

The Qur'ān, of course, sternly repudiates such charges: "Is *this* sorcery or is it, rather, the case that *you* are blind?" (52:15); "Your companion is not possessed—he has seen him [the agent of Revelation] on the clear horizon, who is not niggardly of giving news of the Unseen. Nor is this [the Qur'ān] the word of Satan the outcast [from heaven]—so where are you going? This is but a Reminder to the world" (81:22-27). The accusation of forgery we have already discussed in connection with the "substitution" of some Qur'ānic verses by others and we shall return to it again in Chapter VIII. A particularly disarming reply of the Qur'ān is: "Do they say that you have forged it? Say, If I have forged it, I shall pay for my crime; in the meantime, I am quit of your crimes" (11:35). Here is a summary of most accusations with the comments of the Qur'ān:

> They say: This is but a forgery which he [Muhammad] himself has concocted and certain other people have helped him in this. These people speak unjustly and lie. They say, These are legends of the earlier communities which he has got written down for himself and they are being dictated to him morning and evening. Say [O Muhammad]: Rather, He has sent it down Who knows the secrets of the heavens and the earth; He is the Pardoning one, the Merciful one. And they say, What a [queer] Prophet! He eats food and goes about in the market place! Why has not an angel been sent down upon him, so that he might be a co-warner with him? Or, why has a treasure not been sent down to him, or [why has he not been given] a garden whose fruits he can eat? And the unjust ones say, You [Muslims] are only following a victim of sorcery. Look! What kinds of likenesses they coin for you—they have gone off the way and they cannot find one. (25:4-8)

The Meccans themselves, then, associated some kind of spirit—albeit a harmful one—with the Prophet. The spirit associated with him, however, was undoubtedly not of the kind his opponents attributed to him. It is the same Spirit, the agent of Revelation, that he "saw on the highest or clear horizon" and who revealed the Qur'ān to him. We shall next discuss the nature of this Spirit, the manner of Revelation, the effect of the Revelation in bringing certainty to the Prophet, and the result of the Revelation, the Qur'ān.

The term "angel" is, strictly speaking, not quite accurate for the agent of Revelation sent to Muhammad, for the Qur'ān describes the agent of Revelation, at least to Muhammad, never as an angel, but always as Spirit or spiritual Messenger. Angels (*malak*, plural *malā'ika*) occur frequently in the Qur'ān as celestial beings who are God's agents, carrying out all sorts of tasks from taking men's lives to carrying God's Throne; they can be sent to prophets (for example to Abraham, 11:70, and to Lot, 11:81) and they can be sent down upon true believers to give them courage (41:30), but the Qur'ān does not mention them as agents of Revelation. Indeed, God may also send Revelation (*wahy*) to angels themselves when they are sent to encourage believers in distress: "When [in the battle of Badr] God revealed to [or inspired] the angels [saying], I am with you, so give courage to the believers" (8:12). In the case of the great prophets preceding Muhammad—Noah, Abraham, and Moses—God appears to address them directly, although there is a general statement: "He casts the Spirit from His Command upon whomsoever He wishes of His servants" (40:15), from which we can infer that God's prophets had the benefit of God's Spirit, who gave them Revelation (cf. also 16:2). With regard to Jesus' mother Mary (although she was not a prophet—the Qur'ān does not mention any females as prophets), it is said that she was impregnated by "Our Spirit" (19:17; 21:91; 66:12); and God also infused into Adam, after building his carnal frame, His own Spirit (15:29; 32:9; 38:72). Believers, too, "on whose hearts Faith is firmly inscribed" are supported by God's Spirit (58:22). Jesus, however, was supported with the "Holy Spirit" [*rūh al-qudus*]" (2:87, 253; 5:110) which is also the agent of the Qur'ānic Revelation (16:102). Jesus himself is described as "the Prophet of God, His Word that He cast into Mary and a Spirit from Him" (4:171)—presumably because his mother was impregnated by the Spirit.

There is no doubt that the agent of Revelation to Muhammad is this Spirit. The Meccans, as we have seen, often asked of Muhammad that an "angel be sent down upon him," to which the Qur'ān often replied that angels cannot be sent to humans as prophets (sometimes the Qur'ān also threatened that "We do not send angels except with the final Decision and in that case they [the Prophet's opponents] will not be given respite" [15:8]). It is, therefore, certain that angels did not come to the Prophet—his Revelation came from the Holy Spirit, also described as the "Trusted Spirit" (26:193).

Yet, one should not think that the Spirit and the angels are wholly different. It is probable that the Spirit is the highest form of the angelic nature and the closest to God (cf. 81:19-21 quoted in connection with our discussion of the Prophet's Ascension). At all events, the Qur'ān mentions the angels and the Spirit together in several places: "[On the Night of Measurement] angels and the Spirit descend, with the permission of their Lord; with all commands" (97:4) (we shall speak about this Night below); "The angels and the Spirit ascend to Him in a day the span whereof is fifty thousand years" (70:4); "The Day [of Judgment] when the Spirit and the angels shall stand up in rows [in obedience]" (78:38); "He sends down the angels with the Spirit from His Command upon whomsoever He will of His servants" (16:2). Note that, in the last passage, the Spirit is not something additional to the angels but is something conveyed by them.

When Meccans repeatedly demanded that an angel descend upon

Muhammad and the Qur'ān repeatedly repudiated such demands, it is probable that they were demanding something *they* could see and hear and possibly talk to, while what the Qur'ān continued to emphasize was that the agency of Revelation was the Spirit that came upon the Prophet's *heart*: "The Trusted Spirit has brought it [the Qur'ān] down upon your heart, that you should be a warner" (26:193); this Spirit is identified with Gabriel: "Say: whoever be an enemy of Gabriel, it is He [God] Who has brought him down upon your heart [or it is he, i.e., Gabriel, who has brought it, i.e., the Qur'ān, down upon your heart]" (2:97). That the Revelation and its agent were spiritual and internal to the Prophet is also testified to elsewhere in the Qur'ān, "If God so willed, He would seal up your heart [O Muhammad!], so that no more Revelation would come to you" (42:24). Those Ḥadīth stories, then, where the angel Gabriel is depicted as a public figure conversing with the Prophet whose companions saw him, must be regarded as later fictions.

The view of some modern Western scholars that at first the Prophet thought he was being addressed directly by God and only later came to posit an intermediary agency of Revelation, must also be rejected, since the Spirit and the angels appear in very early suras like 97:4, while even later the Qur'ān continues to employ language where God addresses him directly. As noted a while ago in the stories of earlier prophets God addresses them directly but the Qur'ān does speak of the agency of the Spirit in their cases also (40:15; 16:2). When we discuss the question of the manner of Revelation, we shall quote the categorical Qur'ānic denial that God may speak directly to a human. There is also a suggestion that the Spirit is the actual content of Revelation: "Even so have We revealed to you a Spirit of Our Command" (42:52; cf. also 40:15: "He casts the Spirit of His Command upon whomsoever He wills"). Perhaps the Spirit is a power or a faculty or an agency which develops in the Prophet's heart and which comes into actual revelatory operation when needed, but it originally does "descend" from "above." This is in perfect harmony with a well-known Islamic tradition according to which the entire Qur'ān was first "brought down" to the lowest heaven (i.e., the Prophet's heart, as thinkers like al-Ghazālī and Shāh Walī Allāh al-Dihlawī would rightly say) and then relevant verbal passages produced when needed.

Be that as it may, we must attend to another important fact about the Qur'ānic idiom concerning Revelation. In five verses (16:2; 17:85;

40:15; 42:52; 97:4) where the Spirit is mentioned as descending or bringing something down, i.e., Revelation, it is associated with the term *amr*, which we have rendered as "Command". Except in 97:4 where this term is used alone, it is used with reference to God, and the construction employed is *rūḥ min amrinā* or *rūḥ min amrihī*. The preposition *min* cannot be read as "by," so that these words could mean, "the Spirit by Our [or His] Command," although it is tempting to do so (and the Qur'ān commentators have generally done so in the case of 17:85, which reads, "They [the commentators tell us the reference is to Jews] ask you [O Muḥammad] concerning the Spirit; say, The Spirit is *by the Command of my Lord* and you have been given but little knowledge about it." (Al-Ṭabarī would read, *"belongs to the affair of my Lord,"* i.e., the matter of the Spirit belongs exclusively to the domain of God and nobody else knows about it—a possible but hardly likely interpretation in view of the other cases of the same construction where this meaning is impossible.) Since the construction in this case is identical with that in the other cases, it must have the same meaning: "The Spirit of Our [or His] Command".

But what is this *amr*—rendered by us and many others as "Command"—whose Spirit descended upon Muḥammad or was brought down upon his heart by angels? This "Command" must be what the Qur'ān calls the "Preserved Tablet" or the "Mother of all Books." It is called the "Command" because although it contains everything, the essence of it is its imperatives for man. It is the essence of this Primordial Book or *amr* from which the Spirit or the Holy Spirit comes, enters into the hearts of the prophets, and bestows Revelation thereupon; or whence the Spirit is brought by the angels to the hearts of the prophets. On this interpretation also, the Preserved Tablet, the Source of all Books including the Qur'ān, is higher than angels as the Qur'ān ordinarily speaks of them.

But although one can make these technical distinctions based upon Qur'ānic statements, one cannot stick strictly to them: what the Qur'ān is essentially saying is that God's prophets or human Messengers are recipients of some special or extraordinary power which emanates from the ultimate source of all being and which fills the hearts of these prophets with something which is light whereby they see and know things the way others are not able to. At the same time, this power determines them upon a course of action that changes the lives of whole peoples. This undying and ever renewed Spirit is nothing other than the Agency of all being and life. It is the guarantee that whenever the human race sinks into the moral morass of its own follies, there is always hope for its rescue and renewal. The question now is of the manner of Revelation.

> It does not belong to any human that God should speak to him [directly] except by Revelation [i.e., infusion of the Spirit] or from behind a veil [i.e., by a voice whose source is invisible] or that He should send a [spiritual] Messenger who reveals [to the Prophet] by God's permission what He wills—and He is exalted and Wise. And even so have We revealed unto you [i.e., infused in your mind] the Spirit of Our Command—you did not know before what the Book is nor what Faith is, but *We* have made it a light whereby We guide whomsoever We will of our servants, and *you*, indeed, guide [people] to the straight path. (42:51-52).

What primarily concerns us here is the first part of this passage. What it tells us is that God never speaks directly to a human but He may infuse a Spirit in the Prophet's mind (as the next verse of the passage says of Muḥammad), (1) which makes him see the truth and utter it ("Say: This is my path—I call people [to God] on the basis of a clear perception" [12:108]; "He [Muhammad] speaks not from his own desire—it is but a Revelation vouchsafed to him" [53:3]), or (2) which produces an actual mental sound, not a physical sound, and an idea-word, not a physically acoustic word; or (3) which takes on the form of a Messenger agent "giving" the Revelation to the Prophet. Whatever the agency of Revelation, however, the true revealing subject always remains God, for it is He Who always speaks in the first person and it is He Who speaks even in this passage, informing the Prophet that He has sent the "Spirit of Our Command to you."

That the Prophet actually mentally "heard" words is clear from 75:16-19: "Do not hasten your tongue with it [the Revelation] in order to anticipate it. It is Our task to collect it and recite it. *So when We recite it, follow its recital,* and then it is also Our task to explain it" (see also 20:114). It is also clear that, in his anxiety to retain it or to "anticipate" it in a direction different from that of his Revealing Spirit, the Prophet moved his tongue of his own ordinary human volition, the intrusion of which was repudiated by God. This necessarily implies the total "otherness" of the agent of Revelation from the conscious personality of Muhammad in the act of Revelation. But it is equally clear that the words heard were mental and not acoustic, since the Spirit and the Voice were internal to him, and there is no doubt that whereas on the one hand, the Revelation emanated from God, on the other, it was also intimately connected with his deeper personality. Thus the popular traditional accounts of the utter externality of the agency of Revelation cannot be accepted as correct.

It is not always easy for a person who works with the endlessly complicated twists and enmeshing folds of the materials of history, trying to bend it to a clear and long-range course, to take decisions that are cut and dried. It is easy for an idealist to depreciate or ignore the complications of historical forces and to swim superficially on their surface, without bending history to a definite course at all; it is easier still for a non-idealist to get lost in the folds of historical forces and imagine short-sighted gains to be prodigious. While in his ordinary moments, Muhammad struggled, often successfully, with the forces of history, it was the Spirit of Revelation that enabled him to take definitive decisions on certain issues of major moment where, as we have already seen, as an ordinary human he might falter—despite his exalted natural character (of which, as we have also seen, the Qur'ān gave him a clear certificate). The simple truth is that nowhere in human history is there another man who combined so uniquely and effectively in his person both the idealist and realist factors as did Muhammad, thanks to the unique working of the Spirit of Revelation. The dictates of this Spirit decided clearly and firmly not only between what was true and what was false but also, as a consequence, what was to be done, what was not to be done, and what was to be undone. This is why the work of this Spirit was called *furqān*, "clearly demarcating line" (2:185; 3:4; 25:1), a name which, to an extent, is also bestowed upon previous Revelatons and miracles (21:48; 2:53).

The term *bayyina* ("decisive proof") which, as used for a miracle, we discussed in Chapter IV, is also used in the Qur'ān to mean the Revelatory Spirit—either as a revelatory power within a Prophet or as a divine Messenger to the Prophet:

> What about him [the Prophet Muhammad] who is on a clear proof [i.e., who possesses the revelatory power in the sense of potential Revelation] from his Lord, which is then actually recited by a Witness [the Divine Messenger] from Him, and before him is already the Book of Moses as an exemplar and a mercy? (11:17)

The idea is that the Prophet has a potential Revelation in him, a *bayyina*, a decisive proof for himself that he is God's Prophet, and then the divine Messenger or the active Spirit of Revelation actually recites it to him. In the same sura (11) certain other prophets claim the same for themselves: Noah says to his people, "What if I am on a clear proof [*bayyina*] from my Lord and He has [also] given me a Mercy [i.e., an actually verbalized Revelation] from Him but you are being blinded to it?" (11:28; similarly, the Prophet Sāliḥ, 11:63; cf. also 11:88 in the same vein).

The Revelation or the Spirit of Revelation is then the "clear proof [*bayyina*]." We are told:

> Those who have disbelieved from among the People of the Book [the Jews] and those who associate partners with God [Arab pagans] will not desist [from their enmity towards Islam] until a clear proof [*bayyina*] comes to them [also—as it does to Muhammad], viz., a Messenger from God who recites [to them] Holy Documents containing Precious Writings. (98:1-2)

This certainty and unshakable assurance (*bayyina*) is such that on its basis the religious personalities of the Old Testament are dissociated from the Jewish and Christian communities and claimed for Islam—just as, all prophets have been Muslims: "Or, do you say that Abraham, Ishmael, Isaac, Jacob, and the [prophets of the] Tribes were Jews or Christian? Do *you* know better, or God?" (2:140).

It is the Faith generated by such certainty that is "knowledge [*'ilm*]" and the Qur'ān often contrasts this kind of conviction with other kinds of belief (*zann*: 2:78; 45:24; 3:154; 4:157; 6:116, 148; 10:66, etc.) or guess (*khars*: 6:116, 148; 10:66; 43:20; 51:10). We have already seen in connection with Abraham that there are grades of Faith; the zenith is reached in the Faith produced by Revelation, while at the other extreme, people devoid of Faith claim Faith—like the Bedouins: "The Bedouins say, We believe; say [to them]: You should say, We have surrendered [*aslamna*]; since Faith has not yet entered your hearts" (49:14); or like some Jews who had simulated Faith: "When they came to you [O Muslims!] they said, We believe, but the fact is that they had entered [Faith] with disbelief and they went out of it with disbelief, and God knows well what they concealed" (5:61).

Thus, when this assurance of the Spirit of Revelation came, all thoughts of any compromise or gestures thereto were abandoned, "Say: O disbelievers! I do not serve what you serve, nor are you going to serve what I serve . . . to you, your faith, to me, mine" (109:1-6). We have already quoted 12:108, where the Prophet says that he calls people to his way to God "on the basis of a clear perception," and 6:122, where he is described as a man who was dead but to whom God had given new life. Further, "Say: O my people! go on with your works as you are, I will also continue to do [mine]" (6:135; cf. also in almost identical terms 11:93, 121; 39:39). Again, "Each works according to his own mode of conduct but your Lord knows best who is on a better guiding path" (17:84); and the numerous statements telling the opponents, "Wait [to see who is right] and I shall also wait" (6:158; 7:71; 10:20, 102; 11:122; cf. 32:30). This constitutes the total parting of the ways—the true and the false: "There is no compulsion in [matters of] faith, for guidance has now become clearly distinguished from misguidance" (2:256), but at the same time it has become clear that truth shall triumph over falsehood: "Say: The Truth has come and falsehood has lost ground, for falsehood is, indeed, vanishing" (17:81). (It should be noted that this last verse goes well back into the Meccan period.)

The Qur'ān was first revealed (at least, as we have pointed out, in an implicit or embryonic form—out of which full-fledged details were developed gradually and as occasion arose) on a certain night in the month of Ramadān:

> We have sent [the Book] down on a Blessed Night, since We were going to warn [mankind]. In it [i.e., that Night] every matter of Wisdom is decided upon—as a Command from Us, for We send Messengers as a Mercy from your Lord. (44:3-6)
> The month of Ramadān wherein the Qur'ān was sent down as guidance for mankind and [its verses] as clear proofs for [this] guidance and as *furqān* [i.e., as distinguishing clearly truth from falsehood]. (2:185)

The wording of verse 44:3-4 "We sent it down on a Blessed Night wherein every matter of wisdom is decided upon" bears a striking resemblance to that of sura 97 concerning the "Night of Determination or of Accounting [*qadr*]" from which we quoted in our discussion of the Spirit of Revelation:

> We have sent it [the Qur'ān] down in the Night of Determination, and

who has told you what the Night of Determination is? The Night of Determination is better than a thousand months. In it [i.e., this Night] the angels and the Spirit descend with [decision upon] every matter, with the permission of their Lord. It is all peace till the break of dawn. (97:1-4)

This night, held to be between the 26th and 27th of Ramadān, is solemnly observed every year by Muslims, many of whom spend it in devotional prayers. Since we know that the Qur'ān took about twenty-three years to be revealed, the "descending" of the Qur'ān in that night has been held by many Muslim commentators to mean that the Qur'ān was sent as a whole "to the seventh heaven" and thence it was for the most part revealed in passages as occasion arose. What in some sense corroborates this statement about the revelation of the Qur'ān as a whole is 94:1-3: "Have We not opened your heart and relieved you of the burden which was breaking your back?"; "relief from the burden" was then effected once and for all (although another burden—that of executing the Message—was put in its place). The spirit of Revelation in terms of potentially total Revelation had made its contact with the Prophet's mind.

Although no subsequent event of Revelation was easy, for the Qur'ān itself was a burdensome Call, not only in its content but even in its genesis, nevertheless, this first event of "breaking the ground" ensured that the Message as a whole had a definite and cohesive character. The recurring Qur'ānic term *tanzīl*, as the commentators assure us, often means gradual and intermittent Revelation, or "sending down." The Meccans objected to this gradual revelation of the Qur'ān: "Those who disbelieve say: Why has the Qur'ān not been sent down upon him [Muhammad] all at once? So it is, in order that We give strength to your heart and [also] We have arranged it in an order" (25:32), i.e., it has been arranged according to the occasion. Moreover, "In truth have We sent it down and in truth has it come down. ... A Qur'ān that We have sent intermittently that you may recite it to people at intervals, and We have sent it down in successive Revelations" (17:105).

The Qur'ān testifies both to the crushing burden and to the power of its own Call: "If We had sent this Qur'ān down upon a mountain, you would have seen it humbled and split asunder through fear of God: these are likenesses We cite for men so that perchance they might reflect" (59:21). Again, "If it were possible for a Qur'ān that mountains be moved by it or the earth rent or the dead spoken to [by its power, this Qur'ān would have done it]" (13:31). After all, it was this Message which brought Muḥammad back to life (6:123). Even though the Qur'ān often complains that pagans do not respond to it, yet it also avers that they did not want their people to listen to it for fear they would be influenced by its powerful appeal: "Those who disbelieve say, Let you not listen to this Qur'ān; rather, confuse the hearers, maybe you will win [against Muhammad]" (41:26). It was because of this power that the pagans are said to be "like asses fleeing from a tiger" (74:50). The enemies of Muhammad were often left speechless: "When you see them, their [well-built] figures impress you, but when you listen to what they have to say, they are no more than sticks piled one upon the other" (63:3).

We have said that the Prophet mentally "heard" the words of the Qur'ān; but he also mentally "saw" the Qur'ān being recited by the Spirit of Revelation—"Holy Documents containing Precious Books" (98:2). Again, "Say: this Qur'ān is but an admonition; whosoever will may take admonition from it. [It is contained] in Noble Documents, exalted and pure in the hands of Divine Messengers [Angels or Spirits of Revelation], who themselves are noble and pure" (80:11-15). These are the divine Messages that emanate from the "Preserved Tablet" in the form of the Qur'ān (85:21-22). This "Preserved Tablet," from which all revealed Books take their rise, is also what is called the "Hidden Book" (56:78) and the "Mother of all Books [*umm al-Kitāb*]" (13:39, from which also comes the confirmation or cancellation of revealed verses [and Books]).

There is a vast literature in Islam known as *i'jāz al-Qur'ān* setting out the doctrine of the "inimitability of the Qur'ān." This doctrine takes its rise from the Qur'ān itself, for the Qur'ān proffers itself as the unique miracle of Muhammad. No other revealed Book is described in the Qur'ān as a miracle in this way except the Qur'ān itself; it follows that not all embodiments of Revelations are miracles, even though the event of Revelation itself is a kind of miracle. The Qur'ān emphatically challenges its opponents to "bring forth one sura like those of the Qur'ān" (2:23) and "to call upon anyone except God" to achieve this (10:38; cf. 11:13, which is probably earlier). There is a consensus among those who know Arabic well, and who appreciate the genius of the language, that in the beauty of its language and the style and power of its expression the Qur'ān is a superb document. The linguistic nuances simply defy translation. Although all inspired language is untranslatable, this is even more the case with the Qur'ān.

As we shall further develop in Chapter VIII, the Qur'ān is very much conscious that it is an "Arabic Qur'ān" and, the question of ideas and doctrines apart, it appears certain that the claim of the miraculous nature of the Qur'ān is connected with its linguistic style and expression. Unfortunately, non-Arab Muslims do not realize this enough; while they correctly assume that the Qur'ān is a book of guidance and hence may be understood in any language, they yet not only deprive themselves of the real taste and appreciation for the Qur'ānic expression but—since even a full understanding of the meaning depends upon the linguistic nuances—also cannot do full justice to the content of the Qur'ān. It is extremely desirable and important that as many as possible of the non-Arab educated and thinking Muslims equip themselves with the language of the Qur'ān.

Chapter Six

Eschatology

The standard picture of Qur'ānic eschatology is in terms of the joys of the Garden and the punishments of Hell. The Qur'ān does frequently talk about these, as about reward and punishment in general, including "God's pleasure and anger"—something which we shall have to elaborate in detail. But the basic idea underlying the Qur'ān's teaching on the hereafter is that there will come a moment, "The Hour [*al-sā'a*]" when every human will be shaken into a unique and unprecedented self-awareness of his deeds: he will squarely and starkly face his own doings, not-doings, and misdoings and accept the judgment upon them as a "necessary" sequel (necessary within quotes because God's *mercy* is unlimited). That man is generally so absorbed in his immediate concerns, particularly selfish, narrow, and material concerns, that he does not heed the "ends" of life [*al-ākhira*] and constantly violates moral law, we have had occasion to point out. We stressed in Chapter III that for the Qur'ān the goal of man-in-society is to build an ethically-based order on the earth but that cultivation of *taqwā* or a true sense of responsibility is absolutely necessary for man-as-individual if such an order is to be built. The Qur'ān repeatedly complains that man has not yet come up to this task.

Al-ākhira, the "end," is the moment of truth: "When the great cataclysm comes, that day man will recall what he had been striving for" (79:34-35) is a typical statement of this phenomenon. It is an Hour when all veils between the mental preoccupations of man and the objective moral reality will be rent: "You were in deep heedlessness about this [Hour of self-awareness], but now We have rent your veil, so your sight today is keen!" (50:22). Every person will find there his deepest self, fully excavated from the debris of extrinsic and immediate concerns wherein the means is substituted for ends and even pseudo-means for real means, where falsehood is not only substituted for truth but really *becomes* truth, and even more attractive and beautiful than truth. Man's conscience itself becomes so perverted that, through long habituation with particularized interests and persistent worship of false gods, the holy seems unholy, and vice versa. This is what the Qur'ān terms *ghurūr*, multi-layered self-deception. If man is to be freed from this grave-within-a-grave structure, nothing short of a cataclysm, a complete turning inside-out of the moral personality, is needed. Here are certain utterances of the Qur'ān about this event from the early Meccan years of the Revelation:

> When the sun shall be darkened and the stars fall; and when mountains move, and when she-camels with mature fetuses [the most precious possessions of a Bedouin] are abandoned; and when the wild beasts are herded together; and when the seas boil; and when kindred spirits are united; and when the infant-girl buried alive [as was the practice with some pre-Islamic Arabs] shall be asked for what sin she was slain; and when the deed-sheets are unrolled [before people] and when the sky is skinned off; and when Hell is ignited and when the Garden is brought near—then every soul shall know what it had prepared [for the morrow]. (81:1-14)

This is a typical representation of the grinding pains of that hour. Although, as we shall see below, this judgment will involve communities and their prophets, the judgment itself will be primarily upon individuals. Each individual will be alone that day, without relatives, friends, clans, tribes, or nations, to support them: "We shall inherit from him [man] whatever he says and he shall come to Us alone" (19:80). Whereas a person's wealth and possessions may go to his children or other inheritors, the moral quality of his sayings and deeds is "inherited" or passed on to God and remains with Him until He produces it on the Day of Judgment before the performer himself. On that day, God shall say, "You have, indeed, come to Us [today] alone—as alone as We had created you in the first place" (6:94; cf. also 19:95). This state of not just loneliness but forlornness from all that was worldly association is depicted with hair-raising effect: "[It will be] the day when a man shall flee from his brother, his mother and father, his wife and children—for every man on that day, shall have a preoccupation that will release him from all these" (80:34-37; cf. 70:10-14, which repudiates tribal, i.e., national, ties as well).

On that day, one would wish if one could to buy release with an "earthful of gold," but such offers will be rejected (3:91; also 5:36; 10:54; 13:18; 39:47; 57:15; 70:11). As we have elaborated, the Qur'an both rejects the idea of an intercession and allows nothing else to help a person in that state of helplessness except God's own mercy, which, the Qur'ān repeats, is absolutely unlimited. But, although the Qur'ān, particularly in the early and middle Meccan periods, persistently details the horrors of the Judgment Day for evildoers, the real punishment will undoubtedly be the irremediable pain suffered by those who have perpetrated evil in this life when they realize that there is no "going back" and that they have lost the only opportunity in the life of this world to do good. They will be the real losers (10:45; 22:11; 40:78; 7:9, 53; 8:37; 9:69, etc.): the standard Qur'ānic terms for the ultimate sequel, as we underlined in Chapter II, are not salvation and damnation so much as success (*falāh*) and loss (*khusrān*), both for this life and the hereafter.

This is why the Qur'ān continues to exhort people "to send something for the morrow" (59:18), for whatever accrues to a person is the consequence of previous deeds; it frequently says that whenever an evil strikes someone for what his "hands have prepared for what is ahead," frustration seizes him (see for example, 2:95; 3:182; 4:62; 5:80; 8:51; 18:57; 22:10; 28:47; in connection exclusively with the hereafter: 2:95; 62:7; 78:40; 82:5). Indeed, the essence of the "hereafter" consists in the "ends" of life (*al-ākhira*) or the long-range results of man's endeavors on earth.

"*Al-dunyā*" (the immediate objectives, the "here-and-now" of life), on the contrary, is not "this world" but the lower values, the basal pursuits which appear so immediately tempting that most men run after them most of the time, at the expense of the higher and long-range ends. In Chapter II, we quoted 13:17 to the effect that in a torrent of water rushing down the hills, a higher layer of foam is formed, but when waters pass through the plains, the thick foam disappears without a trace, while that which benefits mankind in a lasting way, i.e., the alluvial earth, stays in the ground. The show of this foam is the "*dunya*," the lasting alluvium is the "*ākhira*." (We also quoted there the verse that criticizes the Meccan merchants' skill at "making money" to the neglect of the higher values of life—the ends of life: "They know well the externalities of this life but are heedless of the higher ends" (30:7).

It is because of *al-ākhira* or the end-values that the "weighing" of men's acts takes on its crucial significance. There is here, of course, sarcasm against the Meccan merchants—in the hereafter, *deeds* shall be weighed, not gold and silver and other trade commodities. Later, the Mu'tazilite theologians took this weighing of deeds too literally and developed a strict *quid pro quo* doctrine; they got themselves into the intractable difficulties connected with any theory of strict retribution. Instead of accepting God's infinite mercy as real and as seriously modifying their *quid pro quo* theory of retribution, they did grave violence to religion in trying to get around it and explain it away. There is no doubt that the Qur'ān speaks of a palpable weighing or scaling, of spreading out people's deed-sheets before them (as is apparent from the following quotations), but there is also no doubt that this is a holistic idea, not a strict *quid pro quo*. There are references galore to weighing of deeds; the following will serve as sufficient illustrations: "So for him whose scale [of good acts] shall be weighty, he shall lead a happy life; but he whose scale is light, his mother shall be the Ditch" (101:6-9). Good people will be given their deed-sheets in their right hands, while the evil will receive theirs in the left hand:

As for him who is given his book in his right hand, he shall say, Come! read my book! I knew that I was going to face my accounting. He shall be in a happy life, in an exalted Garden whose fruit-bunches are nigh [to be plucked]. [It shall be said to them:] Eat and drink to your satisfaction in consideration of what you had left in previous days. But as for him who shall be given his book in his left hand, he shall say, I wish I had not been given this book of mine and I did not know what my account was. I wish death would overtake me. My wealth has not availed me, and my authority [which I used to exercise in life] has perished. (69:19-29; see also 56:27-44; 17:71 ff.; 74:39)

The deed-records, which will speak (23:62; 45:29) and which people will not be able to deny, will be sufficient evidence for and against the doers. More: People's minds will become public so that they will not be able to hide their thoughts, even as graves will empty out their contents (100:9-10). Even one's bodily organs will speak out:

And the day when the foes of God shall be gathered towards the Fire and they shall be driven on—until when they approach it, their own ears and eyes and skins will give evidence against them of what they knew. They shall say to their skins, Why have you testified against us? and the latter shall reply, God Who makes everything speak has also caused us to speak . . . you did not hide yourselves thinking that your ears and your eyes and your skins will not testify against you; on the contrary, you thought that God does not know much of what you do. This miscalculation of yours about your Lord has led you to perdition and you have ended up as losers. Should they resign themselves to the Fire, Fire is, indeed, their abode; but should they ask for forgiveness, they are not proper objects of forgiveness. (41:19-24)

There is, indeed, no refuge from a situation where one's mind becomes transparently public and where one's own physical organs begin to bear witness against one! But, then, this is exactly the state of mind which the Qur'ān wants men to achieve amidst the conduct of *this life*. This is what *taqwā* is, a coalescence of the public and the private life. And this is what the Prophet showed by his own example—while he lived his life in Madina, the closest possible community life, among his companions—and yet he had nothing whatever to hide from others. It is such transparency of the heart that the Qur'ān wants man to achieve, if he is to achieve success and is not to burn in Hell.

Further: There will be a great deal more questioning and answering on that day. The guards of the Fire shall ask its prospective inmates why they were there and whether Messengers had not come to them to warn them against the impending doom:

And those who disbelieve shall be driven in troops to Hell. When they arrive there and its gates are opened, its guards will say to them: Did no Messengers from among yourselves ever come to you reciting to you the verses of your Lord and warning you of this day of yours? They shall reply, Of course, but the judgment of punishment was already ripe upon the disbelievers. It shall be said [to them:] Enter the gates of Hell abiding therein—what an evil abode for the wilful [and the haughty]. Those who had developed *taqwā* towards their Lord shall be carried forward to the Garden in troops. When they arrive there and its gates are opened, its guards shall say, Peace upon you, be you happy, enter it abiding therein. They shall reply, All praise to God Who has kept His promise with us and has given us the earth as inheritance; we will make our abode in its Garden wherever we will—what an excellent reward for those who do good! (39:71-74)

The latter part of this passage is remarkable, i.e., "God . . . has given us the earth as inheritance; we will make our abode in its Garden wherever we will." Although usually Qur'ānic descriptions of the Last Day speak of a general and complete upset of the present cosmos, a dislocation of the earth and the heavens, a complete shaking of the earth—indeed, of "the earth being in His hand-grip on the Day of Resurrection and the heavens being wrapped up in His right hand" (39:67) and "mankind being like scattered locusts and mountains like carded wool"—all these descriptions really intend to portray the absolute power of God. Those who think that the earth and the heavens—the cosmos—is a self-created, unauthored, and ultimate being must understand that is it the all-powerful, mighty, and absolute God Who has brought forth the cosmos out of His sheer mercy; nothing can therefore get outside His control and governance. The Qur'ān talks not of the *destruction* of the universe but of its transformation and rearrangement with a view to creating new forms of life and new levels of being. When it says, "Everything is destructible except His person" (28:88) or "Whosoever is on the earth shall perish and His person alone—the majestic and the noble—shall remain forever" (55:26-27), this, first, speaks not of the universe as a whole but of its contents and, secondly, depicts the absolute and eternal majesty of God.

Certainly, from the verses we are commenting upon, it is quite clear that *this earth* will be transformed into a Garden which will be enjoyed by its "inheritors." That the Qur'ān is speaking not of total destruction of the earth but of its transformation (except insofar as every re-creation or transformation requires a certain destruction), is also clear from such verses as: "The day when the earth shall be transmuted into something else and the heavens as well [i.e., their nature will become different from what it is now]." (14:48) The Qur'ān also repeatedly speaks of a new form or level of creation: "We have appointed for you the death and none may excel Us in that We shall transmute [nubaddilu] your models [amthālakum] and re-create you in [forms] you do not know. You already know the present [form of] your creation, so why do you not take a lesson [from this]?" (56:60-62); "God will then create the next creation" (29:20; cf. 53:47); "Strange indeed is their statement, Shall we be in a new creation after having turned to dust?" (13:5; 32:10; 34:7); "If He wills, He can destroy you [all] and bring out a new creation" (14:19; 35:16); "Have We become fatigued by the first creation that they are in doubt about a new creation?" (50:15, and all those verses that speak about the first creation and re-creation, nabda' al-khalqa thumma nu'īduhū).

Similarly, the females (the houris!) and the males of the next world will be created anew (56:35). Further, about Hell it is said, "It is God's Fire that is blazing and that lights upon the hearts [of men] in lofty columns" (104:6-9). In a passage that speaks of successive peoples and communities entering Hell (the later ones having been misled by the evil legacies of the earlier ones and thus encumbered by them), the Qur'ān makes it clear that the effect of punishment in Hell depends upon the sensitivity of the guilty and hence involves a conscience. The punishment is thus basically moral or spiritual:

> God shall say [to the polytheists:] Enter among the communities that had preceded you, of jinn and humans and into Hell. Every time a new community will thus enter, it shall curse its [preceding] sister, until when all are down in the depths [of Fire], the later ones shall say about the earlier ones, O God! It is these that led us astray, so give them double punishment. Whereupon God will reply, All [of you] *are* getting double [punishment], but you do not realize it" (7:38).

But the happiness and the torture of the hereafter is certainly not just spiritual. The Qur'ān, unlike Muslim philosophers, does not recognize a hereafter that will be peopled by disembodied souls—in fact, it does not recognize the dualism of the soul and the body and man, for it is a unitary, living, and fully functioning organism. The term *nafs*, which later in Islamic philosophy and Sufism came to mean soul as a *substance* separate from the body, in the Qur'ān means mostly "himself" or "herself" and, in the plural, "themselves"; while in some contexts it means the "person" or the "inner person," i.e., the living reality of man—but not separate from or exclusive of the body. In fact, it is body with a certain life-and-intelligence center that constitutes the inner identity or personality of man.

The Qur'ān, therefore, does not affirm any purely "spiritual" heaven or hell, and the subject of happiness and torture is, therefore, man as a person. When the Qur'ān speaks—so repeatedly, so richly, and so vividly—of physical happiness and physical hell, it is not speaking in pure metaphor, as Muslim philosophers and other allegorists would have it, although, of course, the Qur'ān is trying to describe the happiness and punishments as effects, i.e., in terms of the *feeling* of physical and spiritual pleasure and pain. The vivid portrayals of a blazing hell and a garden are meant to convey these effects as real spiritual-physical feelings, apart from the present psychological effects of these descriptions. There are thus literal *psycho-physical effects* of the Fire, without there being a literal fire.

While physical punishment and happiness are literal, not metaphorical, however, the Qur'ān makes it clear that it is their spiritual aspect that is supreme. Thus, we are told, "God has promised believing men and women Gardens, underneath which rivers flow, wherein they shall abide, and pleasant abodes in the Gardens of Eden—*but the pleasure of God with them is greater and that is the great success*" (9:72). While believers and the virtuous have their greatest reward in the pleasure (*ridwān*) of God, unbelievers and evil persons will earn His displeasure and alienation (*sakht*) as their greatest punishment: "Is the one who goes after the pleasure of God like the one who earns His displeasure and whose abode is Hell?" (3:162; cf. 5:80; 47:28; also see verses under *ghadab*, "anger of God," and further verses under *ridwān*, though these do not refer entirely to the hereafter but also to this world). On the Day of Judgment, "God will not so much as talk to or even look at" those who sell God's covenant and their solemn oaths (certain Jews are meant here) for a paltry sum of money (3:77). The faces of the believers on that day will be "fresh with joy and will be looking at their lord" (75:22, a verse from which arose the notorious and foolish controversy in medieval Islam (it lasted for a millenium) as to whether or not God will be literally physically visible to believers in the hereafter; also 76:11; 80:39; 83:24; 10:26), while the faces of disbelievers "will be covered in dust, subdued in darkness" (80:40-41; 10:27; 68:43; 70:44).

To return to the questioning and answering of that day, the people of the Garden, those of the Fire, and those dwelling in "the Ramparts" who are neither in Hell nor yet in the Gardens shall all exchange views and review their past performance:

> The people of the Garden shall call unto the people of the Fire: We have found what our Lord had promised us to be true; have *you* found what your Lord had promised you to be true? They will reply, Yes. Then a crier shall cry between them that God's curse be upon the unjust ones who block the cause of God and would have it crooked and deny the Last Day. [Then] a curtain shall fall between the two.
>
> And upon the Rampart [between the two] will be men who will recognize everyone by facial expression [i.e., whether they are people of the Garden or the Fire]; they shall call unto the people of the Garden, Peace unto you—They would [also] like to enter it [the Garden], but will not be able to. But when their eyes turn towards the people of the Fire, they shall say: O our Lord! Do not put us with the

unjust ones. And the people of the rampart shall call unto some men whom they shall recognize by their facial expression saying, 'The wealth collected by you and your pride has been of no avail to you. Are these [people now in the Garden but who had been poor] the ones about whom you used to swear that God will not bestow [His] mercy upon them [but to whom it has now been said]: Enter the Garden, you have nothing to fear, nor shall you come to grief?

And the people of the Fire shall say to the people of the Garden, Pour some water upon us or something of what God has provided you with, and they shall reply, God has prohibited these things to disbelievers. (7:44-50)

Every community shall be judged by the standards set for them by their prophet and in accordance with the teachings of their respective Revelations—although according to the Qur'ān while they are essentially identical since their source is identical, yet, a community from the ancient past cannot be judged by the standards set for new communities: "How about when We bring out a witness from every community and We call you [O Muhammad!] to give witness upon these people?" (4:41); "We shall pull out a witness from every community and We shall say, Bring your proof [i.e., for your misdeeds, particularly for polytheism which you practiced]" (28:75). The prophets themselves will also be questioned as to whether they gave the Message truly to their people and particularly whether what the latter believed and practiced after these prophets were gone was in accordance with their proclaimed Messages: "We shall surely ask the people to whom missions [of the prophets] were sent and We shall equally surely ask the prophets themselves. And then We shall certainly relate to them [their deeds] on the basis of knowledge [so ascertained, i.e., for the sake of those upon whom judgment is to be passed]" (7:6-7). Jesus will be asked on the Day of Judgment whether he had taught Trinitarianism to his followers, and he shall reply, "Glory be to You! I could not say something that was not for me to say. If I did say it You know it already" (5:116); generally, about all prophets: "The day when God shall gather all the prophets and say, How were you responded to?, they shall reply, We have no knowledge [of this], You are the One who knows the unseen things" (5:109). The last two verses both belong to the last phase of the Prophet's life—as does sura 5 generally—and, therefore, must be considered as a warning not only to Christians and other communities but equally, though somewhat indirectly, to the Muslim community itself. Already in Mecca, the Qur'ān had declared, "And the Messenger [Muḥammad] shall say, O my Lord! my very people abandoned this Qur'ān" (25:30).

Finally, the Qur'ān speaks persistently about a bitter questioning and answering between the socially weak and the rich; the weaker shall accuse the rich and influential of their society of having led them astray by undue influence and threats: those condemned in the Fire shall say to their comrades when a new group of the condemned enter:

> This is a horde pressing upon you; be they unwelcome! [but] they *are* going to burn in the Fire.' [The new entrants] will reply saying, No! Let *you* be unwelcome, it is you who have prepared this [punishment] for us [due to your evil influence]—how evil an abode it is! And they shall add, O our Lord! give these a double punishment in the Fire who have prepared this for us. And they shall [also] say, How is it that we do not see here those whom we used to count as mischiefmakers [the believers, who are, of course, in the Garden]. Did we take them [mistakenly] as a laughingstock or have our eyes missed them [now]? It is, indeed, true—the people of Fire *shall* accuse each other. (38:59-64)
>
> The weak ones will say to those who were big, But for you, we would have been believers. The big ones will reply to the weak ones, Did *we* prevent you from the guidance after it had come to you or were you yourselves guilty? The weak ones shall then say to the big ones, Of course, it was your scheming of day and night, when you pressured us that we disbelieve in God and that we acknowledge other peers unto Him. And they shall [all] be inwardly filled with, but shall try to hide, their remorse when they behold the punishment. (34:32-34; see also 14:21; 40:47; 50:23 ff., where God will say to these disputants, Do not dispute before Me, for I had already sent you the Warning. My words cannot change and I am no tyrant over my servants. 50:28-29).

Resurrection or the final accounting was an idea which the secular Meccan pagans found very hard to accept. In fact, besides the doctrines of monotheism (and the consequent removal of their gods) and of Revelation itself (for they persistently called the Qur'ān a *sihr*, a piece of sorcery, or the result of the Prophet's mental disturbance, etc.), this doctrine was the most difficult for them to accept. It is quite likely that the "changes" they demanded from the Prophet in the Qur'ān included, besides recognition in the new system of their "gods" as intermediaries between man and God, elimination of the Last Day, and particularly of physical resurrection. They said they and their fathers had heard of resurrection before (no doubt, from Jews and Christians) but that this idea was no more than "a fiction of the earlier communities" (23:82; 27:67-68). Still less, of course, would the idea of "moral responsibility" and abstract "ends" of life be comprehensible to them—any more than they tell now upon secular societies of our own day.

For the Qur'ān, the Last Judgment was crucial for multiple, fundamental reasons. First, moral and just as the constitution of reality is for the Qur'ān, the quality of men's performance must be judged, else fairness cannot be ensured merely on the basis of what transpires in this life. Secondly, and this we have underlined in the early part of this chapter, the "ends" of life must be clarified beyond doubt, so that men may see what they have been striving for and what the true purposes of life are. This point is absolutely crucial in the entire doctrine of resurrection in the Qur'ān, since the "weighing of deeds" presupposes and depends upon it. Thirdly, and connected closely with the second point, is the idea that disputes, dissensions, and conflicts of human orientations must be finally resolved. There is little doubt for the Qur'ān that whereas there is such a thing as an *honest* difference of opinion, there is nevertheless very little of it; for the most part, human differences are plagued with extrinsic motivations of selfishness, of group or national interest, of congealed inherited traditions and myriad other forms of fanaticism. And the worst human moral plague is that one often does even good things through wrong and extrinsic motivations. The resolution of these differences of "belief," therefore, will be practically identical with the manifestation of the motivations of these beliefs. Since on that day all the interior of man will become transparent, these motivations will too. But apart from this, truth will show through in that Hour of Truth, and to this the Qur'ān makes frequent reference:

> Say [to the Meccans]: You are not going to be asked about the crimes we are committing, nor shall we be asked about what you do. Say: Our Lord *will* bring us together and then He will decide between us in truth—He is the Decider, the Knower. (34:25-26)
>
> Those who believe [Muslims], and the Jews and the Sabeans and the Christians and the Magians and the polytheists—God shall decide among them on the Day of Resurrection [as to who was right], for God is witness over everything. (22:17)

It is notable that the Qur'ān often calls that day "The Day of Decision" (i.e., between right and wrong, not only deeds, but be-liefs, life-orientations, etc. [37:21; 44:40; 17:13-14; 78:17]. Directly relevant to this point are also the frequent verses that generally speak about the "settling of all matters that were under dispute" (3:55; 2:113; 5:48; 6:164; 16:39,92,124; 22:69; 10:93; 32:25; etc.) It is said, to Muhammad, "You will die and they [your opponents] will, too; you will then dispute before your Lord on the Day of Resurrection" (39:30-31).

To overcome these objections of the Meccans and the difficulties they felt in accepting the idea of Resurrection and the Day of Account-ing, the Qur'ān also brings arguments from God's power in general. The God who created the heavens and the earth and who has created man and innumerable forms of life in this universe is capable of creating man anew, and other hitherto unknown forms of life:

> Did man not see that We have created him from a clot of blood, but lo! he is a manifest disputant. He coins similitudes for Us but has forgotten his own creation: he says, Who will revive the bones when they have decayed? Say: He will re-create them who has created them in the first place and He knows all [forms of] creation—He Who brings out for you fire out of a green tree whence you are enabled to light [your fires]. Is He Who has created the heavens and the earth not able to create their [humans'] likeness?—surely, because He is the Creator Who knows [all manner of creation]. Whenever He wills to create something He simply says, Be! and there is it! Glory be to Him, then, in Whose power is the mastery of everything and to Whom you shall be returned. (36:77-83)

That God can make death and life succeed each other, just as He can bring out sparks of fire from green wood, is also evidenced by the fact that He causes light and darkness, day and night, to follow each other, as indeed He does the rise and fall of nations; and just as these latter two phenomena are "natural" so that we ask no questions about them, so must the phenomenon of resurrection and creation of new modes of life be regarded as a natural fact, given the moral constitution of the universe:

> Say, O my God, the Ruler of the Kingdom! You give rule to whom-soever You will and deprive of rule whomsoever You will, and You bestow power and honor upon whomsoever You will and You debase whomsoever you will [this does not mean, of course, that there are no natural causes for these phenomena]; in Your hands is the Good and You are powerful over everything. You make the night penetrate into the day and You make the day pass into the night and You bring out

the living from the dead and the dead from the living and You bestow sustenance upon whomsoever You will without stint. (3:27; see also 22:61; 31: 29; 35:13; 57:6)

A specific example of reviving the dead given by the Qur'ān is the quickening of the earth in spring after its "death" during the winter: "He quickens the earth after its death" (30:19, 24, 50; 57:17). Here is a translation of sura 50, the theme of which is the resurrection of man and which represents the lengthiest single treatment of the subject in the Qur'ān:

By the glorious Qur'ān! They are rather surprised that a warner from among themselves has come to them, and the disbelievers say, This is a strange thing! When we are dead and turned to dust [shall we be resurrected?]—this is a far-fetched return! We know what the earth takes away of them, and with Us is a Recording Book. Nay! they have disbelieved in the Truth when it came to them and they are, therefore, in a troubled situation.

Have they not observed the heaven above them: How We have built it and beautified it and how there are no rifts therein. And the earth that We have spread out and We have cast firm mountains therein and We have caused all lovely pairs [of male and female—cf. 51:47-49] to grow thereon—as a lesson and reminder to every servant [of Ours] who is sincere of heart. And We send down from the sky blessed water wherewith We cause gardens and crop-grains to grow, and lofty date-palms with ranged clusters—as sustenance for Our servants— and We quicken thereby dead land. Even so shall be the Resurrection [of the dead].

The people of Noah denied [Our Messages] before them, as did the dwellers of Al-Rass, the tribe of Thamūd, the tribe of ᶜAd, the Pharaoh and the brethren of Lot, as well as the people of the Thicket [Madyanites], the folk of Tubba'—all gave the lie to the Messengers. Hence My threat came into operation.

Have We been fatigued by the first creation, that they are in doubt about a new one? Indeed, We have created man and We know what his inner mind whispers to him—We are, indeed, nearer to him than his jugular vein! When the two Receivers encounter him, seated on his right and left, he utters no word, but there is with him a ready observer.

The agony of death shall come in truth [and it will be said to him], Is this what you were trying to avoid? And the Trumpet shall be blown— that will be the threatened day. And every person shall come forth along with a driver and a witness. [It shall be said to the evil ones,] You were [sunk] in heedlessness of this, but We have removed from you your veil, so your sight today is keen? And his companion [angel] shall say, Here is what I have ready [by way of testimony]. [It shall be said,] Throw you two [the driver and the witness] into Hell every ungrateful rebel, who withheld wealth [from the needy], a transgressor and a doubter [of the Revelation]; he who assumed another god besides God. Cast him into an intense punishment. His companion will say, O our Lord! I did not beguile him but he [himself] was far afield in error. God will say, Dispute not before Me, I had already sent to you the warning. My words cannot be changed and I am no tyrant over My servants.

The day when We shall say to the Hell, Are you satiated? and it will answer, Is there any more? And the Garden shall be brought near to those who had the fear of responsibility and will not be very distant [from them]. [And it will be said to them,] This is what you had been promised—it is for every penitent who was heedful—he who was humble before the Merciful in the Unseen and came with a sincere heart. Enter the Garden in peace, this is the day of eternity. They shall have therein whatever they wish, and We have much more.

We have destroyed before them many a people who were much greater in their might than them [the Meccans], who overran lands. [But] was there any escape for them [when Our judgment came]? Therein, indeed, is an admonition for one who possesses a heart or attentively gives his ear, fully witnessing. We, indeed, created the heavens and the earth and whatever is between them in six days but were not touched by fatigue. So hear what they [your opponents, O Muhammad!] say with patience and sing the praises of your Lord before sunrise and before sunset, and also sing His praises into night and after prostrations as well. And listen on the day when the Crier shall cry from a near place [i.e., it will penetrate the ears and the mind effectively—contrasted with 41:44: Those who do not believe, there is a deafness in their ears and they are blind to it (the Revelation)—these ones are being called as though from a *far distant place*]. The day when they shall hear the Cry in truth—that will be the Day of Resurrection. It is We who give life and death, and to Us is the return. The day when the earth shall split away from them suddenly—that is a gathering easy for Us [to undertake]. We know best what they say, but you [O Muhammad!] are no compeller over them, but warn through the Qur'ān him who fears My threat.

Since God is present everywhere and at all times, there is obviously nothing hidden from Him. Man thinks he can hide his thoughts, motivations, etc., from other men and, indeed, he often tries to hide things from himself, does not wish to face the truth of his own situation starkly; but his inner being will become public, for nobody in that Hour will be able to "reserve" anything mentally. All Qur'ānic statements about evidence on that day and about the transparency of one's hidden being lead to the one point that one must bear responsibility for one's deeds, thoughts, and intentions. But that day will be the day of judgment; one will have no opportunity to change anything, to offer a new performance, or to redeem one's failings, for the only opportunity for that is here, now, in this life, which is given only once (for the Qur'ān does not believe in the *karma* or cycles of rebirths and deaths). This *one* life, then, is the only life where man can work and earn or sow those seeds that will bear fruit "in the end."

This is why it is imperative, according to the Qur'ān, to take this life seriously and to recognize fully that no matter how much one may hide one's negative intentions and one's failings, God "is well aware of them," as the Qur'ān often puts it. Hence one must develop that inner torch which can enable one to distinguish between right and wrong, between justice and injustice, which the Qur'ān calls *taqwā*—a crucial term, indeed one of the three or four most crucial terms. Although the final judgment upon man's conduct does lie outside him, as does the final criterion by which he is to be judged—and recognition of this fact is an essential part of the meaning of *taqwā*—such recognition already implies a certain development of the conscience of man to a point where this inner torch is lit. Like torchlight, *taqwā* is undoubtedly capable of gradations, from a zero-point of naive self-righteousness to a high point where one can almost completely X-ray one's state of mind and conscience.

The kind of being "made public" of the inner self so poignantly portrayed as occurring on the Day of Judgment is what the Qur'ān really desires to take place here in this life; for a man who can X-ray himself effectively and hence diagnose his inner state has nothing to be afraid of if his inner being goes public. It is only those who hide their inner being here—largely unsuccessfully, of course, for they really succeed not so much in hiding themselves from others as from themselves—who have every reason to fear the Day of Accounting. This is why the Qur'ān says in sura 50, "You were sunk in heedlessness of this [accounting, X-raying], but now that We lifted the veil from you, your sight today is keen!" The central endeavor of the Qur'ān is for man to develop this "keen sight" here and now, when there is opportunity for action and progress, for at the Hour of Judgment it will be too late to remedy the state of affairs; there one will be reaping, not sowing or nurturing. Hence one can speak there only of eternal success or failure, of everlasting Fire or Garden—that is to say, for the fate of the individual. As Jalāl al-Dīn al-Rūmī puts it:

> If you wish to witness Resurrection, become it!
> For this is the condition for witnessing anything!

Chapter Seven

Satan and Evil

Evil (*sharr*), as the opposite of good (*khair*) and as perpetrated by man, has been dealt with where we discussed individual and collective human conduct. Here we shall discuss the *principle* of evil, which the Qur'ān often personifies as Iblīs or Satan, although the latter personification is much weaker than the former: the Qur'ān, particularly in the Meccan suras, speaks frequently in the plural of "satans"—which sometimes also refer, probably metaphorically, to humans as well: "But when they [the hypocrites] are alone with their own satans" (2:14); "And even so have We appointed for every Messenger enemies, satans from among humans and the jinn" (6:112).

But if the term "satans" is regarded as metaphorical with respect to humans, is it so also with regard to the jinn? In his useful but as yet unpublished study, *The Pneumatology of the Qur'ān* (which discusses angels, Satan, and jinn), Dr. Alford Welch reaches the conclusion in Chapter V that what the Qur'ān calls the "hordes of Iblīs [the Devil]" in 26:95 are the jinn, who say "We touched the heavens and found it full of intensive watch and of shooting-stars. We used to take up secret positions in order to listen [to what transpired in heaven] but anyone who would try to listen now, will encounter a shooting-star guardman" (72:8-9). This is so in view of the repeated statements of the Qur'ān that satans (in the plural) attempt stealthily to snatch news from heaven but are driven away (15:17; 67:5; 72:8-9; etc.).

That the jinn is a creation more or less parallel to humankind except that the former are made of fire whereas the latter are made of "baked clay" is affirmed by the Qur'ān (7:12; 55:14-15). The Qur'ān also states (18:50) that the Devil (Iblīs) was "of the jinn and he disobeyed the command of his Lord." Dr. Welch's view, therefore, does have some plausibility, provided it is made applicable only to some jinn, since the jinn are generally conceived of in the Qur'ān as a genre of creation parallel to man. God's messages are addressed to them also, though perhaps secondarily:

> When We turned some of the jinn to you [O Muhammad!] in order to listen to the Qur'ān, when they attended to its [recitation], they said [to each other], Listen. And when it ended, they went back to their own people as warners, saying, O our people! We have heard a Book which has been sent down after Moses, confirming what has gone before it and guiding to the truth and the straight path. O our people! Respond to the Messenger of God and believe in him, God will pardon your sins and save you from a painful punishment. (46:29-31)

In sura 72 itself, where the jinn say that they *used* to overhear the transactions of the High Council in the heaven but that none can do so now (72:8-9), they say at the very beginning of the sura that they have accepted the Qur'ān because of its excellent teaching. An interesting point is that both in this sura and in the passage we have quoted from sura 46, the Prophet himself is not represented as having heard or seen the jinn directly; it is God who informs him of what the jinn have said or done. Again, in sura 72, from the jinn's mouth, "Some of us are virtuous, while others are below this state" (72:11), and, "When we listened to the Guidance [the Qur'ān], we believed in it. . . . Some of us are Muslims [i.e., have surrendered ourselves to God's will], while others are unjust" (72:13-14). It is, therefore, difficult to believe that all or even most of the jinn are for the Qur'ān "the hordes of the Devil" or fallen angels—although the jinn do appear to be on the whole more prone to evil than is humankind.

There is no mention in the Qur'ān of any messengers having been sent to the jinn directly and from their own kind; from the fact that they believed in Moses and Muhammad, and the fact that they worked as slave-labor for Solomon (34:12, 14), it seems that, despite their fiery nature and much greater physical powers (including the ability to be invisible), they are not fundamentally different from men, except for their greater proneness to evil and stupidity. The Qur'ān often addresses them or otherwise couples them together with humans (6:130; 7:38, 179; 17:88; 27:17; 41:25, 29; 46:18; 55:33, 39,56, 74). From 34:41 and 6:100 it is clear that before Islam at least some Arabs worshiped the jinn and from 15:27 as well as from 7:38 that the jinn antedate the creation of man. Could the jinn represent some earlier stage in the course of evolution? Be that as it may, mention of the jinn ceases in the Madinan period of the Qur'ān, which continues to call itself "guidance for man" and, in fact, never addresses the jinn primarily, or even directly. (As we have said, even in the two passages where the jinn listened to the Qur'ān, the Prophet himself did not experience them but the Qur'ān reported to him about it.)

As for Satan or the Devil, as we underlined in Chapter II in connection with the story of the creation of Adam, as such he is a contemporary of man even though he had been there before Adam in the form of a jinn. This points to a fundamental moral fact, that the struggle between good and evil is reality for man and man alone. The Qur'ān, therefore, portrays Satan as a rebel against God's command but as rival and enemy of man rather than God, since God is beyond where the devil can touch him; it is man who is his aim, and it is man who can either conquer him or be vanquished by him. In metaphysical terms, therefore, Satan is not coordinate with God (as is the Zoroastrian Ahirman, the rival of Yazdān). Hence the constant Qur'ānic warnings to man that he has to struggle with Satan:

> Satan caused them [Adam and Eve] to fall from it [the state of bliss] and be expelled from that [state] in which they had been, and We said to them [to Adam and Eve and Satan], Go down as mutual enemies. (2:36; cf. 7:22, 24)
>
> O people! eat from the earth that which is good, clean, and lawful and do not follow the footsteps of Satan, for he is to you a manifest enemy. (2:168)
>
> O people! enter all of you into peace [i.e., the Islamic brotherhood] and do not follow the footsteps of Satan, for he is your manifest enemy. (2:208; see also 6:143)
>
> Satan is a manifest enemy for man. (12:5; 17:53)
>
> Do you take Satan and his progeny as [your] friends rather than Me, while they are your enemies? (18:50)
>
> Satan is your enemy, so take him as your enemy. (35:6)

The most salient idea that one gets from the Qur'ān is that the activities of Satan are all-pervasive in the human sphere and that man must constantly be alert and on his guard. Whenever the human self relaxes its tension, it is liable to be preyed upon by Satan's "beguiling." Although every human is, to some extent and in principle, as it were, exposed to Satan's tempting or beguiling, people who have *taqwā* (i.e., are on guard against moral danger) do not really lapse into evil but become quickly aware of Satan's machinations. Thus, the Prophet is told, "Should a disturbance from Satan invade you, seek refuge in God—God is hearing, knowing. Those who are on their guard, when a seductive glamor from Satan touches them, they [quickly] remember and thus *see* [once again]" (7:200-201).

This means that the Devil's activity essentially consists in confusing a person and temporarily (or, in the case of evil people, almost permanently) clouding his inner senses. The Qur'ān is emphatic, however, that although no human is in principle totally immune from the touch of the Devil, he has really no sway over those who are on guard against an invasion of their moral integrity. Thus, God said to Satan, "Indeed, upon my servants you will be able to exercise no influence, but only those errant ones who follow you" (15:42; cf. 17:65); again, "He has no authority over those who believe and put their faith in their Lord" (16:99).

Satan's tentacles alone are not strong; it is only man's weakness and lack of moral courage and alertness that make Satan look so strong. According to the Qur'ān, Satan's beguiling activity is rooted in his desperation and utter lack of hope. In Chapter II we quoted Qur'ānic verses to the effect that lack of hope, just like its opposite (pride) is a satanic act. At first, Satan refused to bow down to Adam out of sheer pride, because he thought he was "superior" to Adam; when God condemned him for his pride, he became desperate and came to symbolize the lack of all hope:

> God said, O Iblīs! Why were you not with those who bowed down [to Adam]? He replied, I am not going to bow to a human whom You have created from baked clay of dark mud that has been altered [in its nature]. God said, Out you go from the paradise, for you are cursed, and my curse shall pursue you till the Day of Judgment. He replied, O my Lord! give me respite till the Day of Resurrection. God replied, You have the respite [i.e., you are free to indulge in your activity] till the day of the Appointed Time. He said, O my Lord! since You have condemned me, I shall also embellish for men [their evil deeds] on earth and shall [try to] lead all of them astray—except Your sincere servants. (15:32-40)

This utter hopelessness is expressed by Satan in his desperate strategies to waylay man: "He [Iblīs] said [to God], "Now that You have condemned me to error, I shall waylay their [humans'] straight path to you. Then I shall approach them from their front and their back, their right and their left, so that You will not find most of them grateful [to You]" (7:17).

Iblīs or Satan thus appears more cunning and artful than strong, more deceitful and contriving than forthrightly challenging, more beguiling, treacherous, and "waylaying" than giving battle. This is why he shall say on the Day of Judgment to those who will accuse him of leading them astray, "God made you a true promise whereas I made you a false promise. I had no power over you but only invited you [to error] and you accepted my invitation. Do not blame me but [only] yourselves. I cannot help you, nor can you help me. I declare void your associating me with God [as His peer]" (14:22). As I have said, Satan's power is ultimately to be construed in terms of the weakness of man, for he has little inherent strength. His master-stratagem consists in "embellishing" or "causing to look attractive" the dross of the world as tinsel, or causing to look burdensome or frightening that which is really fruitful and consequential: "Satan has caused to look attractive to them the [evil] deeds they had been perpetrating" (6:43); "Satan made their [evil] deeds look attractive in their eyes" (8:48; also 16:63; 27:24; 29:38; 47:25); "It is only Satan who frightens his followers" (3:175).

It is, therefore, up to man how much power Satan will have and we have discussed man's own weakness at some length in Chapter II. Satan himself is often described by the Qur'ān as a rebel against God (37:7; 22:3; 4:117), but this finally means nothing more than his desperation. We have already seen that he will admit at the final judgment the futility of his endeavors and that he had really no power over humans. The Qur'ān, indeed, says, "Satan promises them nothing except deceit" (17:64; 4:120), which obviously means that there is nothing solid in his "promises." Again, "The believers are fighting in the cause of God, while those who disbelieve are fighting in the cause of the Devil [tāghūt]; hence fight, O Muslims!, the friends of Satan, for the stratagem of Satan is weak!" (4:76). From this conviction that evil is inherently weak and truth strong is born the invincible faith of the Qur'ān that falsehood and evil can and will be vanquished: "These people are the party of Satan—lo! the party of Satan shall be the losers" (58:19); "It is the party of God that will be victorious"

(5:56); "God is pleased with them and they with God; these are the party of God—lo! it is the party of God that will be successful" (58:22).

As we have already seen, then, Satan will betray his "friends" and leave them in the lurch. Further, "Satan *will* forsake man" (25:29). Even in this life, after man has submitted to his machinations, Satan refuses to take any part of the responsibility upon himself: "Like Satan who [first] invites man to commit infidelity to God, but when man does so, says, 'I am quit of you, I fear God the Lord of the world'" (59:16). It is not the strength of Satan, then, but the failure of man himself to show strength against Satan's blandishments, that constitutes the real threat to man. This tinsel so catches his heart and mind that he "gets lost" in the immediate and "forgets" the *ākhira*, the real, solid, long-range and consequential ends, the highest purposes. We saw in Chapter II how short-sighted and narrow-visioned man himself is—indeed, this was found there to be his main weakness. Now, we find that this is precisely what is exploited by Satan. In a sense, then, Satan is nothing but a force that strengthens the evil tendencies innate in man. When both join together, on the surface of it, the conjunction becomes impregnable. If he is to negate this powerful alliance, it becomes all the more important for man to consciously align himself with God in order to strengthen and develop the good tendencies that he carries in himself by nature.

Because of the treachery of Satan's cunning machinations and his ultimate sterility—because in effect, Satan's desperate efforts are counterproductive—man is frequently asked by the Qur'ān not to "follow the footsteps of Satan," presumably because these footsteps lead man nowhere except to self-destruction; Satan *is* the real enemy of man. These "footsteps" of Satan, therefore, mean any evil committed by man, whether it is wastefulness, corruption, war, or any other. "O people! eat of those lawful and good things that are in the earth [i.e., all things that are good to eat or drink], but do not follow the footsteps of Satan, for he is clearly your enemy" (2:168). Again:

> Those are the losers who kill their children out of stupidity and without knowledge and who prohibit what God has given them by way of [good] food by falsely attributing things to God—they have got lost and are not apt to find guidance. And it is He Who has created gardens, terraced and unterraced, and date-palms and agricultural produce of different tastes and olives and pomegranates—[fruits] that both resemble each other and differ from each other; eat from this

fruit when it matures but also give [to the needy their] share when you harvest it, and do not waste, for God does not like the wasteful. [And He has created] from the cattle such as are for carrying burdens and such as are for riding—eat of that which God has given you as [good] food, but do not follow the footsteps of Satan for he is clearly your enemy. (6:141-43; cf. 17:27, Indeed, those who waste are Satan's brothers)

Similarly, on war, "O you who believe, enter into peace, all of you, and do not follow the footsteps of Satan, for he is your clear enemy. And should you lapse after clear signs have come to you, then you must know that God is mighty and wise" (2:208-9). After speaking about the attempts of the hypocrites to sow sedition among Muslims, the Qur'ān talks about moral corruption, "O you who believe! do not follow the footsteps of Satan, for whosoever follows his footsteps, he commands [his followers to commit] obscenity and evil, and but for God's favor upon you and His mercy, none of you could ever be pure, but God purifies whomsoever He wills—He is hearing and knowing" (24:21); cf. also, "O children of Adam! let not Satan seduce you, just as he caused your ancestors to be expelled from the Garden by rending away from them their clothing in order to expose their private parts—indeed, he and his ilk see you whence you do not see them; We have made satans friends of the unbelievers" (7:27).

The idea that a human can or does follow the "footsteps" of the Devil has two main aspects. First, Satan never forces, nor can he force, anyone to do evil but he tries to entice or tempt the possible victim. His enticement consists in presenting the immediate superficial ends or tantalizations of this world's life in such a manner that many people are victimized, most of them temporarily but many permanently, these latter being termed the "friends" or the "party" of the Devil. Secondly, these footsteps lead nowhere but to the destruction of the victim, just as the footsteps of some contrivor might lead a victim to a chasm. It is all-important for man to recognize the footsteps of Satan for what they are, otherwise it is extremely difficult, indeed impossible, for man to save himself from perdition. Thus, the real problem lies within man himself, for he is a blend of good and evil, ignorance and knowledge, power and impotence (cf. the doctrine of human tensions described in Chapter II). The key to man's defense is *taqwā*, which literally means defense but which (see Chapter II), is a kind of inner light, a spiritual spark which man must light within himself to distinguish between right and wrong, seeming and real, immediate and lasting, etc. Once a human does this—and *taqwā* is, of course, capable of gradations—he should be able to see Satan's footsteps for what they are and not be beguiled by them.

The fact that man does carry within himself evil tendencies as well as good tendencies distinguishes him from angels, who are free from evil tendencies and are automatically "good," and puts him close to the jinn, although the jinn are more prone to evil than he is. In any case, there is a struggle between these two trends in man. But the evil trend does become very strong through the objective fact of the existence of Satan, whose machinations have myriad forms (including creation in man of placidity and self-satisfaction in his own virtue) and who, because of man's innate tendency toward the easy and the immediate (compounded further by his dangerous capacity for self-deception), is able to dress up evil as good before him; thus Satan can all but destroy the capacity for inner vision of man described by the Qur'ān as *taqwā*.

It is this conjunction of the evil in man and an objective Satan that makes it necessary for man to join God or ask for God's help. For the Qur'ān, God not only helps but promises that His side or "party" is going to win eventually: "Those who side with God and his Prophet are the believers, God's party shall be the victorious one" (5:56), even as we saw earlier that the "party of Satan will be the losers" (58:19).

This idea of a subjective and an objective evil, as the opposites of a subjective and an objective good, means that the existence of Satan must be objective. As we said at the beginning of this discussion, however, although Satan does not exist "in" man except metaphorically, he is nevertheless a coeval of man, since before Adam there was no Satan and there can be no Satan independent of human nature. Moreover, the workings of Satan are "in" man inasmuch as he affects man's mind through suggestion, temptation, and "invitation": "So Satan whispered into their mind [i.e., the minds of Adam and Eve, to tempt them to the forbidden tree]" (7:20; also 20:120; 23:97). But the mind of man (or rather, his lower instincts) is also represented as "whispering" to man (50:16). Indeed, man's lower instincts are spoken of as not only tempting him to evil but "commanding" him to commit evil: "[Joseph said], I do not acquit myself [of almost being tempted by the Egyptian woman] for the [lower] self ever commands evil except insofar as my Lord has mercy [and saves His servants]; indeed, my Lord is pardoning and merciful" (12:53). On the basis of these and similar verses, some Muslim thinkers, particularly many Sufis, have been of the view that Satan is really "in" man, or is identical with the negative self of man, but probably such verses are to be interpreted as meaning that when the potential evil in man is powerfully aroused by an external evil force, the combination is a veritable "commanding" i.e., a well-nigh irresistible reality.

The question whether Satan is the objective *principle* of evil or is a "person" is, however, more difficult to answer. Certainly, evil is usually personalized, particularly in connection with the story of Adam, where his proper name is mentioned as Iblis: Iblis not only disobeyed God and refused to honor Adam but engaged in a fairly lengthy controversy with God. But later, when Adam and Eve are tempted to eat of the forbidden fruit, their tempter is termed not Iblis but Satan, the normal term for the evil principle, and since the story of the creation and fall of Adam are obviously presented in a dramatized form, it is a question whether the Qur'ān is speaking literally there of "persons." Besides the story of Adam (38:74-75; 20:116; 18:50; 17:61; 15:31-32; 7:11; 2:34), the term Iblis also appears in 26:95: "They [those who are being worshipped as God's partners] and the erring ones [those who worship the former] shall be hurled therein [into Hell], and all the hordes of Iblis" (here "the hordes" is probably used metaphorically to include both evil jinn and men), and, again, in 34:20: "Iblis had correctly judged them [to be his victims], for they did follow him except a group of believers" (the reference is to the people of South Arabia, who were afflicted with the flood of 'Arim and subsequent trials). In this second instance, too, the term Satan (*Shaitān*) could well have been substituted for the term Iblis, since Iblis is used in a much less emphatically personal sense than in the passages connected with Adam's story.

As for the term *Shaitān*, although it is usually employed in the singular, the plural usage is by no means rare. The usage in the plural is in certain cases obviously metaphorical, as in the phrase "satans of humans and jinn" (6:112); or "When they [the hypocrites] meet with those who believe, they say, We [too] believe, but when they are alone with their [own] satans [co-hypocrites], they say, We are with you, we are only joking [with Muslims]" (2:14); indeed, "And by your Lord! We shall certainly gather them [those who deny the reality of resurrection] and the satans" (19:68). Because Satan, in the singular, was given "respite" by God until the Last Day to allow him to pursue his work so that there should apparently be no question of his resurrection. [Note that the term "gathering [*hashr*]" used in connection with the last Judgment *means* resurrection.]

There are many contexts in which "satans" in the plural cannot be taken metaphorically, however, as: "Indeed, they [the disbelievers] have taken satans as their lords [or friends] to the exclusion of God" (7:30); or 7:27, "We have made satans friends for those who do not believe." Again, some satans did pearl diving for Solomon, besides undertaking other works (21:82); although here most probably evil jinn are meant, since jinn served Solomon (27:29).

Indeed, some people—particularly poets who indulged in extravagant image-mongering—received messages from satans, from whom the Prophet Muhammad was immune (despite the fact that no human, including all the prophets, are in principle immune from the approach of Satan), as we read towards the end of sura 26: "Satans have not brought it [the Qur'ān] down nor does it behoove them to do so, nor yet can they do it—they are barred from hearing it [i.e., when the Trusted Spirit or the Angelic nature reads it mentally to the Prophet, cf. Chapter V]" (26:210-212). Further, "Shall I inform you of those upon whom satans descend? They descend upon every liar and sinful person. They listen eagerly [to the voice from the Unseen] but mostly they are liars. As for poets, the erring ones follow them. Do you not see that they wander unbridled in every valley? And they say what they do not do?—except those who believe and do good deeds" (26:221-227). Just as God reveals His Message to His prophets, so satans send messages to their wicked followers; and just as prophets draw strength from contact with the divine, so the wicked draw their strength from satans, except that this strength, not founded upon truth, is unreal in the sense that it cannot withstand the divine strength and thus is *bāṭil*, i.e., both false and defeatable.

Another name used by the Qur'ān for objective evil is *ṭāghūt*, which apparently means simply the evil or ungodly principle (39:17; 16:36; 2:256-257; 4:51, 60, 76; 5:60—in 2:257 it is used with the plural meaning). This term begins to occur in the later Meccan years, where it occurs twice, and persists through the Madinan period, whereas the name Iblīs occurs almost entirely in Mecca and there is only one early Madinan mention of it (2:34). As for *Shaiṭān*, probably all of its *non-metaphorical plural* occurrences are also in Mecca (for it is possible to take 2:102, as well as 2:14—both early Madinan—metaphorically). Thus, in Madina, Iblis disappears, as does the plural of *Shaitān*; *Shaitān* or Satan (in the singular) remains, while at the same time the use of *taghūt* becomes relatively more frequent. *Taghūt* appears to be the objective ungodly principle rather than a person. Satan may well be the same. On the other hand, it is also possible to hold that evil is the force or principle of ungodliness and vice, but that when it becomes related to or affects a given individual, it becomes "personalized" as Satan. (This is not analogous with angels, for angels are not only spoken of throughout the Qur'ān in the singular and plural as persons but some also have names [2:98], although it is possible to argue that *Jibrīl* and *Mikhāl* are not angels, but supra-angelic spirits, as, indeed, we have actually held with regard to *Jibrīl* (Gabriel) while discussing the issue of the agency of Revelation, since it is not identified with any angel in the Qur'ān.)

Chapter Eight

Emergence of
The Muslim Community

In the beginning [wrote Snouck Hurgronje], Muhammad was convinced of bringing to the Arabs the same [message] which the Christians had received from Jesus and the Jews from Moses, etc., and against the [Arab] pagans, he confidently appealed to "the people of knowledge". . .whom one has simply to ask in order to obtain a confirmation of the truth of his teaching. [But] in Madina came the disillusionment; the "People of the Book" will not recognize him. He must, therefore, seek an authority for himself beyond their control, which at the same time does not contradict his own earlier Revelations. He, therefore, seizes upon the ancient Prophets whose communities cannot offer him opposition [i.e., whose communities are not there or no longer there: like Abraham, Noah, etc.]. [1]

Passages like this constitute the classic formulation, at the hands of a great leader of modern Western Islamic studies, of a view of the emergence as a separate entity from the Jewish and the Christian communities of the Muslim community in Madina. The statement, quoted approvingly in the *Geschichte des Qorans of Noldeke-Schwally*,[2] seems to have become a permanent part of the patriarchal legacy for many Western Islamicists who have elaborated it further. The theory invites us to accept (1) that when, in Madina, Jews and Christians (particularly the former) refused to accept him as Prophet, he began appealing to the image of Abraham, whom he disassociated from Judaism and Christianity, claiming him exclusively for Islam and linking the Muslim community directly with him; and (2) that in Mecca, the Prophet was convinced that he was giving the same teaching *to the Arabs* which earlier prophets had given to their com-

1. Quoted in *Geschichte des Qorans* (New York, 1970), Part 1, pp. 146-147.
2. See n.1.

munities. Further elaborations of the theory followed which depict this development as a major, indeed basic, diversion from the Prophet's original stance, culminating in the "nationalization" or "Arabization"[3] of Islam through the change in the direction of prayer from Jerusalem to the Ka'ba at Mecca and the installation of the pilgrimage to the Ka'ba as a cardinal duty of Islam. These latter dissertations will not be treated *per se* in this paper but it will be seen where they are affected by our main argument.

Let it be stated at the outset that the *facts* upon which the classic theory seeks to rest are not wrong; our contention will be that these are not all the facts relevant to our problem and, further, that because they are not all the material facts, they have been distorted and misconstrued. Thus, whereas it is true that the Qur'ān was convinced that its message was identical with those of earlier prophets, it is neither true that its message was only for the Arabs and the earlier prophets' messages only for their communities, nor that when Islam was later linked with Abraham (which happened in Mecca, not Madina), the Qur'ān gave up Moses to the Jews and Jesus to the Christians as their properties because of Jewish (and Christian) opposition.

Nor is it correct to say that the change of Qibla represents either a *rupture* in the Prophet's religious orientation, or its nationalization! One basic trouble lies with viewing the career of the Prophet and the Qur'ān in two neatly discrete and separate "periods"—the Madinan and the Meccan—to which most modern scholars have become addicted. A closer study of the Qur'ān reveals, rather, a gradual development, a smooth transition where the later Meccan phase has basic affinities with the earlier Madinan phase; indeed, one can "see" the latter in the former.

It is clear from the Qur'ān that some Meccans were already desirous of a new religion of the Judeo-Christian type: "Although these people used to say, If only we had a Reminder from the ancients, we would be God's sincere servants, but they disbelieved in it [when it came]" (37:168-70). This situation was in part the result of the penetration of Judeo-Christian ideas into the Arab milieu; it testifies to the existence of a religious ferment among more enlightened individuals and possibly groups. Although there is little historical evidence for the

---

3. For example, F. Buhl, article *Muhammad*, in *The Shorter Encyclopedia of Islam.*

existence of any sizable population of Jews or Christians in Mecca, it is certain that some individuals had come to an idea of monotheism and some had actually become Christians. But what the Qur'ān points to frequently is the existence of some kind of Messianism, a desire for a new Arab prophet: "And they swore with all their strength that if a warner should come to them, they would certainly be better guided than any other community; but when a warner did come to them, it increased them only in aversion" (35:42).

That the Meccans did not want to accept either Jesus or Moses (presumably because they wanted "to do better" than the other two communities; cf. also 6:157-58) is also stated in the Qur'ān: "And when the son of Mary was cited as an example, lo! your people resisted him, and they said, Are our gods better or he? They did not say this except as a [point of] disputation—they are, indeed, a disputatious people" (43:57-58); again:

> But for the fact that a calamity should befall them for what their hands have sent forth and then they should say, Our Lord! Why did You not send us a Messenger so we would have followed Your signs and been among the believers. But when the Truth came to them from Us, they said, Why has he [Muhammad] not been given the like of what Moses was given? But did they not reject what Moses had been given before, saying, Those are a pair of sorceries mutually supporting each other [and adding], We reject both of them. [cf. also 34:31, "And those who disbelieve [in the Qur'ān] said, We shall never believe in this Qur'ān nor in that [Revelation] which came before it."] Say to them [O Muhammad], Then you bring another Book from Allah which would give better guidance than these two [the Bible and the Qur'ān] and I will follow that one, if you are speaking the truth. (28:47-49)

Since these passages date from different contexts during a prolonged and bitter controversy of the Meccans with the Prophet, it would be difficult to fully assess the stance of the Meccans on the issue for the period immediately preceding the advent of the Prophet's mission, for, as the Qur'ān itself says, they said certain things only for the sake of controversy. (Indeed, later in Madina, when Jewish-Muslim enmity became solidified, even the Madinese Jews, at the instance of the pagans, declared the pagan Arab religion to be superior to Islam! [4:51]). Nevertheless, this much is clear: at least some Meccan Arabs were looking for a new religion and a new Scripture which should bestow a certain distinction upon them vis-a-vis the old communities, and they were generally disinclined to accept the earlier Scriptures: "If We had sent it [the Qur'ān] down upon some non-Arab and he had recited it to them, they would not have believed in it" (26:198); again, "If we had made it a non-Arab Qur'ān, they would have said, Why are its verses not clearly set forth? What, non-Arab and Arab? Say, 'It is a guidance and cure for those who believe" (41:43-44). In the phrase "the Arab Qur'ān," we should, I think, see something more than language and nationalism, but *what* is not easy to say; the Arabs themselves probably had only the vaguest ideas of what they wanted, although on the negative side they were much more precise. From the persistent demands of the Meccan leaders during their controversy with the Prophet (10:15; 17:73 ff.) that he change the Qur'ānic teaching, it is also clear that they wanted him to give some place between God and man in his system to their gods. This will make intelligible why they rejected the Mosaic religion, and also why they would not consider Jesus to be superior to their gods.

Let us now consider the position of the Prophet himself. From the times when the earlier prophets begin to be referred to in the Qur'ān, the Prophet is convinced of the identity of his message with theirs: "This is in the earlier scrolls—the scrolls of Abraham and Moses" (87:18-19). These "scrolls," i.e., written revelations, are again referred to in 53:33-37: "Did you see the one who turned his back? He gave a little [of his wealth] and then ran dry. Does he possess a knowledge of the unseen, so he can see? Or, has he not been told of what is in the scrolls of Moses and of Abraham who fulfilled [his undertaking]"? These passages do not, of course, imply that the Prophet knew these scrolls, nor even that he had seen them. (These two are among the very few passages [which probably indicates that there was already a native Arab prophetology] where the term "scrolls" has been used for revealed documents; elsewhere it is applied to the "Heavenly Archetype" of all Revelation or to the deed-sheets of men which will be presented to them on the Last Day.) Later the word "Book" is used and is applied almost exclusively throughout the Meccan period to the "Book of Moses" as a forerunner of the Qur'ān. Also, from the first references to earlier prophets, the Qur'ān uses certain purely Arab figures—the prophets of the tribes 'Ād and Thamūd—in addition to Biblical figures. Jesus (19:30) and other New Testament personalities do not seem to be referred to in the first

Meccan period but appear from the second period onward, while the gospel is mentioned only once in Mecca. (Why the Gospel hardly appears in Meccan period while the "Book of Moses" appears very frequently is a problem for which there is no satisfactory explanation so far, given the fact that Christianity was widespread in Arabia.) These facts also corroborate our statement that the Prophet had little or no acquaintance with earlier Scriptures in the first four years of his Prophetic career.

When opposition starts against the Prophet's theses—that God is one, that the poor of society must not be allowed to flounder, and that there is a final Day of Judgment—numerous detailed stories about the earlier prophets are repeated in the Qur'ān. There can be little doubt that the Prophet heard these stories during discussions with certain unidentified people, and the Meccans themselves were not slow to point this out (25:4-5; 16:103). Muḥammad insisted, nevertheless, that they were revealed to him.

He was, of course, right. For, under the impact of his direct religious experience, these stories became *revelations* and were no longer mere tales. Through this experience, he cultivated a direct community with earlier prophets and became their direct witness: "You were not [O Muhammad!] upon the western side when we decreed to Moses the Commandment, nor were you of those witnessing [at the time]. But We raised up [many] generations [afterwards] who have lived too long [to keep the original experiences alive]. Neither were you a dweller among the Midianites" (28:45). Not only were the points and lessons of those stories transformed through revelation but often their content as well. Shu'aib is represented as admonishing his people against fraudulent forms of commerce—which was Muḥammad's problem at Mecca; Noah is seen rejecting the demands of the powerful in his community that he dissociate himself from his socioeconomically weak followers before the powerful would join his religion—a situation which, of course, Muhammad himself was facing in Mecca. And so on.

Because of this spiritual community with earlier prophets through his revelatory experience, Muhammad was absolutely convinced of the identity of the Messages of all prophets. All Scriptures stem from and are parts of a single Source, the Heavenly Archetype called "The Mother of Books" and "The Hidden Book." This being the case, it is necessary to believe in all revealed books and Muhammad is made to declare in the Qur'ān: "Say: I believe in any and every Book that God has revealed" (42:15). Indeed, the term "the Book" is often used in the Qur'ān not to denote any specific scripture but as a generic term for the totality of revealed scriptures. It was, then, absolutely natural for Muhammad to expect that all communities should believe in the Qur'ān, just as he and his followers believed in all the Books. It is true that the Qur'ān repeatedly emphasizes (16:103; 26:195; 39:28; 41:3, etc.) that the Qur'ān is revealed in "clear Arabic," but this emphasis is addressed especially to the Arab Meccans; otherwise, the truth of a scripture is not circumscribed by being revealed in any particular language.

Let us now consider a different dimension of this issue. From the Qur'ān it is abundantly clear that there were, among the followers of Judaism and (whether orthodox or not) of Christianity, some who affirmed the truth of the Prophet's mission and, in fact, encouraged him in the face of Meccan opposition. History tells us next to nothing about them[4]; nor do we know whether these are the same persons with whom the Prophet held discussions. The Qur'ānic references to them, however, are clear evidence of the presence of Messianism in these circles. In 26:192 ff., we have, "Truly it [the Qur'ān] is Revelation from the Lord of the world, brought down by the Trusted Spirit upon your heart, that you may be one of the warners, in a clear Arabic tongue. It is, indeed, in the Scriptures of the ancients. Was it not a sign for them [the Meccans] that it is known to the learned of the children of Israel?" They are invoked again and again by the Qur'ān as witnesses to the truth of Muhammad's prophethood, being "people whom We had already given the Book," "people to whom the Book or Knowledge had already been given," "people of Knowledge" and "people of Admonition," through the second and third Meccan periods. Even when the Prophet himself, during periods of intense pressure and trial because of opposition, seemed occasionally to lose hope and wonder whether, after all, he should go ahead with his movement, the Qur'ān asks him to seek solace and support from "the people who recite the

---

4. The Muslim tradition usually refers to a delegation of Christians who came from Abyssinia and accepted Islam, but the basis of these reports is uncertain. These verses are for the most part Meccan, but some seem to be early Madinan. In Madina, the tradition refers to certain Jewish converts, the most prominent being 'Abd Allāh ibn Salām, who, however, is often brought in by Muslim commentators in contexts which are clearly Meccan. This whole matter is shrouded in obscurity since the Qur'ān never mentions any names. See Ibn Ishaq, *Sīra*, ed. Muhammad Muhy al-Dīn 'Abd al-Hamīd, (Cairo, 1356/1937), vol. I, p. 320, lines 15 ff.

[previous] Book" (10:94) and not to become a party to the polytheists after "clear signs" and the divine teaching have come to him, which he had never anticipated before his Call (28:85-89).

If God is one and His Message is also one and fundamentally indivisible, surely mankind should be one community. And, particularly in view of the affirmation of his mission by followers of earlier religions, the Prophet hoped to unify the multiplicity of these religions into one single community, *under his teaching and on his terms*; but as his knowledge about differences among earlier religions and sects gradually increased, he soon realized that this was not to be. This undoubtedly set him a theological problem of the first order, which the Qur'ān continued to treat until deep into the Madinan period when the Muslim community was formally established as the "median" and "ideal" community. We are not here concerned with the purely theological aspect of the phenomenon of the diversity of religions in the Qur'ān, but rather with the effect upon the development of the Muslim community of the Prophet's perception of this diversity.

The jolt to the Prophet's idea of a single religious community did not come so much in Madina, as Hurgronje states, as well back in Mecca. We again know very little about who the precise agents were, for the Qur'ān, as usual, names no persons. According to Ibn Ishāq's biography of the prophet, Meccan leaders had once sent a team of two men to solicit the help of the Jews of Madina in their controversies with the Prophet and this team had returned with three questions to be put to him.[5] The Qur'ānic accounts, however, assume much more than this and strongly suggest something like direct controversies between the Prophet and representatives of earlier religions. In these controversies, which evidently demonstrated differences not only with Muslims but also within the earlier religions, the followers of these religions are called *al-ahzāb* (pl. of *hizb*, partisans, sectarians), i.e., those who split up the community of religion. This term had earlier been employed by the Qur'ān on three occasions[6] to refer to ancient nations or peoples who had rejected their messengers and were consequently destroyed by God. In one of these passages (38:11-13), Meccans are invited to ascend to the heavens and witness "there a host of destroyed *ahzāb*,"

5. *Ibid.*, p. 11, n. 3.

6. For reference to these earlier passages I am indebted to Rudi Paret's *Der Koran* (Stuttgart, 1971), p. 233, lines 23 ff.

which are identified as the peoples of Noah, 'Ād, Pharaoh, Thamūd, Lot, and the "people of the thicket," the Midianites. The underlying sense in this usage seems to be of "counter-groups" who oppose the divine message, but then are themselves destroyed.

Every prophet's message, then, acts like a watershed upon people to whom it is addressed; it has the effect of dividing them into the categories of truth and falsehood. But in a later use of *ahzāb*, it means the splitting up into sects of an originally unitary truth. In 19:37, it refers to sectarian differences among the followers of Jesus and his message, differences which distorted his teaching, and the idea grows strong in the Qur'ān, about Jews and Christians in particular but also in general, that "people come to differ only after clear knowledge has come to them" (10:19, 93; 45:17; 2:213; 30:9; 98:4, etc.). Indeed, the original message gets lost over a long passage of time and the sentence, "too long a period has lapsed over them" is repeated (21:44; 28:45; 57:16). It becomes an unusually tormenting thought in the Qur'ān and the Muslims are repeatedly warned—in both Madina and Mecca—against such division, where "every sect rejoices in what it has" (30:32; also 3:103, 105; 6:159). In this connection, the words *ahzāb* and *shiya'* (pl. of *shī'a*, also meaning a party or a sect) are used in the same sense.

When (in the third Meccan period) *ahzāb* is applied to the earlier communities contemporary with Muhammad, it probably has both meanings discussed above: of sects which resulted from splits over the earlier messages, and also (perhaps because of) the splits of counter-groups against the message of Muhammad. In three passages both are sharply distinguished from "those We *had* given the Book," who believe in the Qur'ān as well. The first passage, where the term *ahzāb* is not applied, states, "And even thus have We sent down the Book to you [O Muhammad!]; so those to whom We had [already] given the Book believe in it and some among these people also believe in it" (29:47). The second passage is more explicit, "Those to whom We had [already] given the Book rejoice at what is being sent down to you, but among the sectarians [*al-ahzāb*] there are those who reject part of it" (13:36).[7] This verse suggests that the "sectarians" did not object to

---

7. These verses are mostly, if not wholly, Meccan: Nöldeke-Schwally thinks that all mentions of "those to whom we had given the Book" who are said to believe in the Qur'ān as well are Meccan passages (*op. cit.*, p. 155).

the whole Qur'ān but to a part of it. In the third passage we are told, "And what of him who stands on [the basis of] a firm conviction from his Lord, and then a Witness from Him [the Angel of Revelation] recites it and [already] before it is the Book of Moses as an example and a mercy. It is those [i.e., who have the Book of Moses] who believe in it [the Qur'ān]; but whosoever among the sectarians disbelieves in it, Fire shall be his destiny" (11:17).

The term *aḥzāb* is used once more, but much later, in the middle of the Madinan period (33:20-22), to mean the various parties and tribes (the Quraish and Bedouin tribes and Jews) which had formed a confederacy to war on Madina in the "Battle of the Ditch." But although the Qur'ān no longer uses this term to mean the earlier communities who rejected the Prophet, it continues to speak to them, now as supporting the Prophet and believing in him, now as rejecting or opposing him—in both the Meccan and the Madinan periods. In 17:107, referring to the Meccans, the Qur'ān declares: "Say to them (O Muḥammad!), Whether you believe in it [the Qur'ān] or not, those who have been given the Knowledge [Revelation] before it, when it [the Qur'ān] is recited to them, fall upon their faces in prostration. And they say, Glory be to our Lord! Our Lord's Promise has been fulfilled [in Muḥammad]. And they fall upon their faces weeping and it increases them in God-fearingness." We have it again in 6:115: "Those to whom We have [already] given the Book know that it [the Qur'ān] has been sent down from your Lord in truth—so be not one of the doubters." On the other hand, we are also told, in 6:20, "Those to whom We have [already] given the Book, know it as they know their own sons—those who have lost their own souls because they would not believe [in the Qur'ān]." Both these assertions are repeated in Madina (e.g., 2:121; 2:144-46, particularly the latter), where a protracted religious and political controversy is waged against the Jews, many of whom are accused of unbelief in the Qur'ān and infidelity to their own scriptures as well.

Just as Muḥammad follows upon and inherits the missions of earlier prophets and the Qur'ān receives the legacy of earlier Revelations, so does the Muslim community now inherit the place of earlier communities. This development, too, takes place in Mecca. In 6:89-93, after enumerating eighteen earlier prophets from Noah and Abraham to New Testament personalities, the Qur'ān says:

> That is God's guidance; He guides therewith whomsoever He wills of
> His servants, and if they [the earlier Prophets] had been idolators
> their deeds would have come to naught. They are those whom We
> gave the Book, the Decision, and Prophethood; so if these people
> disbelieve in it, We have already commissioned it to a people [i.e.,
> Muslims in general, particularly those who already had an earlier
> Revelation] who do not disbelieve in it. They [the earlier prophets] are
> those whom God has guided; so follow their guidance. . .They have
> not measured God with His true measure when they said, God has not
> sent down anything on any mortal. Say, Who sent down the Book that
> Moses brought as a light and a guidance to mankind? You [or they]
> write it out into parchments, revealing them, yet hiding much
> [thereof] and you were taught that which neither you nor your fathers
> had known. . .And this [the Qur'ān] is a Book We have sent down,
> blessed and confirming that which was before it, that you may warn
> the Mother of Towns [Mecca] and its environs.[8]

8. This passage, as its context indicates, is Meccan and is basically directed
against the pagans, but certain points have raised difficulties for commentators,
both Muslims and Westerners. Who are meant by the words "If these people
disbelieve in it" and "We have already commissioned it to a people who do not
disbelieve in it"? According to the traditional Muslim view, the "people who
disbelieve" are Meccans, which may well be correct since the context is Meccan;
but "the people to which it has been commissioned" cannot be either Madinese
Muslims or the earlier prophets themselves, as the traditional view holds. Richard
Bell thought that the "disbelieving people" were Madinese Jews and the "people
to whom it is entrusted [or commissioned]" were Muslims, and that the verse is not
Meccan but Madinese. R. Paret notes that the first and the last parts of the verse fit
Meccan pagans while the middle fits Jews; but regards the entire verse as a
well-connected whole. This interpretation in itself appears plausible, but the verse
is obviously not Madinese but Meccan. In the light of our argument on the meaning
of *ahzāb* and the Meccan—Jewish communications on the subject of Muhammad's
mission, the most natural way to understand the verse is that it is addressed to the
pagan Meccans who were supported by Jews and hence the passage hits at the
Jews as well. On this basis 6:92, which has given considerable trouble to commentators and scholars, also becomes intelligible. It makes three related points:
that those Meccans who deny the possibility of Revelation to a human have mis-
conceived God's power; that several Meccans themselves have learnt much from
the Mosaic Revelation which neither they nor their fathers had known before; and
that Jews who copy down the Mosaic Revelation hide a large part of it (the vulgate
has "which *you* write down . . . making it public but hiding much" in the second
person plural, but there is a variant reading in the third person plural, adopted by
al-Tabari, which might be an attempt to smoothe out the text).

Bell (*The Qur'ān Translated*, Edinburgh, I, 124) believes this passage to be
Madinan—in spite of the fact that its first and last parts are obviously Meccan and
could have been addressed only to the Meccan pagans—and regards the words
which accuse the Jews of copying down Scriptures in such a manner that they hide
part of the Scriptures as being an even later insertion by the Prophet. Whereas it is

At the point where Muḥammad clearly realizes that his position is in the direct line of prophetic succession to earlier prophets and that the pagan Arabs are wrong in their idolatry and other communities are wrong in their schismatic character, the Qur'ān describes Muḥammad as a *ḥanīf*, a true monotheist, and his religion as the "straight religion [*al-dīn al-qayyim*]" from which paganism and sectarianism are represented as deviations: "So set your face [O Muhammad!] to the straight religion" (30:43); "So set your face to the religion as a *ḥanīf*; this is the primordial religion on which God has originated mankind... . This is the straight religion ... and do not be [O Muslims!] among those who associate [partners with God], nor among those who split up their religion into sects, each sect rejoicing in what it has" (30:30-32).

That this religion of pure monotheism which is pre-eminently attributed to Abraham was primarily developed against the cult of pagan deities is obvious from 12:37-40, where Joseph declares to his two prison companions, "I have abandoned the religion of a people who do not believe in [one] God and disbelieve in the Last Day and now

true that in its controversies with Jews at Madina the Qur'ān repeatedly accuses them of not representing their Scriptures faithfully, this accusation is by no means limited to Madina. Earlier we drew attention to the fact that some Meccans had heard stories of earlier prophets from the "People of the Book" and had wished for a revealed Book of their own, and that they had not accepted the Mosaic teaching. This is precisely what the latter part of 6:92 is pointing to by saying "And you have been taught [by the People of the Book] what neither you nor your fathers knew." Further, when the Prophet became aware of the differences among the "People of the Book" themselves, he became convinced that whereas the Scriptures were true, these were being manipulated and misrepresented by their votaries. In 29:48 the Qur'ān states, "Before it [the Qur'ān], you [O Muhammad!] did not use to recite a Book *nor were you copying it down with your right hand*, for then those who do not accept you would have been suspicious." This verse has three ideas, the most prominent of which is the reply to the Meccans' charges that the Prophet was being taught the stories of older prophets. The reply is that, had the Prophet been reciting these stories or writing them before his Call, there might have existed some ground for such suspicion. The second idea, also repeated in the Qur'ān (28:86; 42:52), is that Muhammad had never anticipated or made any deliberate effort at being a Prophet, but was called to it suddenly. But, thirdly, there is in the words "nor were you copying it down with your right hand" an obvious sarcasm against the scribes who wrote the old Scriptures and did not represent them faithfully. This idea is, however, squarely Meccan. Also, the verses that follow are clearly Meccan. In order to keep consistent his view that this entire passage is Madinan, Bell takes the phrase "the Mother of the Towns," which the Prophet is exhorted to warn, to refer to Madina, against the weight of all traditional Muslim authorities, who take it to refer to Mecca. Still, this particular substitution of Madina for Mecca is one of the lesser eccentricities of Richard Bell!

follow the religion [*milla*] of my fathers, Abraham, Isaac, and Jacob. It is not ours to associate anything with God . . . . O my prison companions! are several lords better or one all-powerful God?... He has commanded that you not serve except Him alone: this is the straight religion." The image of Abraham as the arch-monotheist is asserted against the Meccan pagans toward the end of the Meccan period where (suras 6 and 12) the stories of earlier prophets except Abraham have ceased and where, in 6:74 ff., after detailing how Abraham arrived at the idea of monotheism after eliminating astral gods one by one, Abraham says:

> O my people! I am quit of what you associate [with God]; I have set my face as a *hanif* unto Him who created the heavens and the earth and I am not one of those who associate [partners with God]. And [when] his people argued with him, he said, Do you argue with me concerning God when He has already guided me? I do not fear what you associate with Him ... . Why should I fear what you associate [with Him] while you do not fear that you have associated [others] with God without any authority that God may have sent upon you—which of the two parties is, then, more deserving of security, if you only knew? (6:79-82).

This is followed by a list of seventeen prophets, including Moses and Jesus, in a passage which states that if these men had committed *shirk*, all their deeds would have come to nothing.

It is, then, in a solidly Meccan context with pagans as its addressees that the Qur'ān develops its image of Abraham as the super-prophet and arch-monotheist; and not in Madina as a consequence of controversies with Jews, as Hurgronje and Schwally say. But the line of monotheistic succession having come from Abraham, through earlier prophets, to Muḥammad, must be kept straight *without any deviation*. The earlier monotheistic communities—"the People of the Book"— have apparently not been able to keep this line straight; otherwise, there would not have been sectarian splits.

In the light of this, it is possible to understand afresh the meaning of the much-debated term *hanif*. In the Qur'ān it probably means not just a monotheist, but a straight, non-deviant monotheist. Neither the pagans nor the "People of the Book" were *hanifs* in this sense, and hence it is on the basis of this straight, Abrahamic monotheism (running, of course, through other prophets to Muhammad) that the

Qur'ān criticizes not only pagans but the earlier communities as well. Towards the end of sura 6, we read:

> Those people who have split up their religion and become sects, you have nothing to do with them; their affair is up to God and He will tell them what they had been doing... . Say [O Muhammad]: As for me, my Lord has guided me to a straight path, an upright religion, the religion of Abraham who was a straight monotheist [*hanif*] and he was no associationist [or idolator]. Say: My prayer, my religious exercises, my living, and my dying are for God, the Lord of all creation. He has no associate; with this I have been commanded and I am the first of those who surrender themselves. (6:160-64)

Important developments do take place in Madina but they do not consist in the Qur'ān abandoning Moses and Jesus to Jews and Christians and linking the Muslim community directly and exclusively with Abraham. This would have destroyed the whole idea of the straight line of prophetic succession as *hanifism*, and the basic unity of religion. Indeed, Moses and Jesus loom large in Madina, just as in Mecca. Also, the earlier Revelation continues to figure and the Qur'ān upholds itself both as its confirmer and preserver. In sura 5, after talking about the Mosaic Revelation and the Gospel, the Qur'ān says:

> And to you [O Muhammad!] We have sent down the Book in truth as a confirmer of the Books [i.e., all Revelations] that have come before it and as a protector over them...For each one of you [Jews, Christians, Muslims], We have appointed a path and a way, and if God had so willed, He would have made you but one community but [He has not done so in order] that He try [all of] you in what He has given you; wherefore compete with one another in good deeds... . (5:48)

One important development in Madina, then, is that earlier Revelations, the Torah and the Gospel, are mentioned by name, whereas in Mecca the Gospel is hardly referred to (although, of course, Jesus and other New Testament personalities are certainly there), while the Mosaic Revelation is always called "the Book of Moses," which repeatedly appears as the forerunner of the Qur'ānic Revelation.

A second major development—as is also apparent from 5:48—is the recognition of three separate communities: Jews, Christians, and Muslims. The Meccan terms "sects" and "parties" (*ahzāb* and *shiya*), used for the earlier communities, disappear in Madina and are replaced with the term *Umma* or the collective term "the People of the Book" (*ahl al-kitāb*), and each *Umma* is recognized as having its own laws. Far from seeking refuge in Abraham in order to validate the Muslim community, the Qur'ān now recognizes in some fashion the validity of the Jewish and the Christian communities. Still, the Muslim community remains the "ideal" or "best" community (*khair ummatin*), the "Median community [*Umma wasat*]," which, over against the "tendentiousness" of the others, is the true descendant of the Abrahamic line. The "People of the Book" are still invited to Islam, however: "O People of the Book! Our Messenger has come to you now, making matters clear to you, after a long interval between messengers, lest you should say, There has not come to us any bearer of good tidings nor a warner; now a bearer of good tidings and a warner has come" (5:19).

We should like to end by discussing briefly the position of the Ka'ba or the *Ḥaram*, with which both the pilgrimage and the direction of prayer are concerned. I find puzzling the statement of Nöldeke-Schwally[9] that the Ka'ba is not mentioned in the Qur'ān at all in Mecca after the very early sura 106. The word Ka'ba itself is, of course, not used in Mecca at all and appears in the Qur'ān fairly late in Madina (5:2 ; 5:95). But if the statement implies, as it apparently does, that the Sanctuary as such went out of the Prophet's attention until the pilgrimage was installed as a Muslim's duty, it is obviously wrong. In 28:57, commenting upon the expressed fears of some Meccans that if they accepted the Prophet's teaching, they would be kidnapped from their homes by his opponents, the Qur'ān says that the territory had been recognized as secure, with the consequence that people were not only secure from attack but traded freely there, resulting in prosperity and abundance. This statement tallies exactly with what had been said earlier in sura 106. This statement about the sacred character of Mecca—thanks to the Sanctuary—is repeated in 29:67, and the Qur'ān complains that, despite its sanctity, people were being kidnapped all around it. Finally, in 7:29 ff., dating from the last years of the Prophet in Mecca, the Qur'ān criticizes the practices of certain pagan Arabs (including some Meccans) who performed the circumambulation of the Ka'ba naked and fasted during the pilgrimage. Nöldeke-Schwally also

9. *Op. cit.*, p. 91.

affirms this,[10] following the overwhelming reports of Muslim Qur'ān-commentators.

This evidence shows that the Prophet not only had never given up belief in the sanctity of the Ka'ba but was involved in the pilgrimage ritual till late in Mecca and was, indeed, interested in certain reforms of the ritual. Reform of the pilgrimage and other religious and social reforms, however, required political control of the Meccan situation, and Meccan opposition to him was in no small measure based on the political implications of his message.

Nor is there the slightest hint that after his arrival in Madina the Prophet had given up the Ka'ba in favor of any other shrine.[11] Indeed, all the evidence is to the contrary. That the Prophet had decided to emigrate to Madina to coerce Mecca to accept Islam is clear from the pact he made with the Madinese in order to come to Madina, which was called the "Pact of War [i.e., with Mecca]." All his political actions after his arrival in Madina—harassment and waylaying of the Meccan trade caravans—are really intelligible only in the light of his over-riding concern to take Mecca—if not through peaceful means, then through economic pressure or, if necessary, war. And within one year of the Prophet's arrival in Madina the Ka'ba was formally declared the pilgrimage shrine of Islam. This concern for Mecca and the Ka'ba can be understood only in the light of the religious, economic, and political ascendancy over the Arabs exercised by the shrine and the tribe of Quraish. What, then, it may be asked, could the Prophet and Islam have gained by placating a handful of Madinese Jews—no matter how important they may have been locally—at the expense of Mecca and the rest of the Arabs?

There was a gap of nearly six months between the ordaining of pilgrimage to the Ka'ba and the change of the direction of prayer (*qibla*) there from Jerusalem, which occurred just before what Western scholars call "the break with the Jews." Now, if the break with

---

10. *Ibid.*, p. 159.

11. That the Ka'ba had been built by Abraham was believed by some Arabs even before Islam. Nöldeke-Schwally (p. 147, n. 3) states, without any specific evidence, that this belief was probably the creation of Arab Jews and Christians, and Christians are even said to have taken part in the pilgrimage to the shrine. In any case, in view of this and the evidence we have given of the continued central place of the Ka'ba in the Qur'ān, the view of Hurgronje and Schwally that 16:36-38 are Madinan must be rejected.

the Jews was so important, as many Western scholars believe, so fraught with ideological implications for Islam and changing its very orientation, how explain this gap of six months between the two events? The logic of such an Islam-shaking break would require that both occur simultaneously, or at least nearly so. On the view I am propounding, the pilgrimage ordinance had nothing to do with Jews or any break with them; there was a continuity between the Meccan and Madinan periods of Islam and the association of Islam with the Ka'ba was made official in Madina because the Muslim community was now no longer in Mecca but in Madina, even though due to the hostility of the Meccans the Muslims had to wait several years to actually perform pilgrimage.

On the question of the *qibla*, however, the continuity was on Jerusalem, not on the Ka'ba. The Prophet had chosen Jerusalem as the *qibla*, not in Madina, but many years before in Mecca itself, as Ibn Ishāq tells us.[12] He adds, though, that the Prophet faced Jerusalem in prayer in such a way that he simultaneously faced the Ka'ba as well. It is obvious from this that the Madinan Jews had nothing to do with the Prophet's choice of Jerusalem as the *qibla* in the first place. It is possible that the choice had something to do with the great sanctity attached to the Mosaic teaching in the Qur'ān, but it seems to me more probable that this choice was made as a protest against Meccan persecution of Muslims, who were not allowed to pray in the Sacred Mosque in the early years. Ibn Ishāq also tells us that when congregational prayers were first introduced into Islam, Muslims used to pray in a hiding place outside Mecca for fear of persecution and that once, when a party of Meccans discovered the Muslims praying there, they jeered at them, upon which a fight ensued wherein Sa'd ibn Abi Waqqās seriously wounded a Meccan with a camel's shoulder-blade: "This was the first blood ever shed after the promulgation of Islam."[13] Muslims could not pray in the Sacred Mosque until well after the Abyssinian Emigration, when 'Umar became Muslim and successfully fought for his right to pray there.[14] Even after that Muslims nor-

12. Ibn Ishāq, *op. cit.*, I:318, line 12 ff.; also II:47, line 3 ff., where it is stated that when the Madinese went to Mecca to conclude with the Prophet the agreement concerning his Emigration to Madina, their leader al-Barā' ibn Ma'rūr, refused to face Jerusalem instead of the Ka'ba when the party prayed on their way to Mecca, while the rest, following the Prophet's practice at Mecca, faced Jerusalem.

13. *Ibid.*, I:275, lines 8 ff.

14. *Ibid*, I:364, lines 14 ff.

mally prayed in a private house for fear of trouble, although the Prophet himself did pray sometimes in the Sanctuary.

After the Hijra to Madina, Jerusalem continued to be the *qibla* in Muslim prayers. The change from Jerusalem to the Ka'ba, therefore, meant a break in practice—unlike the pilgrimage—and had to wait until the official place of the Ka'ba as the central Islamic shrine was well settled in the Islamic system. After this official act made it clear where the Islamic center of gravity lay, the change in the *qibla* was effected. It is to be noted that, as the Qur'ān tells us (beginning at 2:142: "The stupid ones among the people will ask what has diverted them from the *qibla* they have been used to"), trouble over this change was expected not so much from the Jews as from the "hypocrites," who would seize this opportunity to sew dissension among the ranks of the Muslims. We do not wish to deny the importance of the troubled Muslim-Jewish relations but do want to emphasize that the source of the change in the *qibla* lies elsewhere. Muslim-Jewish relations were troubled from the very beginning of the Prophet's arrival in Madina, but these troubled relations by themselves need not have affected the *qibla* question; the Prophet could have kept Jerusalem as the *qibla* while disowning the Jews, just as he kept his Prophetic link with the Biblical prophetic tradition but disowned the Jews as true representatives of that tradition. We must, therefore, seek the real answer in something else, and that is the centrality of the Meccan shrine in the religion of Islam.

Finally, one must question the validity of the concept of the "break with the Jews" itself. There is no single special event or declaration or measure on the part of the Prophet or the Jews that can be taken as the unique referent of this hallowed phrase. We are sometimes told that the change of the *qibla* itself represents "the break with the Jews,"[15] and that obviously begs the question. There were certainly protracted controversies with and criticisms of the Jews of Madina; when the Jews refused to become Muslims, they were recognized as a separate religious community but were asked not to aid the Muslims' opponents in wars—indeed, to help defend Madina against attacks—and they accepted the obligation. When this did not work out, they were expelled and, in the final phase, exterminated. But criticism

---

15. Montomery Watt, *Bell's Introduction to the Qur'ān* (Edinburgh, 1970), p. 12, lines 22 ff.

of the Jews, their recognition as a community, and invitations to them to become Muslims ran concurrently and one cannot assign to them successive periods of time. Which of these phenomena constitutes "the break with the Jews"? Long after the removal of the Jews from Madina, the Qur'an continues to criticize them on religious grounds, along with the Christians (e.g., 9:30).

The Religious Situation of
The Muslim Community in Mecca

Religious conditions in Arabia before Islam have interested many Western writers. For those concerned with the rise of Islam, these conditions have the significance of "explaining" the phenomenon; their immediate object of interest is what has been called "the sources of the Qur'ān." But there is a wide divergence of views among Western scholars as to whether there were Jews or Christians in and immediately around Mecca and if so, to what extent and with what religious consequences.

First, it must be noted that these scholars are so preoccupied by the problems of the relationship of the Qur'ān to the Judeo-Christian religious documents and traditions that they hardly ever discuss the presence of Judeo-Christian ideas among the Meccan *Arab* population before Islam. The field is sharply divided between two camps, one contending, like Richard Bell,[1] that the main historical source of the Qur'ān's teaching was Christianity, the other, represented by C. C. Torrey,[2] insisting that Judaism was the chief historical antecedent of the Qur'ān. Neither discusses even casually the view expressed strongly by the Qur'ān itself that the Qur'ān, with all its historical content, is revealed directly by God.[3] Montgomery Watt[4] holds that Judeo-Christian ideas were generally present in the milieu of Arabia, particularly in Mecca—without adducing specific evidence. We shall attempt below to clarify this situation and to outline the career of Islam

---

1. See his *The Origin of Islam in its Christian Environment* (London, 1926).
2. C. C. Torrey, *The Jewish Foundation of Islam* (New York, 1933).
3. See Chapter VIII above.
4. Montgomery Watt, *Muhammad at Mecca* (Oxford, 1953), Chapter I.

in Mecca in relationship to the Meccans as well as to the Judeo-Christian tradition.

Views differ sharply even about whether there *was* any large Jewish or Christian population in Mecca: Bell and Watt hold that there was no sizable population of the "People of the Book" there, while the less sober view of Torrey posits a "large colony" of Jews on the basis of no particular piece of hard evidence. The main difficulty with Torrey's thesis is that whereas we know very well what happened to the large-scale Jewish communities that existed, for example, in Madina and Khaibar, there is no word whatever in either the Qur'ān or Muslim historical literature as to the fate of any large Jewish community of Mecca. Whether this Jewish community eventually accepted Islam or whether like the majority of Jewish communities in Madina and Khaibar they intransigently opposed it we should reasonably expect to hear about it; but there is nothing on the subject. The opposing thesis that there were hardly any Jews or Christians in Mecca also raises serious problems in view of the Qur'ān's evidence. Some view must be evolved which will do justice to both sides. A satisfactory solution to this problem would also provide us with a materially clearer picture of the career of Islam in Mecca vis-à-vis both the "People of the Book" and the Meccan pagans; would crucially alter some views commonly held by Western scholars on what developments are Madinan and what Meccan; and would provide a gloss on certain key terms used in the Qur'ān.

It is to be noted first that not all Meccan Arabs held identical religious views when Islam appeared among them. Most of them, particularly the mercantile aristocracy, were faithful to their ancestral religion of idol worship, but others—individuals or groups—were in search of a new religion of the monotheistic type. Ibn Ishāq names three Meccans who became Christian, while one, Zayd ibn 'Amr ibn Nufail, "became neither a Jew nor a Christian," as Ibn Ishāq puts it, but died in search of a new religion. 'Uthmān ibn Maz'ūn, one of the early converts to Islam, had also gone through a religious agitation. That many Meccan Arabs had been invited by the "People of the Book" to their religions is obvious from the Qur'ān: in 27:67-68 we read, "And the disbelievers [pagan Meccans] say, Shall we be resurrected after we and our forefathers have turned to dust? We and our forefathers before us have been promised this—but this is nothing but legends of the communities of the past." The same idea recurs in

23:83 in almost identical terms. The words "We and our forefathers before us have been promised this" make it clear, I think, that Jews and Christians had been attempting to proselytize the Arabs—whether on a large or a small scale—for some time.

Indeed, the repeated charge of the Arab pagans that the Qur'ān offered "the legends of the past [i.e., earlier] communities" is a clear proof that many Arabs knew of the teachings of the Judeo-Christian tradition. Further, we have a strong suggestion in the Qur'ān that at least some Arabs had received this teaching fairly systematically:

> And they did not estimate God with correct estimation when they said: God has not sent down anything on a human; say [to them]: Who sent down the Book which Moses brought as a light and a guidance for mankind, which you write down in parchments showing them [to people] but hiding much [thereof], *and [whereby] you have been taught what neither you nor your forefathers knew?* Say: God [sent down that book] and then leave them free-lancing in their discussions. (6:92)

As we have pointed out in Chapter VIII, the words "and whereby [i.e., the Book of Moses] you have been taught what neither you nor your forefathers knew" in the nature of the case must have been addressed to the pagan Arabs and not to either Jews or Muslims. So also can the beginning of the verse, "And they did not estimate God with correct estimation when they said, God has not sent down anything on a human," have been addressed only to the pagan Arabs, who did not believe in any revelation. The question, however, is: To whom is addressed, "Say: Who sent down the Book that Moses brought . . . which you [or according to another reading, 'they'] write down into parchments"? This could only have been addressed to Jews.

But which Jews? Both Nöldeke-Schwally and Bell believe that these words refer to Madinan Jews and that this part of the verse is Madinan, although Bell believes, without a shred of evidence, that the entire verse is Madinan, while Nöldeke-Schwally think that the rest of the verse is Meccan and addressed to Meccan Arabs. But the texture of the entire verse is so closely knit (as Rudi Paret has also pointed out) that it seems absurd to regard it as a composite of Meccan and Madinan parts, just as it is equally absurd to regard it as only Madinan. The verse is Meccan and is jointly addressed to pagan Meccans and Jews. But, once again, which Jews? Answer: The same

Jews from whom pagan Meccans and their forefathers had learnt of the Mosaic teaching, and from whom they had learnt of the promises of Resurrection (cf. 27:68). The language of the Qur'ān implies not just casual encounters but fairly frequent and intimate intercourse between Jews and Meccans. Yet, as we have indicated earlier, we cannot assume a large-scale Jewish presence in Mecca. What is conceivable is that there were a few Jews in Mecca who were visited frequently by other Jews, possibly relatives, from Madina. Also, trading Meccans, when passing through Madina or visiting relatives there, frequently held discussions with Jews and possibly Christians.

Whatever the case, this kind of intercourse was fairly large-scale and systematic. After the Meccans' incessant attempts to contain the Prophet's Message from spreading failed, they sent al-Nadr ibn al-Hārith and 'Uqba ibn Abī Mu'ait to Madina to consult with Jews there as to how to overpower the Prophet in argument. Ibn al-Hārith was also well versed in Persian legends, and when the Prophet sat among members of the Quraish preaching, reciting the Qur'ān, and admonishing them with the fates of past nations, al-Nadr used to take the place of the Prophet when he left and, after telling the stories of ancient Iran, would claim that he could compete with the Prophet in telling stories of the ancient peoples.[5]

This evidence proves beyond doubt that at least some Meccans were eager to learn the lores of neighbouring peoples and were particularly well acquainted with the Biblical lore which they learnt from the Jews. It is also certain that there were some Jews and possibly Christians who had entertained Messianic expectations and who, when the Prophet appeared, supported him, encouraged him in his mission, and believed in his Message. Although these people, usually called "people whom We had given the Book [i.e., earlier Revelations]," or "people who had [already] been given the Book," or "people of knowledge," or "people of admonition," are referred to in Madina as well, they figure much more prominently in Mecca. When Meccans demanded proof from the Prophet that he was, indeed, Allah's Messenger, the Qur'ān said, "Was it not a sign for them [the pagans] that the learned men of the children of Israel recognize him?" (26:197). Later on in Mecca the Qur'ān draws a sharp distinction between these people and the Jews in general who did not believe in the Qur'ān and

5. Ibn Ishāq, *Sira* (Cairo, 1356/1937), I, 320 ff., 381.

were denounced as "sectarians [*ahzab*]"; we have, "And what of him who is on a clear proof from his Lord and then a Witness [i.e. Gabriel] from God recites it, and before it there is already the Book of Moses as a model and a mercy? Those people [i.e., the learned ones of the Jews who were recipients of the Mosaic Revelation] believe in it [the Qur'ān], but whosoever of the sectarians should disbelieve in it, their destiny is Fire" (11:17). Again we read, "Those to whom we had [already] given the Book, rejoice in what has been sent to you [O Muhammad!], but among the sectarians there are those who disbelieve in part of it" (13:36); and 29:47 tells us, "And even thus have We sent down to you the Book; those whom We had [already] given the Book believe in it [the Qur'ān], and among these ones [i.e., the generality of the Jews], too, they are those who believe in it."

But while it is abundantly clear that there was wide diffusion of Jewish and Judeo-Christian ideas and beliefs among Meccans, it is equally clear from the Qur'ān itself that, with very rare exceptions, Meccans were averse to accepting Judaism or Christianity. While the majority of them, particularly the commercial aristocracy, clung to their ancestral religion, those who were going through a more or less severe religious ferment were desirous of a new and special religion which would distinguish them from the earlier communities and make them "excel these in guidance." There is every possibility that the messianism of the People of the Book had influenced the Meccan Arabs as well and that they therefore would rather have a new religion than follow the older ones. After stating that it had been sent because, should Meccans be visited by misfortunes for their deeds, they would try to excuse themselves that no Divine Message had been sent to them to follow, the Qur'ān says, "But when the Truth from Us came to them, they said, Why has he [the Prophet] not been given the like of what Moses had been given?", adding, "But did they not already reject what Moses had been given before?" (28:47-48). The Qur'ān taunts the Meccans; "And they swore with all their might that if a warner should come to them, they would be better guided than any of the [earlier] communities; but when it did come to them, it increased them only in aversion' (35:42); again "And this is a blessed Book we have sent down, so follow it and fear God perchance you may receive mercy. [The Qur'ān has been sent] for otherwise you would say the Book was sent down only on the two communities before us and we were unaware of its teaching, or you would say if a Book had been sent down upon us, we should have been better guided than them [Jews and Christians]" (6:157).

We have made three main points so far: (1) that before Islam there had been contacts between Arabs and the People of the Book, particularly Jews—fairly large-scale and systematic contacts extending over a considerable period, so that Meccans were able to say that they and their forefathers had been told about the Last Day, and the Qur'ān could tell Meccans that they had been taught by the Book of Moses what neither they nor their forefathers had known; (2) that, nevertheless, Meccans in general had rejected the older Semitic religions and many of them hoped for a new religion, a new Prophet, and a new Scripture whereby they could outdo the two older communities; and (3) that from the early days of Islam some Jews and Christians had supported the Prophet's mission, that the Messianism of these learned Jews and Christians had probably influenced certain Meccans who looked forward to the rise of a new religion, and that in the later Meccan period the Qur'ān sharply distinguishes between these Jews and the Jews at large who disbelieved in the Qur'ān and whom the Qur'ān calls "sectarians."

This authentically Meccan situation points to an ongoing controversy, mainly between the Meccans and the Prophet but in which the Jews also formed an important though subsidiary third factor. We must grasp the developing situation in Mecca well in order to pinpoint with sufficient confidence which verses of the Qur'ān can be referred to the Meccan period and which cannot. There appears to be near unanimity among Western scholars that wherever Jews appear as the adversaries of Islam or wherever the term *jihād* and its derivatives or the term *munāfiq* occur, those verses must be Madinan and not Meccan. It is very tempting to hold this view, because in Madina the phenomena of Jewish animosity and of the *munāfiqūn* are both highly prominent. But if one closely follows the developments in Mecca, one is inevitably led to the belief that terms like *jihād* and *munāfiqūn* had begun to be used in Mecca, although their meanings become much stronger and more sharply defined in Madina. Indeed, the very fact that in certain verses their meanings are much less emphatic and less sharply defined argues for these verses being Meccan and not Madinan—supported, of course, by relevant background evidence.

In our commentary on 6:92, we drew attention to the fact that the verse was addressed jointly to Arabs and Jews in Mecca and the latter were accused of writing down the Book of Moses in such a way that they suppressed parts of it from the people. This accusation, though carried over into Madina, certainly begins in Mecca. Indeed, in an obviously Meccan verse, the Qur'ān expresses itself sarcastically about Jewish scribes: "And before it [the Qur'ān] you [O Muhammad!] were not given to reciting any scripture, nor did you write it down with your right hand—for in that case those who disbelieve in you would have reason to doubt" (29:48). In 42:13, while the Qur'ān stresses the unity of revealed religion and the indivisibility of the line of prophetic succession from Noah and Abraham through Moses and Jesus to Muhammad, and declares that the Meccan pagans are particularly opposed to this whole line of prophetic succession, it also underlines its disapproval of divisions and sects among the earlier communities—a phenomenon we have dealt with at some length in Chapter VIII. Then, after stating in 42:14 that these earlier communities, having split up into sects, are exposed to grave uncertainties and doubts, the Qur'ān goes on in the next verse to ask the Prophet to judge among them in religio-theological matters and not social matters (which occurred in Madina). Indeed, the Qur'ān is described as a judge upon those points where the Israelites—which probably includes Christians—differ among themselves: "This Qur'ān [authoritatively] narrates to the Children of Israel most matters regarding which they mutually differ" (27:76). It is strange, therefore, that Western scholars should declare 29:46 to be Madinan; it reads: "And dispute not [O Muslims!] with the People of the Book but with the most polite method, except those of them who transgress."

The reason given by Nöldeke-Schwally and others for calling this verse Madinan is that, in view of the weakness of the Muslims in Mecca, the Qur'ān could not have advocated a non-polite treatment even of transgressing Jews. It is the Islamic situation in its later Meccan phase that we must now clarify in order to understand and correctly evaluate the relative positions of Meccan pagans, Muslims, and Jews. For this, we must briefly sketch out the career of Islam in Mecca, since the indelible impression on the minds of most scholars is that Muslims were an utterly helpless people and that is why they had to emigrate first to Abyssinia and then to Madina—as though their position had remained absolutely static with regard to the powerful Quraish pagans.

This is simply not true. The truth seems to be that although the

Meccans disapproved of the new Faith, they were never able to put up an all-out, concentrated, sustained opposition to it. Muslims were persecuted, and indeed tortured, but this occurred haphazardly. Perhaps because they had a guilty conscience about the accusations that the Qur'ān constantly laid against them—of idol-worship, fraudulent practices in commerce, and exploitation of the poor—or perhaps because Islam gradually appealed to many, including some honorable and influential persons, while the Meccans were jittery on the one hand, on the other their opposition was desultory and half-hearted (consider the immunity of the Prophet himself due to Abū Ṭālib's protection).

After Abū Bakr and Abū 'Ubaida ibn al-Jarrāḥ became Muslims at an early stage and the Prophet launched his movement into the open, some leaders of the Quraish, after two unsuccessful attempts to persuade Abū Ṭālib to dissuade the Prophet from preaching his new message or to lift his protection from him, gathered to think of an effective strategy. But they seem to have harmed their own position rather than benefiting it, because by their propagandizing against the Prophet at the time of pilgrimage all Arabs, including the Madinese, came to know of Islam. The persecution of Muslims seems to have been undertaken in earnest after Hamza became Muslim; that persecution resulted in the first Emigration to Abyssinia, particularly of the weaker members of the Muslim society. But while this Emigration was still in progress, 'Umar became Muslim. Ibn Isḥāq tells us that the Islam of 'Umar and Hamza strengthened the Muslims so much that "they were able to compete with or withstand the Quraish in power [*'āzzū Quraishan*]."[6] This led the Quraish, as though in half panic, to institute a boycott of the Banū Hāshim, which failed after two or three years (as if it was ever possible for it to succeed). Despite the severe trials of some members of the new community at times, the Meccans—even with the support of Jews—never seemed to be able either to silence the Prophet in the debates into which they drew him now and then, or to come to a point where the crushing of the new movement would seem imminent. And as time went on, the Muslims became stronger and stronger through the slow but steady conversion gains they made.

To think of the Prophet and his followers in this situation as utterly

6. *Ibid.*, I:364.

helpless and totally at the mercy of opponents who might kill or destroy them at their own sweet will is certainly at least a half-myth, created, no doubt, by certain later Muslim accounts and impressed upon the minds of modern Orientalists. Hence the dictum of Nöldeke-Schwally that in 29:46 the words "except those [Jews] who transgress" cannot be Meccan. Yet 27:76, wherein the Qur'ān claims to authoritatively set theological points of disputation among the "Israelites," is happily accepted by Nöldeke-Schwally to be Meccan. It is also clear that when, after the death of Khadīja and Abū Ṭālib, the Prophet preached his message to various tribes in the Ḥajj season, and visited Ṭā'if, and eventually moved to Madina, these were not the actions of a helplessly desperate person but of a man who had gained enough following to be confident that, should some outside elements support him, he could sooner or later secure Mecca for Islam. Ibn Ishāq also tells us that on his second meeting at the 'Aqaba with the Madinese before the *hijra*, the Prophet was accompanied by his uncle 'Abbās, who was not then a Muslim but who told the Madinese that Muhammad and his cause were being entrusted to them for aid and were not being surrendered to them, since Muhammad had enough protection at Mecca.[7]

In light of this we may now discuss a passage which some Muslim commentators declare to be Madinese while others consider it to be Meccan and which, with the exception of A. Sprenger, followed by Hirschfeld,[8] all Western scholars believe to be Madinan because it uses words like *jihād* and *munāfiq*:

> Do people, then, think that they will be left alone, after they say, We believe, and that they shall not be tried? Indeed, We tried people before them [Muslims] and God must know those who are true and He must know who are the false ones. Or, do those who perpetrate evil think that they will outstrip Us?—evil is what they judge. ...And who so struggles hard [*jāhada*], does so only for himself—[for] God is independent of the whole world. ... And We have admonished man to do good to his parents, but if they should try their best [put you to trial—*jāhadāka*] that you associate with God that of which you do not know [i.e., if they try to compel you to worship others besides God], then do not obey them—to Me is your return and I shall let you know what you had been doing. ... And among men there is he who says We believe in [one] God, but when he is persecuted in God's cause

7. *Ibid.*, II:49-50.

8. Nöldeke-Schwally, *Geschichte des Qorans* (New York, 1970), Part 1, p. 155, n. 3.

he comes to equate the trial inflicted upon him by people with God's punishment; so if help comes [to you Muslims] from your Lord, these [turncoats] will say, We were with you—indeed does God not know what is in the hearts of men? God, indeed, shall clearly separate those who [really] believe from those who are hypocrites [hypocritical]. (29:1-10)

This passage contains a cluster of three key terms which are closely related. One is *fitna*, which describes a situation where a person is pressured by others—mostly by relatives and friends—to defect from his affiliations or retreat from his views; the weapons used can be either propaganda or mental or physical torture. One element in *fitna* seems to be that, although its victims are usually individuals or families, it is exercised on a fairly large scale and creates a situation where some people do not know what to do and sooner or later simply succumb to pressure, unless they are very strong indeed. The second key term is *jihād*, which means to struggle or try hard for a cause. This word has been used twice, once in reference to a person and meaning to struggle hard to stand up against *fitna* ("Whoso struggles hard does so only for himself [or his own good]") and, secondly, referring to one's parents who try hard to convert him back from Islam to paganism. The third term is *munāfiq* or *munāfiqūn*, i.e., hypocritical ones. Now, if one were to consider only the terms *jihād* and *munāfiqūn*, it would be tempting to regard them as Madinan, since both of these are standard Madinan terms. As for *fitna*, although the term is used in the very early Madinan days to describe the active pressure, including physical violence and even fighting of Meccans to bring back those new Muslim converts who had left Mecca and joined the Prophet in Madina, its standard use refers to the persecution of Muslims by Meccan pagans in Mecca itself. Large-scale *fitna* undoubtedly occurred either just before the Emigration to Abyssinia or during the last phase of the Prophet's life in Mecca, and particularly on the eve of and during the Emigration to Madina. A. Sprenger locates this passage of the Qur'ān during the first persecution.[9] Since most Muslims at that time were not strong enough to withstand pressure, it is unlikely that the Qur'ān would have used such strong language against defectors, particularly the terms *jihād* and *munāfiqūn*.

But Islam gained very considerable strength during the last phase of

9. *Ibid.*

the Prophet's Meccan career. Indeed, Muslims were permitted by the Qur'ān in 16:126 even to retaliate against attacks upon them with physical violence, although bearing persecution with patience rather than violence was still declared better in this verse, *which the generality of Western scholars believe to be Meccan.* Muslims were, therefore, powerful enough to be able to retaliate. If we consider the terms *jihād* and *munāfiqūn* in this Qur'ānic passage, in this *fitna*-background, it at once becomes clear that their meanings are *not* the same as when they are employed later in Madina. We must first note that the verse which speaks of a person or persons who, when subjected to persecution, regard it as though it was punishment from God, cannot possibly refer to Madina, for there subjection of any Muslim to such persecution is unthinkable. This fact in itself should have been enough to deter Nöldeke-Schwally and others from declaring the passage to be Madinan, even though some Muslim authorities have also held this view.

As for the term *jihād* in this context, it obviously means not *jihād* in its Madinan sense but merely a strong-willed resistance to the pressures of *fitna* and retaliation in case of violence; or, in the case of the parents of a son who had embraced Islam, a strong effort to reconvert him from Islam. The *jihād* of Madina refers to an organized and total effort of the community—if necessary through war—to overcome the hurdles in the way of the spread of Islam. Indeed, in Madina, it is often equivalent to *qitāl* or to active war. The meaning of the term *munāfiqūn* here is also much less strong than in Madina, for here it simply signifies people who succumb to pressure and whose faith is not strong enough to withstand that pressure. In Madina, this term primarily indicates a group of people, the clientele particularly of 'Abd Allāh ibn Ubayy, who had deliberately put on the *facade* of Islam as a kind of fifth column in order to subvert Islam and undermine the Prophet's position from within. These people had a more or less definite identity and a kind of secret alliance both with Jews and with Meccan pagans; always, in times of war, they were with the enemies of Islam, at least passively. But in the Qur'ānic passage under consideration, *munāfiqūn* are simply fickle-minded people whose power of faith is weak. In Madina, too, such people probably existed but they were secondary to that hard core of "hypocrites" to whom the term applies in a specific, technical sense. (A parallel to the present verse is in 22:11 which, without using the term *munāfiqūn*, says, "And among men there is he who worships [one] God only as a peripheral matter: so long as good keeps coming to him, he is happy with it, but when a *fitna* strikes him, he turns right around.'')

There is, thus, a continuity of transition from the late Meccan to the early Madinan period, not the clear break projected by so many of the modern writings on dating the Qur'ān and on the life of the Prophet. Western writers seem on the whole to be obsessed by certain Madinan phenomena, especially the Muslim-Jewish hostility and the change in the *qibla*, which many think changed the very orientation of Islam away from Judaism to Arabia. We have argued that these capital misunderstandings occur primarily because the Meccan developments and perspectives are not seen properly. Another capital misunderstanding we have attempted to clarify here is that terms like *jihād* and *munāfiqūn* are seen as invariably Madinan, again because of the lack of a proper perspective, for Islam is seen throughout its Meccan career as totally helpless vis-a-vis both the Jews and the Quraish without due allowance for the continuous changes in the character of the Muslim community in Mecca. The review that we have offered here, though brief, has far-reaching implications for the general modern prevailing view of the nature of the nascent stage of Islam and, indeed, of the formal emergence of the Muslim community.[10]

10. Two further important points may be added concerning the later stages of the development of the Muslim community in Mecca. First, it was when the Meccans saw the increasing spread of Islam that they approached the Prophet and offered to join him, provided he dissociate himself from his weak and socially low-class followers. This fact, corroborated by Ibn Ishāq, has been dealt with by the Qur'ān in 18:28 and 6:52-54, where the Prophet is admonished not to think of abandoning his weaker followers.

The second point has to do with the dating of two mutually comparable verses of the Qur'ān, 74:31 and 22:53-54. In the former it is said, "So that those who have [already] been given the Book should be firmly convinced [of the truth of the Qur'ān] and those who believe should increase in their belief. . .and so that those in whose heart there is sickness [i.e., hypocritical people] and pagans should ask, What did God mean by such an example?" This verse is regarded as Madinan on the ground that it speaks of four types of people—including "hypocrites" which is said to be proper only to Madina, not Mecca. A close parallel to this verse is 22:53-54, also regarded as Madinan on the same grounds. In the light of our argument, which has established that "hypocrites" as a category arose first in Mecca and not in Madina, however, these verses must be treated as Meccan, for otherwise (even according to Nöldeke-Schwally themselves), there is no reason why 22:53-54, for example, should not be Meccan. Indeed, in Madina, there are only three categories, not four, since the category of pagans is hardly there and only Muslims, Jews, and Hypocrites are left.

The People of the Book and
Diversity of "Religions"

Islam's attitude to Christianity is as old as Islam itself, since Islam partly took shape by adopting certain important ideas from Judaism and Christianity and criticizing others. Indeed, Islam's self-definition is partly the result of its attitude to these two religions and their communities.

That there was messianism among certain Meccan Arab circles at the time Muhammad appeared has been amply documented. Instead of accepting either Judaism or Christianity, these Arab circles were looking for a new revealed religion of their own, so that "they might be even better guided" than the two older communities. After the advent of Muhammad as God's Messenger, the Qur'ān repeatedly refers to a group of people about whom it says, "We had already given them the Book [i.e., the Torah and the Gospel] and they also believe in the Qur'ān." These verses clearly show that some Jews or Christians or Judeo-Christians had also entertained messianic hopes and encouraged Muhammad in his mission. The Qur'ān, indeed, taunts the Meccan pagans, saying that whether or not they believed in the Qur'ān (or the Prophet), "those to whom We had already given the Book, believe in it [or him]" (cf. Chapter VIII).

There are several important and interesting issues connected with this phenomenon. For example: was Islam entirely the result of Jewish or Christian "influences," or was it basically an independent native growth that picked up some important ideas from the Judeo-Christian tradition? A number of Jewish and Christian scholars have vied with each other to show that Islam was genetically related to one or the other religion. Recently several Western scholars, among them Montgomery Watt, Maurice Gaudefroy-Demomlyness, and, above all,

H.A.R. Gibb, have argued convincingly that in its nativity Islam grew out of an Arab background, although in its formation and development there have been many important influxes from the Judeo-Christian tradition.[1] But the issue with which we are directly concerned here is not the "originality" of Islam but Muḥammad's perception of himself and his mission, which in intimately connected with his perception of his relationship to other prophets, their religion(s), and their communities.

It is quite obvious from the Qur'ān that from the beginning to the end of his prophetic career Muḥammad was absolutely convinced of the divine character of the earlier revealed documents and of the divine messengership of the bearers of these documents. This is why he recognized without a moment of hesitation that Abraham, Moses, Jesus, and other Old and New Testament religious personalities had been genuine prophets like himself. This acceptance was undoubtedly strengthened when some followers of these earlier religions recognized Muḥammad as a true prophet and the Qur'ān as a revealed book. Hence the falsity of the view popular among Western Islamists (originally enunciated by the patriarchs of Western Islamic studies like Snouck Hurgronje and Nöldeke-Schwally) that in Mecca the Prophet Muḥammad was fully convinced that *he was giving to the Arabs* what Moses and Jesus *had previously given to their respective communities*, and that it was at Madina, where the Jews refused to recognize him as God's Messenger, that he instituted the Muslim community as separate from Jews and Christians (cf. Chapter VIII).

There is no mention of any fixed religious communities in the earlier part of the Qur'ān. True, different prophets have come to different peoples and nations at different times, but their messages are universal and identical. All these messages emanate from a single source: "the Mother of the Book" (43: 4; 13:39) and "the Hidden Book" (56:78). Since these messages are universal and identical, it is incumbent on all people to believe in all divine messages. This is why Muḥammad felt himself obligated to believe in the prophethood of Noah, Abraham, Moses, and Jesus, for God's religion is indivisible and prophethood is also indivisible. Indeed, the Prophet is made to

1. W. Montgomery Watt, *Muhammad at Mecca* (Oxford, 1953), pp. 1-29; Maurice Gaudefroy-Demomlyness, *Mahomet* (Paris, 1957), pp. i-xxii; and H.A.R. Gibb, "Pre-Islamic Monotheism in Arabia," *Harvard Theological Review* 55 (1962) 269-80.

declare in the Qur'ān that not only does he believe in the Torah and the Gospel but "I believe in whatever Book God may have revealed" (42:15). This is because God's guidance is universal and not restricted to any nation or nations: "And there is no nation wherein a warner has not come" (35:24) and "For every people a guide has been provided" (13:7). The word "Book" is, in fact, often used in the Qur'ān not with reference to any specific revealed book but as a generic term denoting the totality of divine revelations (see 2:213, for example).

If Muhammad and his followers believe in all prophets, all people must also and equally believe in him. Disbelief in him would be equivalent to disbelief in all, for this would arbitrarily upset the line of prophetic succession. In the late Meccan period, however, the Prophet became more aware that Jews and Christians would not believe in him, nor would they recognize each other. Recent scholarship has shown that this awareness came to Muhammad in Mecca and not in Madina, as is often believed. At this point, Jews and Christians are called *al-ahzāb* (sectarians, partisans, people who are divisive of the unity of religion and disruptive of the line of prophetic succession), each *hizb* (also *shi'a*) or party rejoicing in what it has to the exclusion of the rest. Muslims are warned not to split up into parties. It is at this point that the religion of Muhammad is described as "straight" and "upright," the religion of the *hanīf* (i.e., of an upright monotheist who does not follow divisive forces) and is linked and identified with the religion of Abraham.

The awareness of the diversity of religions, despite the unity of their origin, sets Muhammad a theological problem of the first order. It so persistently and painfully pressed itself on his mind that from the beginning of this awareness until well into the last phase of his life, the Qur'ān treats this question at various levels. The fact that religions are split not only from each other but even within themselves is recurrently deplored. But a somewhat different point of view on the problem also emerges in the Qur'ān. Humankind had been a unity, but this unity was split up because of the advent of divine messages at the hands of the prophets. The fact that the prophets' messages act as watersheds and divisive forces is rooted in some divine mystery, for if God so willed, He could surely bring them to one path:

Mankind were one single community. Then God raised up prophets who gave good tidings and warnings and God also sent down with them The Book in truth, that it may decide among people in regard to what they differed. But people did not differ in it [i.e., with regard to the Truth] except those to whom it had been given [and that only] after clear signs had come to them; [and this they did] out of [sheer] rebelliousness among themselves. (2:213)

If your Lord had so willed, He would have made mankind one community, but they continue to remain divided. (11:118)

Men were but one community; then they began to differ. But for a decree of your Lord that had already preceded, a decision would have been made with regard to that wherein they differ. (10:19)

In Madina, the terms "sectarians" and "partisans" are dropped, and Jews and Christians are recognized as "communities," although, of course, they continue to be invited to Islam. As we noted earlier, the Qur'ān, in the early stages in Mecca, does not speak at all in terms of communities and certainly not in terms of exclusivist communities. It was the awareness and subsequent recognition of the existence of the mutually exclusive Jewish and Christian communities (and probably equally exclusivist subgroups in Christianity) that led the Qur'ān first to call them "sectarians" and "partisans" and subsequently to recognize them (in Madina) as communities. It was the solidification of these communities that led to the announcement of Muslims as a separate community:

The Jews say, The Christians have nothing to stand on, and the Christians say, The Jews have nothing to stand on,—while both recite the same Book. (2:113)

They say, No one shall enter the paradise except those who are Jews or Christians—these are their wishful thoughts. (2:111)

Jews and Christians will never be pleased with you [O Muhammad!] unless you follow their religion[s]; say [to them]: The guidance of God [not of Jews or Christians] is the guidance. (2:120)

The Qur'ān's reply to these exclusivist claims and claims of proprietorship over God's guidance, then, is absolutely unequivocal: Guidance is not the function of communities but of God and good people, and *no* community may lay claims to be uniquely guided and elected. The whole tenor of the Qur'ānic argument is against election:

When God tested Abraham by some words and he [Abraham] fulfilled them, God said [to Abraham], I am going to make you a leader of men. What about my progeny? asked Abraham; He [God] replied, My promise does not extend to the unjust ones. (2:124)

The whole mystique of election is undermined by the repeated statements of the Qur'an after mentioning Biblical prophets and their people:

> That is a community that is by-gone: to them belongs what they earned and to you [O Muslims!] will belong what you will earn, and *you* will not be asked for what they had done. (2:134, 141)

In conformity with this strong rejection of exclusivism and election, the Qur'ān repeatedly recognizes the existence of good people in other communities—Jews, Christians and Sabaeans—just as it recognizes the people of faith in Islam:

> Those who believe [Muslims], the Jews, the Christians, and the Sabaeans—whosoever believe in God and the Last Day and do good deeds, they shall have their reward from their Lord, shall have nothing to fear, nor shall they come to grief. (2:62; cf. 5:69)

In both these verses, the vast majority of Muslim commentators exercise themselves fruitlessly to avoid having to admit the obvious meaning: that those—from any section of humankind—who believe in God and the Last Day and do good deeds are saved. They either say that by Jews, Christians, and Sabaeans here are meant those who have actually become "Muslims"—which interpretation is clearly belied by the fact that "Muslims" constitute only the first of the four groups of "those who believe"—or that they were those good Jews, Christians, and Sabaeans who lived before the advent of the Prophet Muhammad—which is an even worse *tour de force*. Even when replying to Jewish and Christian claims that the hereafter was theirs and theirs alone, the Qur'ān says, "On the contrary, whosoever surrenders himself to God while he does good deeds as well, he shall find his reward with his Lord, shall have no fear, nor shall he come to grief" (2:112).

The logic of this recognition of universal goodness, with belief in one God and the Last Day as its necessary underpinning, demands, of course, that the Muslim community be recognized as *a* community among communities. Here, the Qur'ān appears to give its final answer to the problem of a multi-community world:

> And We have sent down to you the Book in truth, confirming the Book that existed already before it and protecting it. . . . For each one of you [several communities] We have appointed a Law and a Way of Conduct [while the essence of religion is identical]. If God had so willed, He would have made all of you one community, but [He has not done so] that He may test you in what He has given you; *so compete in goodness.* To God shall you all return and He will tell you [the Truth] about what you have been disputing. (5:48)

The positive value of different religions and communities, then, is that they may compete with each other in goodness (cf. 2:148; 2:177; where, after announcing the change in the *qibla* from Jerusalem to Mecca, it is emphasized that the *qibla* per se is of no importance, the real worth being in virtue and *competing in goodness*). The Muslim community itself, lauded as the "Median Community" (2:144) and "the best community produced for mankind" (3:110), is given no assurance whatever that it will be automatically God's darling unless, when it gets power on the earth, it establishes prayers, provides welfare for the poor, commands good, and prohibits evil (22:41, etc.). In 47:38, the Muslims are warned that "If you turn your backs [upon this teaching], God will substitute another people for you who will not be like you" (cf. 9:38).

According to the Qur'ān, the most fundamental distinction between God and creatures is that God is infinite—All-Life, All-Power, All-Knowledge, etc.—whereas all creatures are finite. God, the Infinite, has created everything "according to a measure" (e.g., 54:49). He alone is the "Measurer [*qadir*]," while everything else is "measured [*maqdūr*]." This idea is ubiquitous in the Qur'ān. This is not a doctrine of "pre-determinism," as many Muslim theologians of the medieval ages understood it to be. "Measuring" in this context simply means "finitude" of potentialities, despite their range. Human beings, for example, are acknowledged by the Qur'ān to be possessed of great potentialities: Adam outstripped angels in a competition of creative knowledge and angels were thus ordered to honor him (2:30 ff.); yet human beings cannot be God.

It is because of the infinitude of God that both absolute mercy and absolute power are both attributable to God alone. God's mercy is literally limitless (40:7; 7:156)—indeed, mercy is a law written into God's nature (6:12). And the very fact that there exists the plenitude of being rather than the emptiness of nonbeing is an expression of the primal act of God's mercy. God's power is commensurate with God's mercy. You may not point to any human being, with delimitations and a date of birth, and say simply, "That person is God." To the Qur'ān, this is neither possible, nor intelligible, nor pardonable.

The severity of the Qur'ān's judgments on incarnation and trinity has varied. There are verses that regard the Christian doctrine simply as "extremism in faith":

> O People of the Book! do not go to extremes in your faith and do not say about God except truth. The Messiah, Jesus, son of Mary, was but a Messenger of God and His Word that He cast into Mary and a Spirit from Him. So believe in God and in His Messengers and say not, [God] is there, desist from this, it is better for you. God is but one and only God—far above He be from having a son; to Him belong whatever is in the heaven and in the earth. . . . The Messiah [Jesus] will not be too proud to be God's servant, nor will those angels who are very near God [disdain to be His servants]. And whosoever should disdain to do service to Him and be too proud [for this], God will gather all of them to Himself [on the Last Day] . (4:171-72; cf. 5:77)

But there are much stronger verses reminiscent of the Qur'ānic statements against idolators:

> Those are infidels who say: God is the Messiah, son of Mary. Say: Who will be of any help against God, if He should want to destroy the Messiah, son of Mary, his mother and all those who live on the earth? To God belongs the kingdom of heaven and earth and whatever is between them; He creates whatever He wills, and God is powerful over everything. (5:117)

Again:

> Committed to infidelity are those who say: God is the same as the Messiah, son of Mary; . . . committed to infidelity are those who say: God is one among three—while there is no God but the Unique one; if they do not desist from what they say, a painful punishment will touch those of them as commit infidelity. Why do they not repent to God and seek His pardon, for God is forgiving and merciful? The

Messiah, son of Mary, was but a Messenger—before him had gone many other messengers; his mother was the truthful one; they both used to eat food [like other men]. Just see how We make the signs clear to them and also see how they are being deceived! (5:72-75)

The Qur'ān speaks in the same vein about and to Muhammad:

Muhammad is but a Messenger—before him have gone many other Messengers. Should he then die or be slain [in battle] will you turn back upon your heels [O Muslims!]? (3:144)

Say [to the pagan Arabs], Tell me, if God were to destroy me and all those who are with me, or should have mercy upon us, who will provide refuge...? (67:28)

Muhammad cannot take it for granted that God will automatically continue to send him revelatory messages:

Do they say that he [Muhammad] concocts lies and attributes them to God? But if God so will, He may seal up your heart [O Muhammad! so that no revealed message will issue forth from it]—indeed, God [not Muhammad] obliterates the falsehood and confirms what is true, through His Words... (42:24)

For the Qur'ān, then, Jesus can be as little an incarnation of God as Muhammad himself or, indeed, any other prophet. But it is true that the Qur'ān speaks with tenderness of Jesus and also his followers (see 5:82: "You shall find the nearest of all people in friendship to the Believers [Muslims] those who say they are Christians. This is because among them there are priests and monks and they are not a proud people"; also 57:27: "Then we followed up [these Messengers] with Jesus, son of Mary, to whom We gave the Evangel, and We put in the hearts of his followers kindness and mercy ...").

This attitude toward Christianity has no parallel toward other communities mentioned in the Qur'ān. Because the Qur'ān is sometimes very mild, indeed highly tender, toward Christians (although at times highly critical of them), some Western scholars have thought that basically Muhammad was a fellow-traveler and perhaps almost a Christian. It has been argued that political motivations prevented him from a full and explicit identification with Christianity. Some have also seen his increasing hostility toward Byzantium as the cause of the increasingly severe criticism of Christianity in the Qur'ān. Some also think that he did not correctly understand the nature of the doctrine of Jesus in Christianity because it was misrepresented to him by Christians. But it is difficult to see how the doctine of incarnation, for example, could be misunderstood. The trouble with the first view is that it is impossible to prove that the severely critical passages of the Qur'ān are necessarily later than other passages. For example, 57:27 seems to be quite late Madinan. The truth, then, appears to be that Muhammad must have encountered various views at the hands of various representatives of Christianity and that the Qur'ān appears to address different groups at different points.

In any case, the unacceptability of Jesus' divinity and the Trinity to the Qur'ān is incontrovertible, as is the fact that Jesus and his followers are regarded as exceptionally charitable and self-sacrificing. The Qur'ān would most probably have no objections to the Logos having become flesh if the Logos were not simply identified with God and the identification were understood less literally. For the Qur'ān, the Word of God is never identified simply with God. Jesus, again, is the "Spirit of God" in a special sense for the Qur'ān, although God had breathed His spirit into Adam as well (15:29; 38:72). It was on the basis of some such expectations from the self-proclaimed monotheism of Christians—and, of course, Jews—that the Qur'ān issued its invitation: "O People of the Book! Let us come together upon a formula which is common between us—that we shall not serve anyone but God, that we shall associate none with Him" (3:64). This invitation, probably issued at a time when Muhammad thought not all was yet lost among the three self-proclaimed monotheistic communities, must have appeared specious to Christians. It has remained unheeded. But I believe something can still be worked out by way of positive cooperation, provided the Muslims hearken more to the Qur'ān than to the historic formulations of Islam and provided that recent pioneering efforts continue to yield a Christian doctrine more compatible with universal monotheism and egalitarianism.

Index

Aaron, as *nabī*, 82

Abraham, and theory of election, 56; arrival at monotheism, 89; as example of filial piety, 42; as founder of pure monotheism, 142-43; development of image of, 132; place in line of prophets, 82, 83; Qur'ān speaking through to pagans, 76; scrolls of, 135; vindication of, 87

"abrogation," 89-90

Abū Ṭālib, besought to withdraw support from Muhammad, 85; pressure for compromise, 87

accounting, difficult for Meccans to accept, 115

actions, of man as based on God, 11

acts, consequences for man's destiny, 34-35; quality as important in religion, 32

'Ād, people as *aḥzāb*, 139; prophets of, 135; tribe of prophet Hud, 82

Adam, creation of, 17-18; infused by God's spirit, 96

agent of Revelation, and true revealing subject, 99-100; as *bayyina*, 101-2; as messenger, 82; as spiritual and internal, 97; enabling Muhammad to transcend history, 100; role in the Ascension, 92-93; work described as *furqān*, 100

Ahirman, compared with Satan, 123

al-aḥzāb, and emergence of Muslim community, 138-39; applied to earlier communities, 139-40; distinguished, 155

ākhira, explained, 106 ff.; forgotten under Satan's temptations, 126; place in Qur'ānic system, 64, 116

Ali, 'Abdullah Yusuf, xii

Allāh, see God

Al-Shamma, S.H., xv

amr, and laws of creation, 23; and laws of nature, 13; and man's free choice, 24-25; as the source of all books, 98; associated with revelation, 98; in relation to purpose of man, 8

angels, as bearers of miracles, 77; as describing agent of Revelation, 95; as related to the Spirit, 96-97; competition with Adam, 17-18; discussed, 95; distinguished from man, 128; not personalized as individuals, 131

Arabs, and the Ka'ba, 145; and the Qur'ān, 135; as worshippers of jinn, 122; contacts with People of the Book, 155; culture as background for Islam, 163; Muhammad's teaching of, in Mecca, 132-33; polytheism of pagan, 5; variety of religions before Islam, 151

Arberry, A. J., xii

arbitration, mandated by Qur'ān, 44

Ascension, of Muhammad, discussed, 92-93

Ash'arites, success in later Medieval

who accepted Muḥammad, 137 ff.

Jibril, as supra-angelic, 131

jihād, defined, 64, 159; implications of term, 160; necessity of, 63; not to be diluted by filial piety, 43; permission for, 62; why created, 63

jinn, see also Satan; discussed, 121-23; proneness to evil, 128

Joseph, Qur'ān speaking through to pagans, 76

judgment, God's role, 9 ff.; of communities, 114; on individuals, 107; of man's actions, 29; in history, 52, 68

justice, and giving truthful evidence, 42; and polygamy, 47-48

Ka'ba, as focus of prayer, 133; centrality of, 145-46

khair, used to describe wealth, 39

khusrān, acts which affect doer adversely, 32; contrasted with salvation, 63

knowledge, as faith generated by certainty, 101-2; creative knowledge possessed by Adam, 18; types Qur'ān is interested in, 34; use of as man's crucial test, 9; worth of empirical knowledge, 34

Korah, symbolism of death for society, 37

kufr, acts which affect others adversely, 32; defined, 21; pride and hopelessness as aspects of, 27

language, of Qur'ān, as forming men's character, 22-23

Last Day, see also Eschatology; described, 106 ff.

laws, difference between physical and moral, 79; legislative procedure, 48; mistakes of legal tradition, 47; of nature as obeying God, 23; ratio legis discussed, 48

legal tradition, fundamental mistakes of, 47

life, as fundamental right, 46

loss, and eschatology, 108

Lot, followers as *aḥzāb*, 139

Madina, see also hypocrites; and emergence of Muslim community, 132 ff.

Madinan period, discussed, 133 ff.

magic, distinguished from signs, 70-74

majnūn, Muḥammad described as, 94

makr, defined, 57

malak, see angel

man, see also resurrection; and temptation, 18-19; as aim of the Qur'ān, 3; as exception to universe being automatically *muslim*, 24; as individual, 17-36; as servant of God, 14; basic weakness, 25 ff.; created anew for next world, 111-12; end is to serve God, 79; fate dependent on right path, 60; Hour of Self-Awareness, 106-7 ff.; in relation to God, 3 ff.; in society, 37-64; knowledge of himself required, 34; man's nature as "inlaid," 25; Muḥammad's hopes to unify, 138-39; must be alert against Satan, 123-24; must be invited to goodness, 33; nature of, 21; pressure from stronger on weaker, 60; purpose of, 8, 79; utility of nature for, 78-79; weakness as source of Satan's power, 124-26

marriage, polygamy, 47-49; of widows with stepsons, 50-51

Mary, and God's spirit, 96

mashūr, Muḥammad attacked as, 94

"mean", as used in Qur'ān, 28

measuring, as applied to God, 167; explained, 12-13; strong holistic bias of, 67

Mecca, and emergence of Muslim community, 132 ff.; as background for Qur'ān, 32; economic structure, 38-42; religious situation of Muslim community in, 150-62; sacred character of, 145; society, 60; surrender to Islam symbolized in 13:31, 77

Meccan period, discussed, 133 ff.

Meccans, asking that angel be sent to Muḥammad, 96-97; demanding miracles from Muḥammad, 77; desirous of new religion, 133-34;